CAT'S OUT THE BAG

CAT HARVEY

BLACK & WHITE PUBLISHING

First published 2021
by Black & White Publishing Ltd
Nautical House, 104 Commercial Street
Edinburgh, EH6 6NF

1 3 5 7 9 10 8 6 4 2   21 22 23 24

ISBN: 978 1 78530 368 5

This book is a work of non-fiction, based on the life, experiences
and recollections of the author. The author has stated to the publishers
that the contents of this book are true to the best of their knowledge.

The publisher has made every reasonable effort to contact copyright holders
of images in this book. Any errors are inadvertent and anyone who for any reason
has not been contacted is invited to write to the publisher so that a full
acknowledgment can be made in subsequent editions of this work.

Use of the Cash for Kids logo by kind permission of
Radio Clyde Cash for Kids (registered charity no. SCO003334)

A CIP catalogue record for this book is available from the British Library.

Typeset by Iolaire, Newtonmore
Printed and bound by Clays Ltd, Elcograf S.p.A.

FSC
www.fsc.org

MIX
Paper from
responsible sources
FSC® C018072

For Dad

Bobby Harvey. Father, inspiration, hero and my best friend. You give me the drive to push through the tough times and the strength to know that everything will turn out okay in the end. 'What's fur ye will no' go by ye,' right enough.

You've taught me that friends, kindness, health, music and laughter is really all we need. Your legacy shall be my happiness.

'The man o' independent mind,
He looks an' laughs at a' that'
ROBERT BURNS

'Reach for the stars'
S CLUB 7

A Note from the Author

Disclaimer! The views in this book are mine alone and absolutely nothing to do with the management of Bauer Radio or Cash for Kids.

They are all much more sensible than I will ever be and probably never carry a kazoo in their bags.

Contents

Foreword – Sally Aitchison 1

Let Me Have My Say, Too – Ewen Cameron 3

Introduction 5

Me 11

The Cast 14

Magic Moments 22

Celebrities 33

These Are a Few of My Favourite Things 43

Cat's Tales of the Unexpected . . . 81

Feline Paw-Sitive – The Purrfect Conclusion 302

The Final Farewell 307

Thank You 309

Foreword

On behalf of everyone at Cash for Kids, I would like to wish Cat success with her new book and thank you for supporting it. Cat has always been the most amazing ambassador for Cash for Kids in Scotland. We fundraise and grant the funds to help children and young people who are disadvantaged or ill.

Everything raised in a local area stays in that local area so people can feel confident they are helping the children of Scotland in an area that matters to them.

At Cash for Kids, we support children and young people affected by poverty, abuse, neglect, life-limiting illnesses and those who have additional needs.

One of our key priority areas is holiday hunger – for many children school holidays are no holiday at all, they can be a living nightmare being away from the support of school and many will be at increased risk of neglect and abuse.

Holiday hunger is a real problem for families on low incomes who normally receive meals during school holidays and one in eight children don't get enough to eat with many returning to school noticeably thinner, according to teachers.

These are sad statistics when children spend 170 days out of school compared to 190 days in the classroom – for up to eight weeks many children will not receive a hot meal and will have no activities to enjoy over the summer holidays. With your support we can help these children.

Cat is an established broadcaster and a very talented woman. The fact that she uses her position for good causes is laudable. Cat has hosted auctions and balls for us, walked the Kiltwalk, and helped us raise thousands of pounds.

Cat is donating all of the royalties from this book to helping children in Scotland. What a wonderful gesture of kindness.

Thank you for your generosity, Cat. And I hope you, the reader, enjoy this fabulously funny and warm-hearted read.

SALLY AITCHISON MBE
Managing Director
Cash for Kids

Let Me Have My Say, Too

Ewen Cameron

Hi, I'm Ewen, Cat's hilarious and devilishly handsome award-winning radio partner.

The following words are inspired by the song 'Opposites Attract' by my teenage pinup Paula Abdul.

This might make more sense if you google the lyrics.

*

Now, here's a little story and you're sure to like it.

Our friends said 'you two ain't gonna last' when we first joined forces and they had good reason to think this, as our personalities and backgrounds couldn't be any more different.

I'm a lightweight and Cat loves to party. She's always the last one standing on a night out and Cat can be found sitting at the piano leading the singsong, while I sit in the corner pinging a tambourine but when we get together, it just all works out.

Even after all these years, people are still amazed how we've lasted this long.

Cat and I together, proving everyone wrong.

It doesn't really matter what others think 'cause we're perfectly matched in every way, but the part of this song that doesn't fit is that we're not lovers and we never will be – because Cat fancies my 22-year-old son Liam more than she'd ever fancy me.

Cat must have money because she pays for our nights out, but that's not surprising with her offshore Rothesay bank account (and my wife looks after my bank cards).

Cat is so much more than my radio wife.

Everyone needs a great friend like Cat in their life.

She's the 'epicentre of fun' and from the first day I worked with her I knew I'd met a cracker.

So, what things do we have in common? Well, there isn't that much, but when we get together, we have nothing but FUN.

It ain't fiction, it's a fact.

We come together coz OPPOSITES ATTRACT.

The End.

*

And that's the reason Cat is writing the book and not me. I'm scared and excited to read what lies ahead. Cat has photos of me in Amsterdam so I'm going to say she's the nicest, most talented person I've ever met. I'm delighted we are back together on-air and creating mischief once again.

Ewen x

Introduction

Forty-two missed calls from my dad at 6 a.m. The morning after the night before. The night I did NOT have a passionate encounter with a Rolling Stone.

The only problem was Ewen Cameron, my radio co-host, told the nation he suspected I had. This was 2012 and the first time I made a mental note to myself that this spectacular misunderstanding must go in my next book.

It's taken me a while to get here. It's been fifteen years since my first book *The Cat's Whispers* hit the shelves. Top ten in Scotland for seventeen weeks apparently. My faither must have spent a fortune.

Cats famously have nine lives; I'm pretty sure I must be up to number seven or eight by now.

So, what is the nature of this book? The difficult number two. Well, it's part memoir, part diary with hopefully plenty of amusing anecdotes to make you smile.

It's little stories about working with Ewen Cameron, radio tales, behind the scenes fun, hilarious encounters with celebrities, fun interaction with our wonderful listeners and everything in between.

Why did I throw water over Susan Boyle? Why did James McAvoy need salt and vinegar Squares crisps? How did we end up in Olly

Murs' dressing room at Hampden with a kazoo? And why is Ewen head over heels in love with Steven Gerrard? All will be revealed.

It's *Ewen and Cat at Breakfast* – the good, the bad and the nonsense!

I'll also explain why a naked incident with then Labour leader Ed Miliband changed the course of my life and why I waved goodbye to Breakfast radio forever in 2014, only to return six years later. (Hey, Status Quo did it a hundred times, why can't I?)

We've all endured a torrid time with Covid and all the subsequent restrictions. I intend to offer a little glimmer of hope. Know that there are good people out there and that laughter truly is a powerful medicine. I'll focus on some of the positive stories from day-to-day life in lockdown Scotland and hope you'll finish this book with a sense of optimism and know you're welcome in our gang anytime.

First things first. Let me clear my name.

I did not, I never have, and I don't intend to ever pump a Rolling Stone!

Ronnie Wood was the band member in question. I'll set the scene.

Ewen and I were down at the Arqiva Awards in London, the commercial radio Oscars of its day. We were nominated for 'Breakfast Show of the Year'. One of the big names we were up against was Christian O'Connell from Absolute Radio, who was hosting the entire event, so we assumed we had no chance. The fact our table was at the fire exit at the very back of the room seemed to confirm this.

Cutting a very long story shorter, we won! We were scheduled to be broadcasting our show live from London at 6 a.m. the following day. Ewen doesn't really drink so he'd thought this was a great idea; I assumed we wouldn't win so agreed to do it.

After the shock victory, my boss at the time said: 'Why don't you let Ewen do 6 to 7 a.m., then you go in for seven, you'll get a bit of a lie-in and can celebrate tonight.'

We all agreed. This is where the seeds of rumour were sewn. I spotted Ronnie Wood at the bar chatting to his wife and a friend. I told Ewen I was going to try and get a selfie.

I didn't know that Ewen was about to leave, so that was the last I saw of him.

The next morning on air at 6 a.m., Ewen told listeners I wasn't in the studio. He said he didn't know where I was and that I was last spotted at the bar with Ronnie Wood, one of the Rolling Stones.

Never ones to let truth get in the way of a good, embellished story, Ewen and Producer Michael kept up this pretence until I rocked in at 6.50 a.m., ten minutes ahead of schedule.

It was at this point I turned my phone on and saw all the missed calls. I also had text messages from friends in Scotland ranging from: 'Please tell me Ewen is joking,' to 'Hope you got some Satisfaction.'

I had to phone my dad and explain what had happened. I felt like a naughty sixteen-year-old trying to pretend I'd not snogged someone I shouldn't have. I was thirty-nine at the time and in a monogamous relationship.

To this day I think he still wonders if I am telling the truth. Well, Dad, it's true. By the time I got to the bar Ronnie and his wife had left. I didn't even get a photo. As Mick Jagger would say: 'You can't always get what you want.'

Ironically, it was at these awards I had my first conversation with Graham Bryce, the big boss of Bauer who I now work for. He was very complimentary and congratulated me on the award. He then smiled and said: 'You will come over to us eventually and I look forward to it.'

I liked him straight away but remember thinking that was a

superbly confident and misjudged statement. I loved Real Radio. I wasn't going anywhere.

Turns out he was completely right.

I could never have foreseen what would happen on that front.

I'd spent many happy years on Real Radio working with Robin Galloway on *Robin and Cat*; however, one morning, egged on by Robin, our producer Barrie Hodge ran naked past Labour leader Ed Miliband during a political interview. Robin filmed it, the Labour Party complained, Robin and Barrie both got sacked and I ended up with Ewen.

I wasn't in the building at the time of this spontaneous incident and knew nothing of it, but out of the blue my radio family was gone. Barrie has just become a daddy and I know he will sit his daughter down one day and explain the story: 'Darling, if you ever google my name you might get a shock. I was front page of all the papers in Scotland for getting naked for a politician.' I know Barrie. This is a badge of honour. I miss his madness but not his desire to be so at one with nature.

I worked with several other great presenters before Bossman Jay Crawford decided Ewen and I were the right fit. I thought Ewen wasn't right in the dome but somehow it clicked.

We worked together on Real Radio for two years, picking up the Arqiva Award for UK Breakfast Show of the Year, a New York Award for World Personality Show of the year and two Sonys. Ha ha, and you just thought we were just a couple of bams! (We are.)

Real Radio was eventually bought by Global and became Heart. We were the Breakfast team there for a couple of months. Producer Michael left first, then Ewen left to go to STV and I had to stay as I'd signed a panto contract meaning I had to stay on air until at least the end of December. Heart just wasn't for us. Truthfully, we were too

Scottish for it. They didn't get our banter. We all chose our moment to leave and it was the correct decision for every one of us.

So where are we now? At the moment we are on thirteen stations all over Scotland. For six years we've been on from 9 a.m. until 12 noon every Sunday on Clyde 1, Forth1, MFR, Northsound 1, Radio Borders, Tay FM and West FM. Now our main focus is on *Ewen and Cat at Breakfast* on Clyde 2, Forth 2, MFR 2, Northsound 2, Tay 2 and Westsound, Monday to Friday 6 a.m. until 10 a.m.

Producer Carnage is at the helm, Producer Michael is our immediate boss and Producer Victoria is in charge of it all. The band, my friends, is officially back together.

Me

Who am I? I wish I knew.

You might know me from the radio or my last book but if you don't, here's the edited highlights.

I'm from Milngavie, Glasgow, I've just turned forty-nine and still have no idea what I want to be when I grow up and I'm weirdly at peace with that.

Many people in my game pretend they are younger than they are; however, I still have the same best pals I've had since I was four years old: Denise, Debbie, Eilidh, Jane, Lynn, Rhona and Angela F and they'd never let me get away with it. Also, our other childhood friend Angela C didn't make it this far because of cancer and we all owe it to her vibrant happy memory every single day to count aging as a blessing.

My dad is a fiddle-playing former barber (that's a variety act I'd pay to see), my mum, who sadly passed away nine years ago, worked in insurance then ran a wee gift shop. My brother Scott plays the banjo, he's married to celebrant Ann, a former nurse who also works with the pensioners in Knightswood, and my two nieces Kirsteen and Jessica are currently both at university, musically gifted and bring more laughter to my life than they'll ever realise.

I have an MA in Scottish Literature, Theatre, Film and TV

and a Merit Certificate in General Philosophy from Glasgow University (I know, hilarious eh?!!), a Postgraduate Diploma in Journalism from Strathclyde University and a Mensa certificate in a drawer somewhere which I'm sure I got for completing a quiz in a newspaper.

I've been a leaflet hander-ooter, I've worked in a coffee shop, played piano in a ceilidh band, then keyboards in an indie band, I've been a band manager, a sportswriter, a sports TV reporter, a football TV presenter, a travel journalist, a newspaper columnist, a radio presenter, a live events host, an after-dinner speaker, a pantomime fairy / fairy godmother / fat monk / bad pirate and turkey smuggler. I've also tried being an actor in several plays and I've written and toured with two of my own, technically making me a playwright too, and yet I find myself once again working with Ewen. He keeps telling me 'it's meant to be'. I now believe him.

My personal life? Do we have to? Where do I begin? If you read *The Cat's Whispers*, I was with a lovely man affectionately nicknamed Mr Cat. We were at school together and somehow hit the friend-zone. We parted amicably and still send yearly Happy Birthday texts, which is nice. He's met someone else and I'm genuinely happy for him.

Months after we went our separate ways, I met 'The One'. Turns out he wasn't. We had nine great years together before he broke my heart in 2018. I've far too much love for his family to explain here what happened. Let's just say my ability to trust has been totally shattered. Maybe one day we will be friends again but, right now, I still hurt. That said, if Bradley Cooper wanted to give me a call, I'm sure the healing process could speed up a bit. Time will help and I know I must look forwards not backwards. Can you tell I've read far too many mindfulness and self-help books?

And so, I spend most of my time taking my dad on wee jaunts. He's my comedy sidekick and we have such a great laugh together.

I have the best circle of friends and thank my lucky stars daily that I've so many truly wonderful people in my life. You know who you are. They say that a lot in books, don't they? I used to think it was a cop-out because the person can't be bothered listing them individually. I tried, really, I did. I started naming each one individually but then deleted the massive paragraph for the fear of missing out someone out by mistake and being a big disappointment (I need to stop trying to be such a people pleaser). So yes, my wonderful mates, you do all know who you are.

I am still Partick Thistle and Scotland daft and can't wait for the Tartan Army to be allowed out on full manoeuvres again. I'm always trying to lose weight and I'm doing okay at the moment thanks to my daily walks of 15,000 steps. However, this will never be easy for me as I can smell chocolate from a mile away. My dream date is a jar of Nutella and a big spoon.

I love travel, hillwalking, swimming in the sea, clouds, the moon, stars, food, bevvy, animals, live music, I'm an enthusiastic karaoke participant (this means decent performer with questionable vocals), and I love Dick Van Dyke and having a right good laugh. This is also the worst Tinder profile of all time.

I'm honoured to be able to chat for a living and I'm so full of gratitude to my mum and dad who raised me with the prevailing principal of kindness and the ability to find humour in everything. They taught me bugger all about cooking or filling in tax forms, but I've got some cracking stories.

So, there you have it. As they'd sing in *The Greatest Showman*: 'This is me.'

The Cast

EWEN

Where do I even start with the enigma that is Ewen Cameron? Loud, energetic, annoying, hilarious, kind, caring, genuine, frustrating, loud again and possibly one of the most misunderstood bampots in Scotland.

Ewen likes to play the daft wee laddie, but trust me – he is far more intelligent than he likes people to believe. It vexes him that I know this.

Producer Michael and I affectionately once called him ALF. An acronym for A Loveable Fud. Sums him up perfectly. He wears his 'fud' badge with pride.

Ewen's childhood was beyond traumatic but that's his story not mine. All I will say is the fact he's turned out to be a loving husband, great father and wonderful friend is a testimony to his incredible survival skills and determination to succeed.

During the hardest times in my life, he has been there as a constant support and I can't thank him enough for this.

On air we're a great team. We are both ideas people, so life is never dull. Not all of them work, but we have great fun trying.

I remember the first time Bossman Jay at Real Radio put us together on air, I thought: 'Oh naw, he's an eejit.' Then I clocked how he operated. Gregarious, fun, outrageous but deep down relatable and empathetic. Don't get me wrong, he can be a massive pain in the arse as he is NEVER wrong, but I admire his strength of character in believing his own mind.

Most of all he makes me laugh. Really laugh. I never have any idea where we are going with any link as he's so spontaneously aff his heid. Tangents are his speciality. This keeps me on my toes. Nothing we do is ever scripted, as anyone who has ever heard our chaotic chat will be able to tell.

It's natural and I can't pin-point why, but I feel like it just works. I'm glad we are back together at Breakfast even if my Zen, calm and inner peace has been shattered with his relentless energy. We are exactly the same age and I can't wait to see what nonsense we get up to on air as we grow old disgracefully together...

CARNAGE

Paul Carlin. Producer Carnage. CARNAGE. The third part to our little Monday to Friday dysfunctional radio family. Talented, creative, genuine, obsessively hardworking and one of a kind is the best way to describe our Carnage. He can seem quiet and reserved to begin with, but he certainly comes alive on a night out. Like adding water to a Gremlin.

I feel that the time is right to share the story of where his name originated. It is a curious tale involving a glitzy awards do, Chris Tarrant, burly security guards and an imaginary salted peanut.

December 2008. Carnage, or Paul as he was known then, was producing 'Robin and Cat' on Real Radio. We'd been nominated for Breakfast Show of the Year at the GMG Awards in London. I couldn't go because I was playing the fairy in the Pavilion Pantomime in Glasgow.

I remember being dressed in a full fairy costume complete with wand and wings and picking up my phone at the interval on the off chance someone had news. I had twenty-eight messages.

Yes, we'd won which was marvellous, but every message contained either an 'OMG', 'You are not going to believe what happened' or a 'He was removed by security'.

Here is the story as I was told it from several witnesses. Robin and Paul went up on stage to collect the prestigious award from *Who Wants to be A Millionaire?* host Chris Tarrant. It's fair to say they'd both had a glass or two of the good stuff.

Robin accepted the award, shook Tarrant's hand and got into position for the obligatory photo. Then it happened. In slow motion. Paul approached Tarrant. He stood far too close. Cupped the TV star's face in both hands, then inexplicably licked it from chin to forehead. Yes, licked it!

The strapping security guards at the side of the stage could only see Tarrant from behind, trying to frantically brush off this invading slavering Glaswegian and assumed it was some form of assault. Paul was quickly and powerfully escorted off the stage and Carnage was born.

Once the dust had settled and the former *Tiswas* presenter's face had dried, we eventually made Carnage explain what was going through his mind to do such a crazy thing.

I expected him to be riddled with the 'fear', but he wasn't, he just calmly explained: 'I don't know why I did it. I was on stage, he was in front of me and for a moment his face just looked like a giant salted peanut, so I licked it.'

So, there you have it, Carnage by name, occasionally carnage by nature.

I love him. Don't go changing pal ...

PRODUCER MICHAEL

Michael has produced Ewen and me on Breakfast at Real Radio, Heart and our Sunday show.

Michael is the calm to our storm. Apart from being one of the nicest people you could ever hope to meet (everybody LOVES Michael), he is amazing at his job and I'm not just saying this now that he's somehow become our boss.

Michael is the content controller of Forth 1 and 2, plus all of the Scottish stations on the Greatest Hits Network, which is Clyde 2, Forth 2, MFR 2, Northsound 2, Tay 2 and Westsound.

This means he's very important. Which is funny because we've been on so many wild nights out over the years, and I have all the photos and videos.

Michael generally remains in control on these occasions, which makes me even prouder of the moment at the Bauer Awards lunch in London two years ago, when I heard singing from a far corner of the crowded concourse.

'Oh, Inverness is wonderful, oh, Inverness is wonderful. It's got a bridge and a castle – oh, Inverness is wonderful.'

He's very proud of his hometown.

Michael's flat in Wester Hailes became my second home for years during the Edinburgh Festival or any time I was covering for Arlene on *Boogie in the Morning* on Forth 1. (Boogie, Arlene and Marty are a phenomenal Breakfast team and I genuinely love the fact we're now all great friends and playing for the same side).

I was heartbroken when he sold his flat. I couldn't believe he didn't ask me if it was okay!

Seriously though, I am immensely proud of Producer Michael and know he's destined for great things. Right, that's enough; that should secure me at least a tenner pay rise in my new contract if we've not been sacked by then . . .

WEE VIXEN

Wee Vixen, Producer Vic or Victoria Easton-Riley as she's known in the industry. The pint-sized wee lassie fae Falkirk is now basically running everything as content director for Bauer Scotland.

By her own admission she is a teeny toatie wee thing but wow, does she pack a big punch.

Do not ever underestimate this lady. Sharp, ambitious, creative and switched on, she is exactly the right person to be leading this band of merry waifs and strays.

Wee Vixen and I go back a long way. We were both part of the Real Radio madness. Producer Vic, her other title, was working on the Football Phone-in with Ewen and Roughie when I was on Breakfast with Robin.

We have a shared love of being the last person standing at any party and as such naturally gravitated towards each other, recognising kindred spirits (usually vodka for me, rum for her).

It was no surprise to anyone when management made Vixen and I share a room on a work trip to Benidorm. We were the perfect fit. So much so, we did the same again when we ended up in Torremolinos a few years later. What happened in Spain stays in Spain although after a day out with Vixen, I did gatecrash a Spanish wedding at 2 a.m. wrapped in a Saltire, wearing a sombrero and ended up slow dancing with the bride's octogenarian grandfather.

Producer Vic left Scotland to work for Radio 1; it had always been her dream. She worked on many award-winning shows before becoming the producer of Grimmy on the Radio 1 Breakfast Show.

We are lucky to have lured her back north of the border and she's already making a massive difference to the future of radio in Scotland. She's determined to bring through new talent; she's coaching the young team and is heavily involved in promoting diversity and inclusion. She is also all over every show and presenter working for Bauer. Quite frankly, I don't know how she does it.

We all have so much respect for Victoria Easton-Riley but I am never happier than when Wee Vixen comes out to play.

That's the main cast covered. I am so lucky to be working with gifted, ambitious professionals focused on delivering relevant, entertaining content. And Ewen.

MY DAD

I guess it would be remiss of me not to add my dad to my cast list. He is my comedy inspiration and so many of my tales and travels involve him.

My dad, Bobby Harvey, was the Scottish Fiddle Champion in 1962 and 1963. He became an EMI recording artist and toured the world with the White Heather Club and then his own Ceilidh Band.

He is now eighty-six and still full of nonsense. There will be many tales about my dad peppered throughout the book.

In October 2020 after shielding for months we had the following exchange in a garden centre:

Me: What do you want?

Dad: Two cakes.

Me: Do you not want soup?

Dad: No. I want two cakes.

Me: You can't have two cakes.

Dad: HOW NO'?

Me: . . .

. . .

. . .

He had a point. How no' indeed. I relented and his date slice and almond finger were delivered. This was the moment Bobby 'two cakes' Harvey, the world's friendliest gangster name, came into prominence and made Twitter smile. Turns out over 125,000 of you were on his side.

I hang off his celebrity coattails because in 2020, my dad, then aged eighty-five, became a worldwide internet sensation. TV cameras were on his doorstep and he ended up in the national press including the *Sun*, the *Daily Record* and the *Daily Mail*.

Why? He was playing his fiddle on his doorstep for the NHS.

During the Thursday night clap for carers movement, where everyone was encouraged to go outside their homes and show their appreciation for the NHS and key workers, Dad decided to add his own twist just for his neighbours.

He popped on his tartan waistcoat and played a few tunes. His neighbour Ian Lavrie filmed it on his phone, and sent it to me. I popped it on Twitter and BOOM.

For six weeks he put on his doorstep concert, performing many Scottish classics like 'I belong to Glasgow', 'Northern Lights of Aberdeen', 'Flower of Scotland', 'Amazing Grace' and some alternative choices: 'Mary from Maryhill', and 'We'll be Coming Down the Road'.

His neighbours loved it. A bit of fun and a wee socially distanced sing-along.

My Twitter pals eagerly awaited the video each Thursday and they shared it far and wide. They've now had over two million views with reactions coming in from Europe, Canada, New Zealand, Australia and South America to name but a few.

The media were quick to cotton on. 'Cute old pensioner playing songs dressed in tartan' makes for a good 'and finally' story.

My dad is nothing if not loyal. My university pal Nichola Kane produces the news for STV; she phoned and asked if they could film him. He said yes as he is very fond of her. The footage of him playing closed their 6 p.m. news programme all over Scotland. The very next day the BBC called to see if they could film him the following week. He said no. His reason: 'I wouldn't do that to wee Nikki, it's her story.'

That didn't stop SNS, a national photography agency getting in touch too. He was fine with getting photos taken as he was very keen to raise awareness of the NHS and the incredible treatment he's had from them over the years. Every session he dedicated to his medical team at the Beatson who have been treating his prostate cancer for nine years.

I received a message from my friend Emma in Toronto who'd seen a clip of him online. Her parents live in the same street as my dad; I found it hilarious that she'd seen his performance and they hadn't.

For a few years he's been known as 'Cat's Dad'. Now things have returned to how they used to be and how they always should be. Once again, I'm asked: 'Are you Bobby Harvey's daughter?'

I am. And I'm privileged to be so.

Magic Moments

Ewen and I have had so much fun on air over the years, it's difficult to remember all of the capers we've got up to / got away with.

In no particular order here are some of our magic moments.

BEEP THE SHEEP

The day Ewen stopped traffic. Or his wife did. Ewen and Teresa had been playing pranks on each other for weeks. Teresa has a terrific imagination and proved to be a more than equal contender.

It started when Ewen put all the clocks forward in the house. Teresa got up and dressed at 2.30 a.m. thinking it was 6.30 a.m.

As revenge, she popped a laxative in his curry (keeping the marriage spicy I guess!). After this, Ewen decided to unleash his A-game.

This took a lot of work and advanced planning.

With the kids and Teresa tucked up in their beds on a frosty winter night, he texted his neighbour and they met on his driveway in the dark armed with plastic water bottles and over 3,000 balls of cotton wool.

In silence they crept round Teresa's car and got to work. They wet each individual cotton wool ball to stick to the metal bodywork on her car and repeated this process over and over again. With the temperature well below zero, the balls froze to the car in seconds. They didn't stop until her entire car, apart from the windows, was one big ball of cotton wool fluff. It took over an hour.

The next morning, Ewen and I were on air from 6 a.m. as usual and he could not hide his excitement. He knew she had to take the kids to school and would have to use her car with no time to scrape off the woolly topping.

He watched his phone during the songs, the news, the adverts. Waiting. Waiting. Waiting on the message. Then it arrived. 'YOU F***ING A******E.' I think she took it well.

Ewen was delighted but made it SO much worse by telling the nation on air what he had done. He also encouraged anyone who passed her on the road to 'beep the sheep'.

And so poor Teresa had to drive her mortified weans to school getting beeped at by cars, vans, buses and lorries. We called her when she got to the school gates and we all ended up crying with laughter as we could hardly hear her speak for the cacophony of vehicle horns.

Apparently, people were abandoning their cars in the street to get out and take a selfie. Our mobile sheep stopped traffic. He's baa'd but he's not called EWE-n for nothing.

TOMMY BUM DRUMS

Always one of our favourites, Tommy Cunningham, the legendary drummer from Wet Wet Wet, was in the studio one Sunday. Tommy is one of the funniest guys in showbiz and always game for a laugh.

Ewen asked Tommy if he's always loved to drum, to which he replied: 'Aye, I can pretty much drum anything.'

By this he meant that from an early age he was always bashing out a rhythm on anything he could find – tables, plates, empty boxes and, every wean's favourite, the upturned pots and pans kit.

Ewen asked him to drum the microphone, which he did with his just his fingertips. It sounded great. Ewen then asked him to drum the desk, which he did with the palms of his hands and it also sounded fabulous. Then Ewen asked him: 'Can you drum Cat?' He burst out laughing and tried to work out how best to tackle this prospect without getting lifted.

I'm not good with pain so the thought of a muscly drummer skelping any part of me to make an audible drum roll gave me the fear.

Tommy was eyeing up suitable surfaces: my head, my forearm, my knees. So, with my full permission and nothing remotely dodgy going on, I found myself bent over a chair with one of my childhood heroes playing my bum with his hands to their track 'Sweet Little Mystery'.

He certainly had a large surface to deal with and declared I was definitely more a bass drum than a snare.

His bum-drum solo was impressive. It did sting a bit, but it was worth it. Spontaneous moments like these – you can't beat it! I'm adding 'Human Bongos' to my CV.

P.S. What did the drummer call his twin daughters? Anna one, Anna two. Sorry, but it's one of my favourites.

ROLLERCOASTER SPAGHETTI

Back in our Real Radio days, Ewen wanted to recreate his favourite childhood TV memory by eating food on a rollercoaster.

As ridiculous as this sounds, we were inundated with listeners who also thought this would be a hoot. Miraculously, the management at M&D's Scotland's Theme Park in Motherwell offered us the rollercoaster and said they'd even provide all the food and a power-washer at the end.

Thousands of people wanted to join us, but we could only have about twenty for numbers. the *Daily Record* found this on-air narrative highly amusing and asked if they could send a snapper to capture our upside-down adventure.

For maximum impact it was decided that we would all be treated to a two-course meal and two spins on Tornado, the rollercoaster. Spaghetti Bolognese to start, followed by strawberry milkshake. You can imagine.

What I learned about gravity, velocity and sheer bampottery that day, is that no matter how hard you try, you have NO control over food in a paper bowl when being wheeched along and turned upside-down at 80 m.p.h. over 1,000 metres of twisting track.

Within seconds my spaghetti Bolognese splashed over my face and my hair. A large chunk of it flew backwards and skelped the listener sitting three back full on his face. We were all covered, and I mean *covered*. Ewen couldn't even see as he had so much spaghetti sauce in his eyes.

Sides sore from laughing, voices sore from screaming, we came back into the docking bay to be handed a large strawberry milkshake each. We might as well just have poured it over our heads the state we all ended up in.

Despite the power hose at the end and several showers, I could still smell milk on my skin a couple of days later.

The audio and video we recorded on the rollercoaster was a hilarious mix of screams, laughter and splats. Ewen has some crazy ideas. This one was certainly loopy!

WHY DOES IT ALWAYS RAIN ON HIM?

It's always a delight when we get to host small intimate gigs for winners with a big-name act or band. On this occasion the radio station had secured a gig for competition winners with Travis in The Caves in Edinburgh.

This was a big deal. The winners were delighted, and the entire night was geared round seeing Fran Healy and the boys perform their greatest hits. I was on holiday during this particular gig, but I've heard all the stories from everyone present. I've also heard the audio recording of the big moment.

Ewen came on stage and wound up the crowd, getting them to cheer and building the excitement. He's great at this and you can always hear the buzz in the room.

Then in his best presenter's voice: 'Ladies and gentlemen . . . The moment you've all been waiting for . . . Make some noise for one of the best Scottish bands of all time . . . It's . . . Texas!'

Yes, in a gig dedicated to the greatness of one band, he actually introduced them as another. Thankfully they saw the funny side and came out laughing at his genuine mistake and played a storming set.

Almost as good as me being introduced onto the main stage at the Race for Life in Glasgow Green in front of 16,000 disappointed women, as 'Cat Deeley'. I could see it in their eyes: 'Oh, she's let herself go since leaving Ant and Dec . . .'

LAPLAND

Along with all the work we enjoy doing for Cash for Kids, we've also been on several trips with the charity When you Wish Upon a Star.

They make the wishes come true for children with life-limiting conditions.

On two occasions I've been the singing elf on chartered planes to Lapland to visit Santa. I got to use the on-board announcement phone to sing Christmas songs through the plane for all the children and their parents to join in.

The planning behind this trip is immense as each child can need their own personal medical team.

Seeing their eyes light up when landing in Lapland is wonderful as there is always snow. Then it's off to the magical forest where they are met by proper elves and allowed to roam freely and have hot chocolate round fires, a sleigh ride with reindeer, go on a fast husky sled or be whisked through the forest on the back of a carriage pulled by a skidoo.

There's hot dogs, entertainment and fireworks before everyone is bussed to a local hotel for dinner and the big one – meeting Santa and Rudolph. They come into the hotel as it is too cold for the children outside. He is a very well house-trained reindeer!

This part is so emotional. I know what every single parent is thinking when their child goes up for their present and cuddle from Santa and it breaks my heart, but this is a day of memory making and joy.

On the way back to the airport we stop off at the Arctic Circle shopping village, decked out with lots of twinkly lights and Christmas decorations.

The last time we visited, we were just back on the bus when the courier looked up to the sky and said: 'I think we are about to get a show.'

It was as if the Universe knew these families deserved something special and we were treated to a dazzling display of the Northern Lights. Back on the plane, about twenty minutes into the flight, the captain said we were about to fly through them so dipped the cabin lights. The effect was magical. Gently flashing turquoise, deep green, bright purple, pink, violet colours like the best light show you've ever seen. The plane was totally silent. Many of the children were sleeping and their parents watched the greatest show in nature. I looked at Ewen, and, like many others, there were tears trickling down his face. As the father of three children, I know how hard this trip is for him, but we have to be the happy ones.

These families deserve these special moments, and I will never forget this flight and the strength of emotions felt. I like to think this flight home was nature giving every single one of those parents a big cuddle and the strength to carry on . . .

WHAT'S IN EWEN'S ATTIC?

Like a classic soap opera, this saga ran on and on over our Sunday show for months. Ewen and his wife were struggling to sleep because something was in their attic.

Nobody wanted to go and see what it was. Ewen recorded audio of the clanging noises and our listeners all had an opinion. Mice, birds, squirrels, rats, bees, big spiders and even a lost bird of prey were suggested.

Ewen asked me what I thought it was and I said with confidence: 'It's clearly a small Victorian child.'

I had no idea how much this throwaway line would come back to, ironically, haunt him. For weeks everywhere Ewen went, the bank, the shops, the supermarket somebody would shout, 'Alright Ewen, how's your small Victorian child?' or 'Have you still got that small Victorian child in your attic?' You can imagine the looks from those not in the know. To this day we never found out what was making the noise. They eventually paid a man with a torch to investigate but he found no trace of anything.

My theory stands; they should just be glad that little Mary-Euphemia is a friendly sort.

THAT GAME!

It was all thrown together very last minute. Producer Vic and Producer Michael thought it could be fun for Steven Mill and Ewen, who present the *Big Saturday Football Show*, to host a one-off live special for the Serbia versus Scotland game – the play-off game for a place in the Euros. I was asked to join the presentation line-up as the token member of the Tartan Army. I've followed Scotland for years and I've got plenty of fun stories to share, even if my memories of what happened in the actual matches are a bit hazy. Standard, for the typical foot-soldier.

With social distancing firmly in place, we set up a makeshift studio in the former canteen. We were to discuss the game live but not commentate on the action. What happened was a succession of hilarious stories, incidents and the highest level of drama you could imagine.

I'm not sure how we got onto the topic but at one point I told the story of being stuck on a minibus in London during Euro '96 – the police wouldn't let traffic move for hours. Steven asked the question I feared: 'What happened if you needed to go?' I would like to apologise to my friend Fiona, who skilfully had to utilise an empty Irn Bru bottle at the back of the bus, for sharing this story. Her three children were appalled. Her husband found it hilarious and quite a talent!

Then at a vital moment in the match our TV screen died. We assumed the feed from Serbia had gone down but no, I spotted that Producer Michael had inadvertently walked past the TV the wrong way and pulled the plug out with his leg! Imagine if we'd missed a goal. Most people will know how that night turned out. Scotland were 1–0 up until the dying seconds and, just as a country was about to party, the killer blow, they equalised, 1–1. Extra-time was the longest in the history of football and when the game went to penalties, we all assumed we would go out. Turns out Scotland are magnificent at penalties and David Marshall made the save which turned him into a hero.

The audio for this historical save, and the realisation that we had finally qualified for a tournament after years of disappointment, is pure raw emotion. You are in the room with us. We don't hold back. We can't. It's real. We had no idea that this single moment would lead to two things 1) A big radio award nomination and 2) The worst hangover of my life.

Number one I shall address later in this book, number two I shall deal with right now. Oh dear. Talk about not being match fit! I love a night out, but I'd not been drinking in nearly a year. I need people to party with, so I never drink in the house. My lockdown has been teetotal. Until this night. Well, we partied. Hard. In the canteen, miles apart from each other, we sat in our own wee corners and cracked open the bevvy. We were euphoric. Then it was 6 a.m. and we were still there. Then it was 11 a.m. and I was on a couch sleeping in a frozen conference room. I later discovered that Steven Mill was in reception sleeping on a couch under a saltire flag. Ewen, who had the sense not to drink and had gone home, slept and came back for the Breakfast Show, kept checking up on both of us with water and treats. I got a taxi of shame home about lunchtime and didn't eat solids for another twenty-four hours.

Management, thankfully, turned a blind eye as we hadn't really broken any rules (well, apart from sleeping on the couches) and we had the best excuse in the world: 'It's the first time we've qualified for anything since 1998! Cheers to that!'

RANDOM FUN STUFF

Also, in the endless search for amusing radio content:

* I attempted to sing the fat landlady Madame Thénardier part in *Les Miserables* in front of 3,000 people at the Armadillo. Thankfully it's a comedy role so I think I got away with it.

* Ewen and I both tackled a charity shark dive at Deep Sea World. The tiger sharks were more terrified of Ewen's teeth than vice versa.

* Ewen popped on heels and a tight-fitting dress to host the Cash for Kids little black dress lunch. Despite the Chewbacca legs, he certainly had a finely turned ankle.

* I've trekked through the Thai jungle to Burma with listeners, and also tackled the Great Wall of China for charity too.

* Alan Logan, one of the nurses from Glasgow Children's Hospital who I met on the Great Wall of China, is Mel C's biggest fan. I invited him into the radio studios to record a pretend interview about 'fundraising'. He had no idea Mel C was about to turn up, who was in on my prank. His reaction was priceless. He was stunned, star-struck then managed to hold down a decent conversation about her albums, tours and future plans. They got lovely photos together before Mel C left and Alan screamed and ran out the building to phone his mammy.

* Ewen and I took very opposing sides on our Sunday show when he revealed he was going to book an apartment in the same resort as his son Liam on his first boys' holiday to Faliraki. They need to make their own mistakes like we did. In 1991 in Santa Ponsa I learned never to drink a shot called 'brain damage' ever again. My other friend eventually learned that the Spanish waiter she fell deeply in love with was not 'her' Juan. He had in fact many!

To this day Ewen still gets chastised, mostly from dads in the supermarket, about wanting to spy on his son. He eventually didn't go. Liam did. He returned in one piece, just like Aunty Cat predicted!

Celebrities

We've been lucky enough to interview many household names from the world of music, theatre, comedy, TV and film for our show. Some of them have been our heroes (Kelly Jones) and some were just fulfilling contractual obligations (Mark from Westlife).

In no particular order here are some of my top picks over the years.

SHARLEEN SPITERI

My first Texas gig was in 1989 in the Glasgow Pavilion with Gun as the support act. Over thirty years later they're still delivering new music and touring with as much gusto and enthusiasm as they did back in the day.

Much of the success of Texas is down to the talent and personality of lead singer Sharleen Spiteri. She's incredible. People either want to date her or to be her, and she's a hoot on a night out.

We once ended up having a random night on the sauce with the band in a hotel in Wales. She'd been booked to play a set at a radio conference we were attending. Ewen was star-struck. I could tell he fancied her as he went all awkward and giggly. Sharleen sensed it and wound him up to perfection. She has such a sharp wit, it was a joy to watch. We sneaked in a quick interview for our Sunday show and she was on brilliant form. She revealed her only diva-like dressing room demand is for a nice Diptyque candle. Ewen, all gushy and trying to impress said: 'I'll buy you one.' To which she shot him down with, 'I know what you're like, you'd knock it from a chapel.' Boom!

Later that night we met the band in the hotel bar, and she invited us to join them. We laughed lots and Ewen stole her chips.

I told her my brother had bought her old car years ago. Once she realised it was a true story, and I wasn't from some Texas-obsessed stalking family, our professional friendship was back on track. Ewen and I love having her on the show. She's sassy, self-deprecating and ultimately brilliant fun. I can't wait for the now twice-rescheduled gig at the Hydro. Hope she still has chips and a smelly candle.

JAMES McAVOY

The A-list Hollywood actor came to join us on our Breakfast Show at Real Radio live, the morning after the night before. What were his PR people thinking?

It was the morning after *Filth* premiered in Edinburgh; writer Irvine Welsh came to the studios, too. I have no idea what time that pair finished partying, but our resultant interview was as dangerous as it was hilarious. After the show finished James asked if he was okay to hang out with us in our studio for a while as he couldn't face going on the road again. We weren't going to knock that back and so I ended up buying him everything I could think of from our vending machine to help his hangover. It's not all lobster canapes, this media lark. He was desperate for a cup of tea and was over the moon to see I'd also sourced salt and vinegar Squares crisps, which he scudded with delight.

SUSAN BOYLE

It's not every day you get to pour a bucket of water over a global superstar in a swimsuit, but we shall get to that later.

Susan Boyle, or SuBo, has popped into our studios many times since finding fame on *Britain's Got Talent* back in 2009. She always brings chocolates and is a sweet lady who is really too nice to be near the crazy world of show business apart from the need to share her incredible talent.

I once interviewed her in her dressing room at the Kings Theatre in Glasgow after an amazing sell-out show. She was shattered and happy and asked me if I had my famous kazoo with me. (There is usually always one in my bag.) She asked if she could have a shot (she did) and then when I told her she could keep it, she was so excited and genuinely grateful. It was like I'd given her a million pounds. Worried management types poked their head through the door in shock at the commotion; I can only assume they thought I'd given her some kind of mad drug pipe.

My favourite Susan Boyle story was during the Ice Bucket challenge phase in 2014. I was nominated by a friend and decided to nominate Susan for a laugh, never thinking she would actually be game. Back then her pal Sadie looked after her; she sent me a text after hearing me on the radio. 'Susan is up for it. Do you want to come to her house?'

At this point Susan was a mega-star on both sides of the Atlantic with number one albums and adoring fans.

Yet, I found myself in the back garden of her parent's old house in Blackburn surrounded by friends and family. Kirstie the local butcher was there along with Margaret and John who put her bins out if she's away filling stadiums on world tours.

Susan emerged in a dressing gown carrying an American flag; turns out her hero and new pal Donny Osmond had also nominated her. She plonked herself down on a chair in the middle of the garden, stripped off the dressing gown and sat in her green floral swimsuit awaiting her freezing cold shower.

Before I upended the water she said: 'Thanks to Cat and Donny Osmond for the nomination.' It felt as wonderfully surreal as it sounded.

With a small rubber duck balanced on her head, Susan sang her iconic audition song from *Les Miserables*, 'I Dreamed a Dream' before I poured gallons of icy water over her. The angelic notes were replaced with howls of laughter.

After drying off we went into her house for pizza. Susan showed me her new skills on the piano; she'd had a few lessons. She knew that I play a bit and what unfolded was one of the most unexpected but fun musical sessions of my life. I played the piano, she stood at my shoulder and sang. We played some Burns songs, *Les Mis* and 'Caledonia'. She was still dripping wet from her soaking and her friends were more interested in the buffet than the pair of us. It was like Hogmanay in the 1970s. Glorious.

As I drove away in my car, I saw her running up the street after me. I thought I must have left something so I reversed and wound down my window. She then gave me a bottle of posh Champagne and said with genuine gratitude: 'Thank you so much for coming out to do that.' She really is a wee star . . .

THE STEREOPHONICS

Oh dear. Not my finest professional moment. The problem was that I've been in love with Kelly Jones the lead singer since they first came on the scene in 1992. Those eyelashes, those eyes, that voice. You get the drift.

When I was told to record an hour-long Christmas special with the band, I pretended I had all the muso knowledge required to handle them.

On the day Kelly and Javier, the drummer, were sitting in the studio opposite me, I'd put on a full face of make-up and even brushed my hair.

He is utterly beautiful in real life and has an aura that is so hypnotic I found myself daydreaming and, this is embarrassing, just staring at him.

Producer Carnage was in charge of the technical side of things (yes, we've worked together a long time), and at one point had to gently skelp me on the back of the head to get things started.

The problem, you see, is that I genuinely thought I'd asked Kelly my opening question and was waiting for his answer. In my head I had. Unfortunately, in real life I hadn't. I had simply smiled at him adoringly.

Thankfully, he was so unfazed by my ridiculous fan-girl behaviour he just laughed and once we were up and running it turned out to be a brilliant interview.

He told me about the time he ended up by chance playing a gig in the same city as 'a couple of my pals'. They ended up at the same hotel for late-night drinks. As they kept getting mobbed by fans, the trio decided to take a couple of bottles of Jack Daniels and their guitars and went to a local park where they sat on the grass in the dark getting very merry and having a great jamming session. I can only imagine how incredible it would have been to have walked past Kelly Jones, Noel Gallagher and Paul Weller giving it laldy. This is without doubt the coolest show business story I've ever heard, and it made me love him even more. Will he ever realise I'm his perfect woman? 'Maybe tomorrow.'

THE PROCLAIMERS

I love these guys. Their music, their sense of humour. Ewen and I were invited to the filming of their 'Spinning Around' video. It was directed by *Little Britain* star Matt Lucas, and everybody made us feel so welcome on set. It was lovely to see everyone in action, even though Craig and Charlie were both dressed as sweet old ladies.

I've played my trusty kazoo with them at T in the Park; okay it was during an interview backstage but it's still a cool claim to fame. They also invited me and my friend Joyce Falconer from *River City* backstage at their gig in the ABC a few years back. I remember they offered me a large whisky which I accepted because I didn't want to appear rude. I hate whisky but I remember thinking you don't get much more Scottish than this – a dram with The Proclaimers! I'd walk 500 miles for that . . .

BOYZONE

In another Christmas Special I had to interview Ronan Keating and Stephen Gately. They were hilarious and like naughty brothers full of nonsense. Their camaraderie was so clear to see and they told tales about each other with such love and affection. It broke my heart when Stephen passed away a few years later and I saw footage of Ronan at the funeral.

We talked about their best Christmas ever and Stephen said he had great fun at Ronan's house one year playing with his daughter's new Barbie. He laughed, 'He should have known then what I was like.'

They were in no hurry to get back on the interview trail and, like several others before, asked if they could stay in the studio with me for some respite. I got them some juice and treats, and we sat for at least another half hour just talking absolute nonsense. They were great fun and lovely people.

OLLY MURS

I have no real recollection of how it came to pass that Ewen and I were in Olly Murs' dressing room at Hampden before he went on stage to open for Robbie Williams. I am sure he must have had a new album out or something.

We were met by his people at the reception and whisked down to the pitch-level corridors I knew so well from my previous life as a trackside reporter for STV.

Olly was charming, hyper, nervous and very welcoming. He told us to help ourselves to anything we wanted. I liked the look of his laptop but Ewen said he meant from the fridge. He only had beer and water. As I don't like beer, in a role reversal from the norm, Ewen had beer and I had the water.

Ewen mentioned I was talented on the kazoo and did he want me to join him on stage. Olly said maybe not this time, but he was happy to do a dressing-room duet. I delved into my bag to pull out my kazoo and we recorded a good minute of 'Troublemaker' before we both burst out laughing. Technically I've now played Hampden!

GARRY SPENCE AND STEVIE G

I've been friends with Garry Spence for years. Even when he's worked at rival radio stations we were always pals. We met through mutual friends at T in the Park about fifteen years ago and just clicked. He's funny, kind and has proven to be a strong friend through the good times and the bad.

Garry now presents the biggest drivetime show in Scotland. He's a cool club DJ and has interviewed some of the biggest stars in the world. He also knows absolutely *nothing* about football.

July 2020. We are allowed into pubs, socially distanced, and have drinks brought to us if we've booked a table and given contact details in advance.

I'm out day-drinking with Garry and our other pal Louise

Robertson, another truly awesome person and extremely talented news producer at the BBC.

We walk into the Chip in Ashton Lane where we have a table in the corner. However, to get to it, we pass Partick Thistle boss Ian McCall, Rangers boss Steven Gerrard and Rangers assistant and former Scotland legend Gary McAllister sitting at a table.

I've known Ian and Gary for years through working in football, so I stop for a socially distanced chat. Stevie G introduced himself, which I thought was lovely and he proved to be a very nice man indeed.

Louise and Garry join the chit chat. I did mention we had been drinking. I'm talking to Ian about Thistle and all I can hear is Garry Spence having this overly excited chat with Gary McAllister.

'I'm Garry with two rs like Barry and Larry. How many rs do you have?'

I can tell our new pals are on their first drink and decide it's time to wish them a pleasant evening and usher Garry with two R's over to our corner.

He's buzzing and says he knows nothing about football but has pals in Inverness who are Rangers daft. I start talking to the barman and Garry disappears, I assume to the loo.

But no. The coolest DJ I know is over asking Stevie G for a two-metres-away selfie. I mouth, 'Sorry' to Ian McCall.

Fast forward an hour or so and we go to leave. I stop to say bye and Garry is once again magnetically drawn to former England captain Stevie G. (Ewen will be so jealous. He loves him too.)

Garry almost reclaimed his dignity by apologising for the selfie before destroying his street cred by dropping this now-legendary line: 'Honestly, Stevie, the transport links in Bishopbriggs are second to none.'

I'm not sure if he was trying to persuade the Liverpool legend to be his next-door neighbour or was merely sharing his awe of his hometown's proximity to the M8 and M80.

Either way there was only one conclusion – time for the final whistle and UP THE ROAD!

THE NICE ONES

Most celebrities fall into this category. I've liked most of them to be fair. Many of them are on a relentless tour of UK media outlets and are frazzled by the time they get to Scotland. We've interviewed the Saturdays, One Direction, The Wanted, JLS, Sarah Harding and Cheryl Cole from Girls Aloud, all of whom proved to be good fun. James Arthur was a little prickly with Ewen, but I liked him.

Take That were fantastic, Katy Perry was bonkers but fun, James Blunt is a brilliant interviewee and very self-deprecating, while the veterans are always grateful to be relevant again. Rick Astley, Gabrielle, Tony Hadley, Go West and Beverley Knight were all a joy. Interviewing Jason Donovan was a hoot as this time it was Ewen who was totally star-struck.

Most of the time the celebrities are great craic, but their 'people' can be difficult. They are basically just trying to protect their artists and I get that, but they are often much more aggressively negative than is required.

I remember interviewing Little Mix and their 'people' arrived half an hour before the band to brief us on what we could NOT ask. That week rumours were rife that Perrie Edwards had split up from then fiancé Zayn Malik from One Direction. Under no circumstances were we to broach the subject. Until we agreed to this, we were not allowed to meet the band. Obviously, we said that we would play ball, and as is so often the case, the artist did not have the same rules. We played the game and did not ask and within the first three minutes Perrie jumped right in and said: 'I bet you want to ask me about Zayn – well, we have split up and are no longer together.'

We could see their London PR people weeping into their soya milk decaffeinated lattes, but we'd done nothing wrong. Sometimes they really just want to talk.

THE GRUMPY ONES

This is a short list as generally most people have been nice. I only have two on my list that I don't ever wish to meet again. Mark from Westlife was one. I had to record an hour-long Christmas special with the band. He read an *OK!* magazine throughout our interview, flicking the pages loudly. On mic I asked him if he was bored as I was so cross at this blatant waste of my time. Thankfully his bandmate Nicky more than made up for him and was super lovely. Maybe Mark was just having a bad day.

Heather Small from M People is the other one. She seemed really snappy the day we met and I thought she was pretty mean to the stage crew at Big in Falkirk. In my opinion, that's not okay but, again, things might just not have been going well. I'll give her the benefit of the doubt too, but I now can't listen to M People (my life is surprisingly okay for this).

These Are a Few of My Favourite Things

One of the best things about being a former columnist in what was Scotland's largest-selling paper, the *Sunday Mail*, for nearly a decade is that I have a thorough archive of my life in the form of wee short happy stories.

I joined in February 2010 and finished up in March 2019, a whopping 471 columns later. I never missed a single Sunday and worked under three editors, lasting way longer than I thought I would. The day my final column was published was the week my first play opened. The world moves in mysterious ways.

In my column I shared stories about my friends, my work, Ewen, a lot about Ewen, and even more about my dad. He became my comedy foil, and he loved every second of it. As Mickey McMonagle, my final magazine editor, commented: 'You know wee Bobby is the real star and talent of your family?' I know my place. He is right.

Lorna Hughes, the current *Sunday Mail* editor has kindly agreed for me to share some of these old columns because this book is for Cash for Kids.

This is a lovely way to have a quick trip down memory lane. It is not, in any shape or form, a devilishly cunning cut and paste technique to up my final book word count. It is not. I promise.

So, before we get to the daily diary detailing the emotional stress and joy of working on *Ewen and Cat at Breakfast*, let's have a look back at a few of my favourite things . . .

15 JANUARY 2012 – CELEBRATING MY 500TH PANTOMIME PERFORMANCE AT THE PAVILION

Last night at 7.30 p.m., I stepped onto the stage at the Pavilion Theatre in Glasgow for my 500th consecutive pantomime performance.

In the last six years, over half a million people have seen me in fairy wand-waving action and I'm beyond grateful for the opportunity.

This has been an incredible theatrical journey for me. I've been a fairy five times and even loved being the fat monk Friar Nip 'n' Tuck in *Robin Hood*.

As a child I was obsessed with panto and could only dream of witnessing at first hand the glittery costumes, energetic dancing, boos and laughs the goodies and baddies generate.

I've reached this milestone with Scotland's finest dame Dean Park. He's played the dame all over the country for years and goes through more make-up a season than Kim Kardashian on holiday. In six years, he's had over 3,500 costume changes.

We had a wee chinwag in the wings and ended up crying with laughter at some of the fun times we've shared.

My top ten include:

1. Dean as the dame in a tilted bed with design stars and panto debutants Colin and Justin sliding uncontrollably on silk sheets in every direction except the way they wanted to go.

2. *High Road* hottie and *Wizard of Oz* star Derek Lord waving goodbye in his normal clothes at the stage door heading for his train and suddenly realising we'd not done the finale walk down yet.
3. The performance for the hearing-impaired when the flamboyant interpreter got the giggles attempting the correct sign language for a 'wee jobby'.
4. Jim Davidson and Billy Armour as Robin Hood and the Sheriff of Nottingham in the archery scene after they'd both been given several Hogmanay drams. Comedy ad-libbing at its best.
5. Des McLean and Steven Purdon dressed as the Tinman and the Strawman standing in Renfield Street for a sneaky fag between shows when a drunk asked for a cigarette, took it, thanked them and walked away as if it was the most normal thing in the world.
6. Choreographer and lead dancer Lynsey Brown nearly decapitating herself with a wig strap while trying to impress a hot schoolteacher sitting in the front row with an overambitious flip.
7. Writing naughty words on my hand and showing them to make Shellsuit Bob, Steven Purdon, giggle during the finale dance.
8. Panto-hater and *Daily Record* sports guru Jim Traynor's dismay when I made him sing 'head, shoulders, knees and toes' in front of 1,500 baying children.
9. Joyce Falconer as the Wicked Witch of the West getting stuck in a ten-foot mechanical chrysanthemum. Her broad Doric accent muffled by laughter: 'I cannae get oot the flooo-errr' as her wee stripy leg tried to kick through a leaf.
10. Derek Lord again as the Wizard of Oz emerging upwards from the stage trapdoor wearing two hats by mistake and still holding and reading from his script!

Panto can be tough, that rare tumbleweed moment when time stands still as that forgotten line refuses to appear is horrific and I'd like to gloss over my shameful tequila-flavoured hangover in *Pinocchio* 2009 where I had to have a 'moment' between scenes dressed as the blue fairy.

Nothing makes you assess your lifestyle as much as having to squeeze into a toilet for a tactical spew between scenes wearing sparkly wings, roller boots and a tutu. The shame!

However, nothing makes you feel more alive than seeing people smile, laugh and simply join in. Special needs children and pensioners particularly adore the show and I well up when I see their joy.

I'm sure Dean and I would both like to thank everyone for allowing us to make OUR dreams come true. Bring on the next five hundred, we can handle it – oh yes, we can ...

Update: To date I've performed in over seven hundred pantos at the Pavilion, in my humble opinion one of the finest theatres to play in the world. In my last two roles, I was cast as a bad pirate followed by an evil turkey smuggler. Where are my Cinderella days? They're behind me!

Ewen joined the panto cast in 2016 for *Elfie's Magical Adventures* alongside Liam Dolan, Stephen Purdon and Grado to name but a few. It will come as no surprise to anyone who saw these performances that Ewen and Cat the panto double act did not make a return. He was a hoot in the cast, but he'll be the first to admit that remembering lines and acting did not come naturally to him. We were cast by manager Iain Gordon as 'Smart Cat and Useless Ewen'. On this occasion, the theatre critics might have agreed. Ewen knows he will not be up for any Oscars, Baftas or Tonys anytime soon, but he's certainly entertaining and many football fans still boo him in the street, so don't ever write him off. I still think there might be potential.

For the last few years, I've found my wings again and perform in 'Michelle McManus's Winter Wonderland'. I play Fairy Bampot and write and perform comedy sketches and songs with Michelle. We have the fabulous Soundsational Choir on stage with us which sounds epic, and it is a night of Christmassy magic with all your favourite songs and some fairy mischief along the way. Not only is Michelle my friend, I can honestly say she's one of the nicest, hardest-working girls you'll ever meet, and I defy anyone not to have tears in their eyes at her version of 'Holy Night'. World class!

20 JANUARY 2013 – EWEN AND I ARE LOOKING FOR NEW CHALLENGES
Sax in the city and a trip to A&E.

It's nearly three weeks into January and most of us are clinging onto our New Year's resolutions and teetering on the precipice of defeat. I was fascinated to read the survey revealing the UK's top ten aims for 2013:

1. Spending more time with the family. I'd have thought after the festive period spending LESS time would have featured, too!
2. Fall in love. Turns out we all want a bit of romance after all.
3. Help others achieve their dreams. I recently told my pal NOT to use the 3 a.m. picture of her clutching chips and cheese, tongue out and crossing her eyes as her internet dating photo thus potentially helping her achieve number 9.
4. Quit smoking. Top advice for all but those in the Arbroath fish industry.

5. Learn something new and exciting. More of this later.
6. Get fit and healthy (yawn).
7. Live life to the fullest (let's party!!).
8. Spend less and save more (instantly negating point four).
9. Get organised. I have a brilliant Feng Shui book if only I could find it amid my clutter.
10. Predictably, losing weight.

Recently on Real Radio Breakfast we were discussing these and decided point five – the ambition to learn something new and exciting was the most interesting one of all.

My co-host Ewen Cameron and I agreed a challenge to learn something new and exciting within a period of ONE month before revealing our new skills together to a select audience.

Quick to respond, our darling listeners suggested we embarked upon everything from decorating cupcakes, pole-dancing, juggling, wing-walking, riding a unicycle and hand-gliding.

A special mention must go to Rikke Pederson who offered to teach us Danish in Denmark (Internet radio listening can provide interesting banter), Margaret Lumsden who suggested we learn Torvill and Dean's ice-skating classic *Boléro*, and Mark from Airdrie whose textual suggestion tried to hit the spot. 'Try Tantric sex.' Er, no.

Several people suggested learning sign language, which is a fabulous idea but wouldn't really work too well as a radio feature.

Eventually we chose an individual challenge which will make for a bizarre 'big reveal'. Despite never having lifted a brass instrument, I'm going to learn the saxophone and entertain a crowd with the famous solo from Gerry Rafferty's 'Baker Street'. I've got two weeks left to complete my challenge and I'll only say one thing: being adept at the kazoo has not helped. It's difficult!

Ewen, on the other hand, inspired by the Olympics and Tom Daley in trunks, had opted to make a splash by learning how to swan dive from the top platform at the Edinburgh Commonwealth Pool. His bravado is diminishing. He can dive bomb from the pool edge brilliantly, but the biggie is ten metres or just over thirty-two foot high and he's discovered a new fear of heights.

And so the plan is that in a fortnight (date yet to be confirmed as health and safety issues to sort), I'm going to be dressed in an evening gown standing on top of the high platform at the Commonwealth pool playing 'Baker Street' on the sax as my co-host, wearing only a hint of Lycra, plummets to a standing ovation or a trip to casualty.

Already the ridiculous prospect is giving me the heebie-jeebies, although I reckon that's more to do with seeing Ewen in Speedos than the actual challenge.

Please wish us luck with this madness, we shall either sink or swim with this one.

Update: Thanks to a lesson from a student at The Royal Conservatoire in Glasgow, I managed a recognisable rendition of the famous Sax solo on air. It wasn't nice to listen to, but you could at least hear what it was meant to be. The controlled blowing technique is a lot harder to master than I thought.

Ewen's diving career plummeted spectacularly during lesson one. He belly-flopped into the pool while attempting a one-and-a-half somersault from the lowest board and did in fact end up in A&E with cracked ribs and a crushed ego. His medical team told him NOT to resume this challenge. Dramatic as ever, he certainly caused a big splash . . .

30 JUNE 2013 – MY FIRST PROFESSIONAL MODELLING ASSIGNMENT

It has been said many times before, but Ewen and I have the perfect faces for radio. Still, for this one-off special assignment it was game on . . .

There are some professions in life you're just never going to excel in – I have decided after a brief sojourn into the heady world of modelling I'm going to leave it to the professionals.

While I am sure this will come as a massive relief to the likes of Naomi, Claudia, Kate and Cara, I've given it a go and it really isn't for me.

It was a sobering reaction to how one is aesthetically perceived when my work colleagues heard of my task.

Once the laughter had subsided and astonishment kicked in, they began to ponder just who would be desperate enough to ask me to model, and what. Guesses ranged from shoes (despite being a disaster from neck to knees I have a finely turned ankle, don't you know) hands (I have two) to tents (how those out with the camping fraternity would describe my general style of fashion!).

It gives me great pride to reveal I was asked by the club I've supported since I was little, Partick Thistle, to help with the new strip launch. I was to 'model' in the photo session for the press and television cameras with three first team players showcasing the new and rather splendid red, yellow and black striped garment.

I'll not lie; this offer was made and accepted at 2.30 a.m. one Saturday night in a chips and cheese shop on Great Western Road. I'm sure this is how Vivienne Westwood nurtures her muses too.

My mate Michelle had been working for Thistle in a PR capacity and I can only conclude that she reckoned if she got me onside, I'd mention the new strip on air with Ewen and in this *Sunday Mail* column. She's not daft.

She has known me for years and is very aware of my modelling limitations. I'm sure she must have bought the chips as somehow, I agreed.

Fast forward several weeks, launch date arrives and I have the fear. You see, despite the fact I have my photo taken often through my job, I am physically incapable of posing for a sensible snap.

Six years as a panto fairy means I generally stick up my wand arm (the right) in the air, or seek some form of comedy prop. In the absence of this, I either do 'jazz hands' or point at something or someone with both index fingers extended like ET.

I had three diva-like demands:

1. Under no circumstances would I be seen in shorts.
2. My top had to be a baggy XL man's one just in case of an unflattering cling.
3. No clichéd players lifting the bird shot (imagine the guilt of injuring your own team).

The shoot location was the Kelvingrove Art Gallery and my fellow models were Jags stars Stephen O'Donnell, Scott Fox and John Baird.

With lip gloss on, I nervously joined the boys for our shoot. The snappers were very polite and encouraging for the first few snaps. I was to act like a fan with arms splayed, yes, I can do that, and then they asked sweetly if it would be possible to remove me from the set-up – and this was the photo most papers used the next day!

The dreaded 'lift' question was raised but I turned the tables and offered to lift one of the players instead. I'd like to apologise, Mrs

Baird: that is how I ended up giving your husband John a piggyback in the national press.

While I love my club, I'm going to leave it to the boys next time. It turns out vertical stripes are not as flattering as fashionistas would have you believe.

Update: Eight years on and I still can't pose for a sensible photo. With lifelong body issues hiding under baggy tops, I'm beyond awkward and now accept that there is only one way for me to go. Jazz hands all the way baby, jazz hands all the way.

20 JULY 2014 – BYE BYE BALADO

My final T in the Park at its second, but finest, home. I tried for years to persuade Ewen to join me, but the thought of mud and the portaloos kept him away. In retrospect this was probably for the best. T in the Park was about endurance. I'd have had to tuck him up in his tent after two beers in the middle of the afternoon!

It's exactly one week since the last musicians played the final chords at the finest festival venue in the world.

Okay, so I've yet to experience Glastonbury, Coachella or Woodstock, but for years T in the Park at Balado has been my favourite weekend of the year and by all accounts the bands and artists loved it just as much as I do.

I've survived sixteen out of eighteen Ts at Balado and have watched with admiration as the festival has grown in size, stature and success.

Over 2.7 million people have enjoyed the site and I know the good people of Kinross are gutted that a health and safety directive about an underground pipeline has brought it all to an end.

The camaraderie, festival fun and camping capers are often just as memorable as the blistering performances on stage.

Musically there are several stand-out moments for me. In 2001, Noel Gallagher's impromptu acoustic duet with Paul Weller; in 2004 Snow Patrol's Gary Lightbody breaking down in tears as the audience sang 'Run' in the King Tuts Tent; Primal Scream in the same tent in 2008; and being pleasantly surprised by Lady Gaga in 2009 and Beyoncé in 2011, neither of whom are really my thing.

I've lost count of the number of times I've danced to The Killers, the Stereophonics, Travis, Biffy Clyro and Paolo Nutini and watched them progress through the years from small venues to main stage acts.

For sing-alongs you'll never beat The Proclaimers, although Deacon Blue's greatest hits in 2013 was incredible as second-generation teenage fans belted out the words that meant so much to their parents.

I've been lucky enough to experience all sides of T in the Park at Balado, from the crammed Citylink bus to the site (affectionately known as 'the jakey bus') to the VIP area and media village to interview bands.

I've worked hard and partied harder. I've danced lots and slept little.

Since 2009 I've camped with one of the local farmers, Jim Patterson, and his wife May, in their front garden at the Gallowhill campsite after an impromptu meeting with their daughter Fiona Hynds and her husband Stephen (both brilliantly bonkers). After a 'special juice' too many, she suggested I camp with her family who live on site. I agreed. I don't think they ever expected me to turn up!

However, I did and since then they have become my surrogate T family. Both in their late seventies, they out-party us every year and provide a constant stream of breakfast rolls, homemade dumpling, and a rousing Scottish singsong whenever we are fading. I will miss them as much as Balado and have already promised to return to 'T in the caravan-park' – a new one-day festival for, er, us.

I've loved Balado. Playing my kazoo with The Proclaimers singing along during a live radio interview remains a golden moment, putting Tennent's big boss George Kyle in a comedy headlock after sampling too much of his product and telling him he had 'lovely knees' one best forgotten.

Moving T will logistically be a momentous task, but DF Concerts are the best in the business and will pull it off.

Auchterarder should embrace the chaos and the town will reap the benefits. The Kinross locals were crying at a farewell thank you presentation.

So, 2015 Strathallan Castle it is then; if the owner wants to get in touch to sort out a wee spot on his grass near a flushing loo then I'd be very grateful.

Bye bye, Balado – you rocked.

Update: I attended the two years of T in the Park at Strathallan Castle. They tried. It was sh***. Sorry, but it was. TRNSMT, the new kid on the block at Glasgow Green, has been great though and is the way forward.

11 OCTOBER 2015 – TRAVEL ADVENTURES WITH FAITHER

Taking Dad along for the ride on some of my BBC Travel trips proved comedy gold.

As misunderstandings go this was his best yet.

I'd taken my eighty-year-old dad Bobby on a day trip to Mull. We meandered down the main street in Tobermory, window shopping at leisure.

Suddenly he stopped to read a large whiteboard in a shop doorway and started muttering with discontent. After several angry grunts and genuinely upsets groans he grumbled, 'Och, that's just not right.'

We were standing outside the Hebridean Whale and Dolphin Trust shop where they have a board pinned to their front door listing recent sightings.

On the sign included common dolphin, minke whale, harbour porpoise, sunfish, bottlenose dolphin and basking sharks.

The only problem was they share the same doorway with the Crystal Palace, Mull's Chinese restaurant.

Without his reading glasses Dad assumed it was the menu and began cursing the influx of tourists for their extravagant and exotic tastes.

I'm sure I laughed a tiny little bit of wee, it was that funny.

Once I explained they'd been spotted in the bay or off the shores of nearby islands and not in a sweet and sour sauce, he too buckled into hysterics.

It was the first incident in a week of comical happenings, which is why I love taking him away.

We lunched in the Gallery, a converted church. I chose soup as usual while Dad, never one to shirk a challenge, ordered crab claws in garlic butter.

Now I am not telling tales but he's the only person I know who needs to wipe sauce off his FOREHEAD after BBQ spare ribs. This was never going to end well.

The pliers and skinny fork were not doing the job, so he asked the waiter for a hammer. With said implement in hand, Faither set about destroying the claw, his plate and the solid oak table beneath with one mighty blow.

The old lady at the next table nearly keeled over with fright while I had to pick chunks of buttery crab meat off my jumper and out of my fringe.

With his triumphant cheeks glowing under a film of garlic butter and shell-mageddon all over the table, an immaculate wee wifie approached.

I was sure we were going to get a lesson on seafood etiquette. Instead, she said, 'Are you Bobby Harvey?'

Disaster – recognised in his hour of greed.

'I saw you in the Calum Kennedy show in 1956 in the Palace Theatre in Dundee and you were marvellous.'

Well, Margaret Kemp and her husband got a warm garlicky handshake from my infamous fiddle-playing dad as they disappeared down memory lane.

The following day as I was staring out to sea on the CalMac from Tarbert to Portavadie, the captain came down and asked: 'Are you the lassie from Twitter that likes ferries?' I'd posted a picture of us heading to Mull earlier in the week. 'Would you and your dad like to see the bridge?'

Well, I've never seen him move so fast. The gammy knee forgotten as he hauled himself up three flights of vertical steps to see Skipper Duncan McGougan and Colin McNicol at work in their new hybrid ferry.

They patiently explained the new electric-diesel system and showed him how they steer and dock with a small joystick.

He was overjoyed at this wonderfully kind gesture from the crew and was in his element looking out the large floor-length windows on the bridge with his binoculars over the sea.

I'm hoping he was looking at the glorious coastline and NOT searching for a minke whale to stir fry for his dinner.

Update: Along with providing occasional holiday cover on *Off the Ball*, *Out for the Weekend* and *The Afternoon Show* for BBC Radio Scotland, since 2017 I've also worked as a freelance travel reporter on the Kaye Adams show. Kaye has a wicked sense of humour and I've loved sharing my travel stories with her.

I've been lucky enough to visit America, Canada, Croatia, Cuba, the Czech Republic, Denmark, Hungary, Ireland, Italy, Jersey, Poland and Vietnam. Honestly, I still can't believe it and I keep expecting to be found out as a 'wee chancer' soon.

However, the best and most memorable trips were the local ones where I managed to fling my dad in the car to join me for an adventure.

Together we've walked alpacas in Dumfries, kissed sea lions at Blair Drummond Safari Park, made chocolate in York, learned how to fly broomsticks like Harry Potter in Northumberland, explored the glorious beaches in Islay and the Western Isles, met some wonderful people and eaten an awful lot of lovely grub. Here's some more of our escapades.

29 APRIL 2018 – BOBBY HARVEY AND WANDERING WILLIE!

One of my fun jobs at the moment is jaunting up and down Scotland finding the perfect 'Wee Day Out' for BBC Radio Scotland.

While this is taking me to previously unexplored corners of our glorious country, I've learned as much about my travelling companions as I have my new surroundings.

Sometimes I travel alone, sometimes I have company. The journeys with passengers are proving the most rewarding.

My wee 83-year-old dad Bobby has joined me on a couple of jaunts. The first was to Inveraray in Argyll. I wanted to visit the Loch Fyne Oyster Bar, the castle and the jail but promised him lunch in the George Hotel if he behaved himself.

Dad's accordion player of over sixty years, Ivor Britton, was from the town and they've played the local club on many occasions. I think he met everyone who'd ever attended in our one morning!

Just as we were leaving for home he said: 'We need to go and see Wee Aggie.'

This was not on my carefully prepped itinerary.

'Who is wee Aggie?' I asked.

'Och, you know her fine, WEE AGGIE,' he replied. He does this a lot. Insists I know people he met before I was born!

Anyway, Wee Aggie used to be a Highland dancer in my dad's Scottish show. She was excellent, apparently, and the daughter of Pipe Major Ronnie McCallum, who was the Duke of Argyll's piper.

She started dancing in his show when she was seventeen, and Wee Aggie has now had her free bus pass for several years.

Dad led me up into the garden of a house overlooking Loch Fyne that 'may or may not be Wee Aggie's'.

We rang the bell and waited. I just hoped Wee Aggie, who he hadn't seen in years, was still with us!

Thankfully, she very much was. A beaming bundle of energy opened the door and yelped with joy. She was delighted and surprised in equal measures.

An hour of reminiscing, tea, cakes and laughs later, we left. Her son Stewart is now the pipe major of the Inveraray Pipe Band — world champions no less. Dad's trip was made.

His next excursion with me was to Gatehouse of Fleet in Dumfriesshire. Neither of us had been before, or so we thought.

Driving down the M74 just after Abbington, he told me the story of the day he flew down this route between the hills with Scottish entertainment legends Calum Kennedy and Will Starr because they'd missed their train from Dundee.

They'd a gig in Blackpool and only hours to get there. Calum knew a guy with a small plane and persuaded him to fly them down. Visibility was poor so they flew just above the motorway.

They had to get the train home and didn't have any money as they'd spent it all on whisky. The three of them hid in a sleeper carriage and got off at Gleneagles as there would be no ticket inspector there. They hitched back to Dundee, standing at the roadside resplendent in kilts with their instruments. This is incredible when you remember how famous Calum was back then.

When we got to Gatehouse, one of my tasks was pottery painting near Mossyard Beach. We arrived early so took a wander onto the small, hidden beach.

'I've been here before,' said Dad with utter conviction.

Turns out he'd filmed an STV drama back in 1969 called *Red Gauntlet*, based on a Sir Walter Scott novel. He thought he'd played the part of 'Wandering Willie'. I was scared to ask.

Turns out, he was the local fiddle player, hence his casting. The smile on his face, standing on the golden sand watching the waves thinking back to happy times, was better than any expensive exotic holiday.

Driving Dad on the open road for him to walk down memory lane has been a joy; we should all try to make these journeys more . . .

NOTE: Not all my travel trips run so smoothly. I've been sick over the side of a boat in Orkney, the feathered occupants of the Bass Rock have left me several presents on my hair and jacket, and I've been mauled by midges in Aberfoyle and Glencoe.

I'm always game to give anything a go but I should maybe have reined it in on this next trip to Kinloch Rannoch.

8 AUGUST 2018 – I'LL GIVE ANYTHING A GO JOUST ONCE

It's quite an achievement ticking off a bucket list item that you never knew was on your bucket list in the first place.

Learning to joust on a rehabilitated racehorse is the perfect example.

Before I did this completely by surprise, I never realised how much I wanted to do this. Not even for a second did I contemplate learning such a skill that would've been a marvellous addition to your CV three hundred years ago.

Every part of this story makes me smile. Particularly because we never saw it coming – not a good phrase now that I'm nearly a professional jouster.

I was visiting Kinloch Rannoch in Highland Perthshire (utterly beautiful by the way) as part of my 'Wee Day Oot' feature on BBC Radio Scotland.

My pal Fiona suggested a pony trek as she'd spotted an online advert for the Rannoch Equestrian Centre.

The last time Fiona and I were on horseback was nearly twenty-one years ago on two lovely fat plodding Highland ponies. I know the timescale for a fact as her daughter turns twenty-one this year and we never knew at the time she was already in her tummy! We even signed disclaimers confirming no pregnancies.

As we drove into the yard, I looked at the beautiful horses in the field. They were lithe, athletic and enormous! (All over seventeen hands if you speak fluent horsey.)

We were greeted by Andy Dewar McCabe who owns the centre.

He was once head of horsemanship at Sandhurst, training all the elite military horses.

I pointed out that I couldn't see any trekking ponies and he laughed: 'There aren't any, I rehabilitate racehorses.'

Now Fiona and I are game, we can ride a bit and by that, I mean we can sit on a horse and maybe trot without tumbling off, but ex-racehorses are different beasts.

I was introduced to Ed, my trusty steed for the day. To give you an idea of size, the top of my head was halfway up his body. Ed used to run at Cheltenham. Ed looked fast.

At Andy's place he teaches horsemanship, so you have to groom your horse to bond before heading out.

It was at this point we learned our fate.

'We'll walk down to the loch and back then I'll teach you how to joust.'

I honestly thought he was joking.

'Do I get a lance or a sword?' I laughed.

'Both, but not at the same time,' he replied.

It was then he brought out the massive replica sword and the three-foot solid wooden jousting pole. He wasn't kidding.

How do these things happen to me? I'm sure my life is on a hidden camera show somewhere.

And that's how I ended up in a remote Highland field with a wonderfully eccentric military mastermind learning how to kill on the move.

Okay, so we were walking, he was holding the horse's head as simultaneous steering and thrusting is multiskilling not for begin-ners. I'm delighted to report both Fiona and I hit the target both times. The wooden shield on the pole is called the quintain. We may have been slow, but we were accurate.

We then mastered how to remove an elevated rope ring with a sword while moving. Again, the hand–eye coordination is crucial; remembering not to fall off also helps.

Andy told us he can chop a cabbage in half with a sword at twenty miles per hour, galloping on his horse in an impressive move he calls 'The Coleslaw'.

We didn't have time to see this in action as we took up too much time spearing things, but I totally believed him.

Fiona and I both loved the unexpected randomness of our jousting experience. If you see me cycling through Partick with a washing pole under my oxter, don't call the police, I'm just horsing around and honing my new skills.

Update: We survived. We probably won't be trying this again anytime soon. Amazing memories, though.

27 AUGUST 2017 – AY LADYBOYS, MAGIC TRICKS AND A STANDING OVATION FROM A BAFTA WINNER.
It can only be our misadventures at the Edinburgh Festival Fringe.

Tomorrow marks the official end of the seventieth anniversary of the Edinburgh Festival Fringe. The city will soon start returning to normal, the buzz will subside, and you'll no longer see dragons reciting Shakespeare wearing body glitter.

Due to work commitments, I only managed one visit this year, but I crammed in enough ridiculous incidents to form the basis of a show.

I started the day watching my radio co-host Ewen Cameron present his STV2 *Late Show from the Dome*. Guests were Amy Macdonald and the host of Irish *Blind Date* and stand-up comedian Al Porter.

I laughed when he admitted that, at twenty-three, he still lives with his mum because nobody of his generation can afford to get on the property ladder. He said the only way they can get houses is to inherit them, adding cheekily, 'Every time my mum coughs I think – ooh, I'll redecorate the bathroom.'

Our next show was the hilarious Jason Byrne, truly one of the funniest guys on the circuit. The previous night, Ewen had a night out with him and John Bishop; Jason was meant to be joining us for a pint on the night I was there but had to cancel as 'I've got my bike'.

Somehow, I imagined all the big names would have blacked out limousines with drivers not mountain bikes.

In one of the bars, we met top Canadian comedian Tom Stade and his wife. I was crying with laughter at his not-for-the-family newspaper tales.

By this point Ewen, who is not a drinker, was on beer number three. He was getting sentimental and gushy, much to the delight of our radio Producer Michael and me. I will never let him forget the moment he told the entire room in all seriousness: 'I want to be Cat. She is the EPICENTRE of fun. I want to be the epicentre of fun.'

Fuelled with three-beer bravado, he decided we would go to the Abattoir, a VIP bar for performers.

As we rocked up, Ewen strode confidently to the gate. The large Australian bouncer was imposing.

All fingers and thumbs, he couldn't find his VIP card (he does actually own one), and resorted to the pleading line, 'I've got my own TV and radio show, mate.'

The big bouncer smiled politely and replied: 'Sure you have, that's what they all say.'

I'm sure Producer Michael and I could have been more helpful but at that point we were bent double laughing.

Ewen's dignity was saved when *Live at the Apollo* comedian Stephen K. Amos appeared and asked why he was standing outside. Stephen had to vouch for the three of us and we were allowed in. I'm sure he regretted that decision later.

Our next hilarious encounter was with phenomenal TV forensic mind-reader Colin Cloud, who once reached the last stages of *America's Got Talent*.

I'm not sure why I thought it was a good idea to dazzle him with the card trick from a Christmas cracker that I carry in my purse, but he was polite enough to tell me I had potential. Watch out Debbie McGee. He then showed me a faster way to do my trick.

The end of the evening is fuzzy (tiredness obviously). Apparently, I tried out my new improved magic on the next table. I'm told they included BAFTA, Golden Globe and Academy Award-winning actress Emma Thompson, who had also had a sherry or two and was so taken by my skills she gave me a standing ovation.

If I was to review our day out, I'd give it five stars – and a can of Irn-Bru for the morning after. Bravo, Edinburgh, *bravo*.

Update: We always have fun at the Fringe and have had at least one epic night out every year. Ewen's obsession with the Ladyboys continues. He's starred on stage with them in full drag (he has worryingly impressive legs in high heels). If you've never seen the show, it's a visually stunning camp carnival of utter joy. If you can imagine one big high energy hen night in a marquee for seven hundred people, you'll get the idea.

One year we even took esteemed Scottish actor Gavin Mitchell aka 'Boaby the barman' from TV hit *Still Game*, who'd been Ewen's guest on the STV *Late Show*.

Poor Gavin thought he was joining us all for a quick after-show drink. Little did he know, we'd take him to the tent of fun and that three hours later the chunky comedy character ladyboy, resplendent in a floor-length gold sequinned gown, would pick him at random and drag him up on stage (pardon the pun) to dance a slow erotic routine with him in front of a full house.

The laughing ladyboy didn't know quite how to react when the bold Gav gyrated and wiggled every bit as good as the star.

The tantalising Thai turn also seemed bemused with the numerous excited shouts of recognition from the floor of 'LOOK IT'S BOABY', a rightly confusing statement given the nature of the show.

It was just one of those wonderful unplanned moments of madness the Fringe can throw your way. It also proved that Gavin Mitchell is definitely Still Game, *very* game in fact. We have photos, video and memories to prove it.

12 MARCH 2017 – AMY MACDONALD

This is the first full column I wrote about the legend, talent, global superstar and friend we call Amy. She is a welcome and integral part of our team and a nicer lassie I swear you will struggle to meet.

It's very pleasing when home-grown Scottish musical talent makes an impact on the international stage – but it's even more enjoyable when you've had that very superstar in a drunken headlock while wearing a Santa hat.

Singer-songwriter Amy Macdonald is scheduled to headline many big festivals this year and is currently number one in the charts all over Europe with her fabulous new release *Under Stars*, her fourth studio album.

Having sold over nine million records worldwide and picked up music industry awards in Poland, Switzerland, Germany and

Scotland, I'd just like to say – I knew she was going to make it!

This fact riles my radio co-host Ewen Cameron more than anything.

Eleven years ago, a fresh-faced seventeen-year-old Amy visited Real Radio where we were working at the time with a record plugger. She looked like she was dogging school to be there but there was an inner confidence and a sparkle in her eyes.

She played two acoustic songs in our boss's office and gave all the presenters a CD with three tracks on it.

When she left, I was humming the chorus all day to one of the songs she'd played. This was a good sign, a song that becomes an 'earworm' will almost certainly be a hit.

That night I played her demo CD over and over again and fell in love with her unique rocky vocals and catchy melodies. The rough versions of the songs I'd been given went on to be her first two hit singles 'This is the Life' and 'Mr Rock & Roll'.

Ewen thought she was just another nice wee lassie with a guitar and didn't even lift her CD from the office table. I said she would be a superstar, he said she'd never make it. Amy does holiday cover for me on our Sunday radio show now and reminds him of this over and over again. It's priceless.

She came on air with us a few weeks ago and let me duet with her on my kazoo; she now joins The Proclaimers, Olly Murs and SuBo in that musical club. I've quite the compilation album in the pipeline.

Amy is never far from the headlines as she's a feisty, intelligent, opinionated woman, never afraid to speak her mind on any subject from politics, football, health and fitness to her beloved cars. I love this about her. She'll never play the 'what is expected of a generic female pop star' game. She is also genuinely a very funny, sweet and lovely lass.

If this sounds like I have a gushing fan-girl crush on her, it's because I do. If only Amy and my other love Paolo Nutini would have babies – think of the future of Scottish music!

We've had several days and nights out together including a trip to the set of *Still Game* where she was star-struck by the entire cast and a boozy post-panto Christmas party where I woke up the next day with the fear.

I'm quite sure at one point I had her in a headlock while wearing a bobbly festive hat telling her just how much I loved her music, her face, her fashion and just her in general.

As I tentatively flicked through the photos on my phone the morning after, my fear was justified. It was like the end credits of *The Hangover*. The headlock was as real as the pint of pink flaming 'zombie' in my other hand.

Fame is a fickle beast, and she handles it brilliantly. Any international recording star who graciously accepts your apology with the words: 'Don't worry, you were really funny' deserves ALL the success in the world.

Update: Since this shameful night, I can confirm I have been every bit as badly behaved in her company on many other occasions. I've ended up dancing on her kitchen table not once but twice at separate house parties. On both occasions I've told her: 'Remind me to go home at 11 p.m. as I'm working in the morning.' On both occasions she joined me on top of her robust kitchen table for dancing and laughter and I've left about 4 a.m. after having had an absolute blast with her friends and family. She's come to see Ewen and me in panto, and I've been backstage in her dressing room at the Barrowlands after a bouncing sell-out gig. She ordered in Domino's pizzas for all the band and her pals. Would Beyoncé do this? Would she? Not a lobster in sight!

One of our favourite days out ever was a trip to the *Still Game* set with Amy. She is such a massive fan of the show (even using it as her specialist subject on *Mastermind*) she jumped at the chance to join Ewen and me on location. It was hilarious to see her so star-struck by Jack, Victor, Isa, Navid, Boaby, Tam, Winston and Eric. To this day, it is still my favourite selfie. Ellen DeGeneres's 2014 Oscar selfie doesn't even come close!

In 2021 Amy released *The Human Demands*, her fifth studio album. She's now sold over twelve million records and sells out stadiums all over Europe. On 17 December 2021, she will play the SSE Hydro. I can hardly explain how proud this makes me feel. She also comes on our show and has listeners in hysterics with beautiful descriptions of how she makes the perfect roast potatoes. The wee seventeen-year-old who nervously played us her songs is rocking her career. We are all lucky to call her our friend and I look forward to many more nights of fun to come. 'This is the Life' indeed . . .

10 FEBRUARY 2018 – THE GAY BALL

I've had the pleasure of 'working' at this event for several years now and I am truly grateful to the LGBT+ community for making me feel such a welcome part of their wonderful family.

I know I go on about it every year but the Gay Ball, which always takes place on a wintery Monday night in Glasgow, remains one of the highlights of my working year.

While the rest of the world is tucked up indoors, the LGBT+ community and their friends have the most fabulous, flamboyant and friendly shindig you could wish for.

There are feathers, sparkles, dancing showgirls, five different live acts and all hosted superbly by the vision of loveliness that is drag queen Cheri Treiffel.

Since we last worked together, Cheri has become an internet sensation. She gatecrashed my friends', Peter McConnachie and Peter Deaville's, wedding in the summer, theatrically belting out the song 'It Should've Been Me', marching up the aisle just as they were about to say their vows.

The two Peters (for that is what they are collectively known as) of course co-ordinated this hilarious intervention but forgot to tell their families. The clip went viral all over the world and has been seen by over 40 million people.

Thankfully, Ms Treiffel remains grounded and still works alongside those less famous like me. I just host the auction and raffle on the night but truthfully can't class it as work when I have so much fun.

The twenty-fifth anniversary of the ball was organised superbly by Glaswegian singing legends May and Robert Miller, along with Cheri and a host of other volunteers. The work they put in pulling it all together is breathtaking. They even buy and put up all the table decorations for a room with six hundred people.

All the money raised goes to Kilbryde Hospice and TIE, a charitable campaign group promoting inclusive education in Scotland.

It is truly the only night I work at where over four hundred people are already on the dancefloor during the soup!

One of the highlights is always Natalie Scott's world-famous tombola. I asked her once why it was world-famous and was told: 'People from England, Ireland, Wales and Drumchapel have previously bought tickets.' Who am I to argue with that logic?

Natalie, a transwoman, is an inspiration. She's worked as a counsellor and delivers incredible motivational speeches about her life. She was the Attitude Pride Award Winner 2017 and has picked up numerous LGBT Icon awards but more than anything, she's a lovely person with a brilliant sense of humour.

The tombola consists of hundreds of prizes all kindly donated and ranging from the sublime to the ridiculous. There are fabulous treats to be had and then there are the prizes my friend, entertainer and panto favourite, Liam Dolan, ends up with.

His luck, or lack of it, is now legendary.

The first year he won a small individual-sized bottle of Babycham. The following year he spent £40 on tickets and won a Dundee cake. This year he was the proud winner of 'Pop and Hop', Tesco's own brand version of the board game Frustration, a state of mind he'd be entitled to as he stood with his new toy watching everyone else cooing over their extraordinary hauls of exotic vouchers, luxury spirits and posh candles.

Keen to keep him on side, May and Natalie, unbeknownst to Liam, arranged for him to have the final winning ticket at the raffle at the after-party in the Waterloo Bar the following day.

He celebrated his turn in fortune and made his way to the stage to collect his star prize – a bag of cheese and onion crisps.

May, always the joker, even auctioned the unicorn slippers Natalie wore to host her tombola and raised another £55 for the charity pot.

I didn't make the after-party this year. It wasn't the 5 a.m. finish after the ball sitting up chatting to Andrew Agnew, PC Plum from *Balamory*, that ruled me out, it was the fear of what chaos might ensue.

The only time I made it to the next day bash, the revellers, who are a sharing caring bunch, passed round a bottle of Limoncello left over from the raffle to share.

I thought it had a funny aftertaste and was the only person to read the label and realise it was Limoncello-flavoured bubble bath.

Next year's bash is already a guaranteed sell-out. I'll maybe have recovered by then . . .

Update: In 2019 I was left truly gobsmacked when I won the Pride Awards Journalist of the Year. My dad's first question was, 'Are you now a lesbian?' I replied 'no' and he said 'Toots, you know it's totally fine if you are.'

That's why I feel lucky. I was brought up in a family where this would never have been an issue. My dad worked in entertainment all his days and has had as many gay friends as I do, back in a time when they were shamefully forced to keep quiet.

The judges' notes said I was a strong and powerful ally to the LGBT+ community through my writing, plays and radio work. I honestly cried a little as I had no idea that I'd made any sort of impact.

I'm proud that Scotland is constantly striving to be a welcoming diverse country where you can love who you want and be who you want to be.

The two Peters continue to be a source of joy to me with their zest for life, and hopefully next year May and Robert Miller and Cheri Treiffel will be able to bring the Gay Ball back to life post pandemic. It was fabulous before – the return will be nothing short of spectacular . . .

8 APRIL 2018 – THE HORSE WITH NO NAME

The story that's too bizarre not to tell. There is neigh way I could make this one up.

Today I'm going to share a little tale I'm entitling 'The Curious Incident of the Horse in the Night-time'. A story of mystery and intrigue involving two stags and a straggly but loveable abandoned horse.

The stags were my two gay friends who were getting married

71

in a fortnight. They'd opted for a joint stag do in Aviemore and had invited several couples including (shock horror to many men) lassies!

This was my first-ever stag do and it didn't disappoint.

Research shows there's a big increase in mixed celebrations before a wedding because people nowadays have as many male as female friends, and vice versa.

We hired a house that slept twelve and our line-up consisted of three gay couples, two straight couples and two single guys.

I can honestly say I have never stayed with a more house-proud bunch. On previous hen dos, the squabbles have been over who has to clear up, on this Sten or Hag do (both actual names for this) people got up early so they could do the cleaning. Marvellous.

On our big night out, we had dinner in a local restaurant, a mini pub crawl and then hit the Vault, the local nightclub which lets you in free on a Friday.

Our stags, one dressed in 1970s disco gear and the other (a bank manager) dressed as a giant pink baby, were surprisingly loving life in their new clobber.

It was around about now the mysterious horse trotted into our lives. We meandered home in dribs and drabs. I was last (naturally, as I love dancing!) and when I got into the kitchen was greeted by a three-foot rust-coloured toy furry horse standing upright and sturdy enough to be used as a seat. She looked like she'd been through the wars. Scruffy main, a tear on her rump and no rails to rock on.

She was christened 'The Horse with No Name'.

Our brave friend Fergie told us he'd climbed into a river to save her. The following morning Teresa (who was way more sober than Fergie) revealed it had been spotted next to a puddle in an underpass. Never let truth get in the way of a heroic story.

I was worried he'd pinched it from some heartbroken child's garden, but our fluffy friend was soon to gallop into the annuls of local history.

The following day, two more friends arrived for lunch. One was Jodie McCluskey, an Aviemore local and radio presenter on MFR. As soon as she walked into the kitchen her eyes popped out her head: 'What is *that* doing here?'

She looked stunned.

Turns out a month previously, The Horse with No Name was abandoned outside her front door by a drunken pal of her husband's as a gift for their new baby.

Since then, it's been spotted all over Aviemore. Nobody knows who shifts it, nobody knows where it came from.

Jodie laughed: 'It's been moved between the Tesco car park, the train station and the local play park for weeks.'

At least the horse was now warm and loved.

My crazy radio partner Ewen Cameron put it in his car and took it home to Falkirk after the weekend was over. Pictures then followed of his dog sitting on top of it before he made a stable for it in his hut (yes, really).

The plan is The Horse with No Name will make a spectacular appearance at the wedding. We are hoping to add a place to the top table.

It will have a bespoke outfit fitting of the occasion before our Producer Michael does the right thing and returns it to Aviemore under the cloak of darkness.

There's neigh denying it, horsing around can be a lot of fun.

Update: The Horse with No Name had pride of place at the altar on the big day when the boys got hitched. Ewen's wife had even made a beautiful silver tulle frock for her – we somehow decided she was a wee lady horse – and combed her straggly locks, adding pretty floral clasps. After this story was printed in the paper and we talked about it on air, a lady from Aviemore got in touch. The Horse with No Name had, as I originally feared, been removed from her kid's garden months previously in a drunken prank. Her wee girls were heartbroken. Producer Michael, forever a knight in shining armour, drove The Horse with No Name from the wedding in Glasgow to his flat in Edinburgh then back to Aviemore and left it at their front door under the cloak of darkness so the mystery could continue. We then received a photo of the happy family reunion. What an adventure our wee pony had been on. Far too much horsing around in my opinion.

18 NOVEMBER 2018 – THE SUPERMARKET CAR PARK, LOO ROLL AND A NEW CAREER
A story so fanciful it should be turned into a play!

Every now and then I like to reinvent myself and try my hand at something new. Sometimes it works and sometimes it doesn't, but it does mean that my life is very rarely dull.

While I'd love to claim this is a carefully structured ever-evolving life plan, I'm honest enough to know it's because I don't know what I want to be when I grow up and I'll have a bash at anything.

My new vocation has emerged at this time in my life, completely unexpectedly, through a drunken misunderstanding, a lifelong dream and a trip to Morrisons supermarket.

Let me set the scene. I'm sitting in the car park and the rain is battering my car roof. I'm waiting for it to ease off to make the mad dash from car to shop. Until it does, I footer with my phone and check emails. There's a new one from Raymond Anderson, who works with arts venues for South Lanarkshire Leisure and Council Ltd. He also produces plays and has hired me for the last three years every February to be part of his touring productions.

The email read: 'May tells me you have a script we could use in February. Can you send it over please?'

Now this is where the drink comes in!

The May in question is May Miller, singer and all-round hilarious entertainer. She's been in all the plays for SLLC with me alongside Liam Dolan, Johnny Mac, Andrew Agnew and Michelle McManus.

Now May and I enjoyed a wee sherry or two a few weeks ago. She mentioned Raymond was looking for a play to put on and I think I said: 'I've got an idea for one we could do.'

By the time May relayed this information to Raymond, he heard that I'd written the play, it would be perfect for our cast and that it was good to go. Only it wasn't. I only had a title.

Sitting in the supermarket car park I pondered my options:

A. Lie and say I had a script.
B. Tell the truth and blame the bevvy for this unfortunate theatrical misunderstanding.

In the end I chose a bit of both. I told him I had an idea for a script that wasn't quite finished yet. He didn't know that by that, I really meant *not even started*.

He quickly replied: 'Okay, send me the synopsis.'

And so, in the Morrisons car park, in my car, in the rain, on my phone, I wrote a three-paragraph story outline with succinct character breakdowns. I'm sure Steven Spielberg must have done this in a Walmart parking lot at some stage in his early career.

The reply was instant. 'Love it, can you have it written for 1 December.'

I wondered if he meant December 2019, but no, I agreed to write my first-ever play and to have it finished in less than a fortnight.

While this is complete insanity on every level, I'm not scared. I've had ideas about this for several years but just never forced myself to begin. Now I have no choice.

We took cast photos, and I wrote the promotional blurb for the venues' brochures before a single word of the play was written.

'Love Me Tinder – A Date for Your Diary', a brand-new comedy about internet dating in 2018 incorporating many real-life hilarious dating tales, courtesy of my poor unfortunate mates, will tour in February 2019. Hopefully. If I get my finger out and finish it.

I'm now focused and determined to deliver a cracker, which is good news for all concerned given that tickets are now on sale! (What an ideal Christmas gift.)

On opening night I'll be a bag of nerves and will always remember that fateful trip to the shops for chicken breasts, Jaffa Cakes and loo roll which raised the curtain on my next new career . . .

Update: The gods of creativity were shining on that supermarket car park because *Love Me Tinder* became a total sell-out. In fact, here's the story I wrote after the final performance.

3 MARCH 2019 – *LOVE ME TINDER* – THE AFTERMATH

Today I'll probably be lying in a dark room reflecting on the glorious adrenaline-filled fortnight that's been the journey and delivery of my first-ever play.

You may recall a month or so ago I told you I'd somehow agreed to write a play after a drunken misunderstanding when a producer thought I'd already written one when really I only had an idea and a title.

Cutting a long story short, I wrote *Love Me Tinder – A Date for Your Diary* in eleven days. It's a comedy about internet dating and finding love and quite frankly I had absolutely no idea if it was mince or not. I googled how to write a play just to make sure I was on the right lines.

Thankfully my amazing cast helped me get this up and running in possibly the shortest rehearsal time of a new piece of writing in history. Due to budget constraints and availability issues, we put the play from paper to stage in five days. Theatrical types will now be hyperventilating with the Fear.

Trust me, on the opening night, when we'd only finished the technical side of the show with ninety minutes to go and had NOT had any time for a dress rehearsal, I think everyone of the cast and crew wanted a hug from their mammies.

The phrase 'it'll be alright on the night' was coined for this evening. I've truthfully no idea how we did it but, from the moment we began to the rapturous standing ovation at the end, we survived.

Every subsequent show got slicker and more confident and I'm still shell-shocked to reveal that every single performance in the run sold out with lengthy waiting lists for tickets.

So, thank you panto legends Johnny Mac and Liam Dolan, PC Plum from *Balamory* Andrew Agnew, singers May Miller and Michelle McManus and my fabulous friend Joanna Kaczynska who plays the Polish yoga temptress to perfection.

I did have to laugh after one of the performances when a guy called Gary spoke to Joanna at the end and commented on how good her fake Polish accent was. When she laughed and replied 'thanks', he

CAT'S OUT THE BAG

asked if she was 'one of those actors who always stays in character'.

We had to convince him that she actually is Polish.

Apart from the fun we have on stage, rehearsals, while intense, were an absolute hoot too. The problem with working with your friends is that it's too easy to get distracted and want to chat about fun stuff. Liam, who was directing, had to enforce a firm 'save it for lunch' rule. He would even take a note of the topic we veered onto, so we never missed any hot gossip.

Lunch breaks in Rutherglen Town Hall were legendary. I wish I'd recorded them. Hilarious chat and fantastic soup, cake and pieces.

Some of the subject headings we discussed included: Do you think dogs know their own names? Why are cows the only animals with pats? And, can you ever have a happy relationship with a mayonnaise guy if you are a salad cream girl?

Truthfully, I can't thank Producer Raymond Anderson and everyone at South Lanarkshire Leisure and Culture enough for being brave enough to give us the opportunity. Apart from believing in me, they fed us so well my trousers hurt and Colin the big boss even gave all the cast bottles of Prosecco.

We were all buzzing when queen of comedy Elaine C. Smith, from *Rab C* and *Two Doors Down* popped in too with presents, advice and kind words. I'm just learning, so support from bosses and people who know far more than me means the world.

I'm going to look into the logistics of possibly touring and getting the cast back together again. The feedback has been a dream come true and I've met so many lovely people who read this column who came to support me and for that I am truly thankful.

The world needs to laugh right now and I'm pleased my wee play, thanks to the phenomenally talented cast, has delivered a fun night out.

I'm just waiting for Broadway to call, although I'd probably need to do a bit of a rewrite. I don't think the good people of Manhattan would know what getting a winch is, do you?

Update: *Love Me Tinder* with the original cast was booked for a Scotland-wide tour in May and June of 2020. It was cancelled because of Covid and rescheduled for February and March of 2021. This was also cancelled as Scotland was forced back into lockdown. The theatre industry has been crushed by the pandemic and we must all hope that live entertainment can soon be allowed to safely continue and recover. Please support your local theatres and music venues. I have the best cast in the world and a play good-to-go. We are just waiting for the green light to start planning again but it still feels like a long way away.

My second play 'One Singer – One Song', a comedy about a Glaswegian entertainment agency, opened in February 2020 just before the industry was frozen. It was also a total sell-out and I really can't thank everyone who bought a ticket enough. I'm genuinely humbled and grateful to you all.

Again, my writing was saved because my cast were so phenomenal: Edward Reid, Stephanie MacDonald, May Miller and Tom Urie were directed by Andrew Agnew. He saved the day as some of my ideas were a bit 'out there'.

I remember Raymond the producer phoning me full of concern on one occasion: 'I've just read the script. It says you are going to electrocute the entire cast with a lightning bolt. You do know we are putting this on in Rutherglen Town Hall and not the SECC?'

'Yes,' I replied confidently, 'it will be fine.' Truthfully, I had NO idea how to make this work, but that's why I had Andrew. His vision is brilliant.

With some comedy cardboard cut-out lightning bolts on garden canes, some crackling sound effects and simple strobe lighting, he made it happen and no actors were hurt in the making of this production.

I am very much a beginner when it comes to writing plays. I've had fun so far, but there's so much more to learn and I'm excited about creating more madness in years to come.

There is a wonderful creative team at SLLC who are not scared to take a punt on new work by new writers. Previously, I've also worked with them on the *Vagina Monologues* with May Miller and Michelle McManus and our full ensemble was together twice for *Gone But Not Forgotten*, a comedy about the funeral of a very colourful Glaswegian father.

Without intending to sound smug or preachy, I'd love to say to anybody who has a dream to try something creative to just give it a go. It won't always work but amazing things can transpire. Starting is by far the hardest part, so if you ever need a call while you're in a supermarket car park to get the ball rolling, just say the word.

Cat's Tales of the Unexpected...

Hopefully you've enjoyed some of my memories; now it's time to read the 2021 memoirs. My daily diary of my return to the airwaves as Scotland battles through the pandemic.

There's good times and sad times but most of all fun times. I'm privileged to be able to share these with you and know that Cash for Kids will benefit. Once again thank you and to Teresa Cameron, Ewen's long-suffering wife and truly one of life's kindest and best, I'm sorry for what is about to unfold...

MONDAY 11 JANUARY

Today's the day I thought would never happen. A return to breakfast radio and a succession of loud jangly alarms ringing at silly o'clock.

Don't get me wrong, I loved my years on previous breakfast shows; I just wanted to sleep more.

However, the stars have aligned for this to happen and I'm up, dressed and out the flat in less than twenty minutes. One of the joys of radio is being able to rock into the studio with a look fashionistas would generously describe as 'an aesthetic riot'.

Covid and numerous lockdowns highlighted several things to me.

One was my need for people, interaction and laughter and the other was how many cups of tea I was drinking a day. As the months have dragged on, my need for fun and nonsense has become even greater than my constant need to pee.

With theatres closed for the foreseeable future and both the plays I've written on hold until further notice, I finally agreed to rejoin Ewen Cameron full-time. I'll question the sanity of this decision as time and this book goes on.

We are now on the Greatest Hits Network 6 a.m. until 10 a.m., Monday to Friday. That's Clyde 2, Forth 2, MFR 2, Northsound 2, Tay 2 and Westsound (we still are on the 1's on a Sunday).

My bosses and pals Michael, Victoria and Graham made it all very easy and I'll always be grateful to them for this opportunity to create happy havoc once again.

With any new show, the first day is always a bit crazy – working out what to slot where and how many new features to introduce.

Scotland needs to smile. The weather is miserable. The country is in lockdown and parents are in emotional tatters as home-schooling recommences.

Keen to ramp up the feel-good, this morning we introduced 'Song with a Story' to our listeners – an upbeat tune that takes you back to a happy memory. To demonstrate how it works, I was allowed to go first.

My song of choice has been my karaoke song for twenty-one years. The story of how it became so, is so ridiculous that even my dad asked if it was true. It is. It's the song that saved me and my friend Nichola Kane (Head of Edinburgh, Politics and Diversity at STV) a kicking on the other side of the world.

Let me explain. It was the year 2000 and we were working in New Zealand covering the Edinburgh Tattoo's first overseas show. Over three hundred performers and a life-size stunning theatrical slat of Edinburgh Castle made the experience surreal yet uncannily like the real thing. Nichola was reporting for the television, I think I was pretending to be her producer.

On our day off we travelled to a little town called Nelson. New Zealand is famous for wine. We spent the day sampling the goods.

At night we ended up in a bikers' bar. I've no idea how that transpired, it just did. Clusters of motorbikes outside and a bustling bar crammed full of leather-clad, tattooed beardies and us.

They were having a karaoke night and believe it or not, neither of us had ever been to one before.

Nichola, fuelled by the grape, put herself up for a song. I giggled uncontrollably at the bar as the normally sensible news girl bounced on stage.

Two seconds into the intro of her song I thought we might die: 'YMCA' by the Village People.

'Do-do doo, do do do do-do do do.' Pint glasses were placed on tables as a host of hairy people tried to work out if she was taking the piss or not. The atmosphere was charged and not in a good way. There is, of course, a very camp biker in the famous video.

To this day neither of us has any idea why she picked this song. Even at the end, after a one-woman-all-the-actions performance, there was a deathly silence.

Instead of heading for the door, I thought the best way to survive was to win them over. Did I mention we'd had a few?

'Rock. I need to sing something that's rock.'

And so, it came to pass that Guns N' Roses' 'Sweet Child O' Mine' became my karaoke song and still is to this day. For after that first musically questionable rendition, along with theatrical air-guitar actions from both of us, our sceptical audience warmed to the clearly sparkled Scottish lassies and ended up giving us a standing ovation. Never judge a book by its hairy cover – the bikers turned out to be a lovely bunch, just not overly fond of 1970s disco.

A bit later on in our show we played Al Green's 'Let's Stay Together'. Ewen revealed it was one of twelve love songs he recorded onto a mix tape for his wife Teresa when they first started winching.

He asked me: 'If I was to make a mix tape of love songs for you, what would be on it?'

My reply: 'MC Hammer – You Can't Touch This.'

Still got it.

TUESDAY 12 JANUARY

Day two and the reality of early starts kicks in with a half-inch-thick layer of ice on my windscreen to try and clear quietly to avoid waking my neighbours.

Have you ever tried to scrape a windscreen quietly? It doesn't help my stealth cause that the drive at my flat is made up of red chuckies and every step delivers a deafening icy crunch in the heavy silence of the dark morning.

That said, I'm wide awake and perky.

Today is National Kiss a Ginger Day. I love these silly days, I'm sure they invent them just to give radio presenters something to talk about in quiet months.

I instantly think of my friend, *Pop Idol* winner Michelle McManus. We shared a dressing room in panto one year and I remember as clear as day her declaring: 'I just want to meet someone nice and have a wee ginger baby.'

Her dream came true in a story that involves too much drink, a bar after a Scotland game (we lost) and pakora sauce. Lots of pakora sauce.

On the night Michelle first met her husband-to-be in the bar, my mate Rhona ending up spilling her spicy pakora sauce all over him in a taxi. He laughed and helped her clear it up. Michelle and I caught eyes. We both thought the same thing – he's a keeper!

Anyway, cutting a very long tale shorter she married the loveliest, most handsome ginger man imaginable and has the most beautiful wee ginger baby in the world. Never give up on your dreams, folks. I hope they're celebrating today.

Most parents in Scotland are frazzled as day two of home-schooling commences. Day one, due to a Europe-wide problem with Microsoft Teams, was apparently shambolic.

Live feeds were crashing, children couldn't see or hear their lessons and parents everywhere probably decided a bottle of Merlot was the ideal mid-morning play piece.

We asked people to sum up day one of home-schooling in five words or less.

Stuart Watkins revealed: 'Nobody speaking in my house.' Gary Burns said: 'Glad I opted for dogs.' Sarah Lynagh joked: 'Tendered my resignation to Head'; at least I hope she was joking. Lynn Grattan enquired: 'Alcohol? Asking for a friend.' And Halinka Rands made us both laugh with: 'Should have used contraception.' She did add seven laughing emojis, so we know she was only teasing.

Parents, grandparents and guardians up and down the country are becoming well versed in the technical intricacies of online teaching with camera and mute buttons mastered.

Turns out every day is a school day after all . . .

WEDNESDAY 13 JANUARY

Another yellow weather warning for ice and snow today makes me wonder what it must be like to work on air in Tenerife.

Imagine falling out of bed and instead of dressing like Nanook of the North with a de-icing kit in hand, your biggest sartorial decision is which pair of flip-flops to pop on. But I do love Scotland and wouldn't change it for the world. As Billy Connolly once said: 'There's no such thing as bad weather – just the wrong clothes.'

Momentum is gathering this week for a statue for the Big Yin to be commissioned. I'd be all for that, the anecdotal stories I hear about him from my dad are hilarious. They used to gig together years ago. Apparently, Billy and his banjo would turn up to the Cross Keys in Milngavie for sessions (music AND bevvy) wearing pyjamas. This was way before the Asda mums cornered this market. The Cross Keys is the same bar which, in the 1950s, regularly had Charlie the Elephant tied up to a post outside while his handler, Ibrahim, enjoyed a lunchtime pint before walking him back to Craigend Zoo, now Mugdock Country Park. Dad tells me Charlie loved sucking the froth off the top of a pint of Tennents and then spraying it over anyone standing near enough with his trunk. Like most of Faither's tales, he revealed this detail with a glint in his eye, so it may or may not be true.

Today, 13 January, is known as Discovery Day – the day in the year the highest percentage of couples find out they are pregnant. Experts say it's a result of celebrating over the festive period, which is ironic really.

Globally – it's National Rubber Duckie Day. Told you people made these up to have a laugh when times are grim. Ewen asked his social media followers to send photos and videos of their rubber ducks; the best would be put into the final of 'Duck Idol' which I would judge. Hard to believe I have two university degrees and a Mensa Certificate.

We were inundated with rubber duck pics from all over Scotland with the most wonderful names; Duck Berry and Quack Efron were my favourites. The contest was a squeak-off. Yes, people actually recorded and sent in audio of their rubber ducks squeaking. With Producer Carnage masterfully creating high tension with a drone music bed, Scarlett Quackers belonging to Ailsa Crone was my winner. Her squeak had a clarity and sweetness of tone reminiscent of early Celine Dion.

We are delighted so many people wanted to take part. It's clearly not just Scarlett that's quackers . . .

THURSDAY 14 JANUARY

Aye or naw?

Our very simple take on a true or false game. Sometimes getting the name right can make the difference between a feature catching on or appearing briefly and disappearing into the radio abyss.

Ewen and I are both unashamedly Scottish. We celebrate our heritage and during our ideas bashing session both loved the informal nature of the question as it sounds like something your pal would ask you. Ultimately, without wanting to be cheesy, that's our number one aim, to be your radio pals.

Today's question was a right sneaky one. I like making them tricky, so the obvious answer is not always the right one.

On Monday I asked: the Sultan of Brunei once spent £20,000 on Irn-Bru for a Burns supper. Over eighty per cent said 'aye'. Ewen and Producer Carnage were adamant this must be true as it was too ridiculous and random for me to have just made up. Welcome to my head everyone. I made it up: the answer was 'naw'.

Others included: The World's Shortest Street, measuring just six foot nine inches, is in Scotland – seventy per cent said 'aye', which is the correct answer. *The Guinness Book of World Records* have given that title to Ebenezer Place in Wick.

Did Hollywood star Gerry Butler train as an accountant before becoming an actor? Seventy-one per cent of you said 'aye' – wrong! The answer is 'naw'. I knew this might trick you as he actually trained as a lawyer and, in fact, was the president of the Law Society at my alma mater, Glasgow University. Kind of gutted he was long gone by the time I'd started. I'm pretty certain I'd have tried to snog him in the student union once some fifty pence pints of cider bravery had kicked in.

Today's question was a bit of a sneaky one: Did Queen Victoria smoke cigarettes on her trips to Scotland to get rid of the midges? A whopping eighty-three per cent said 'aye'. Wrong again… (did I mention I like to win?). Queen Victoria was notoriously anti-smoking (thanks Google). So much so, when she passed away, her son Edward VII had to open up a smoking room in the palace. However, I was a bit sleekit: on her trips to Scotland she did make *other people* smoke near her to get rid of our wee biting beasties.

My dad told me flailing wildly to get rid of midges was how Highland dancing was invented. Was he telling the truth? Aye or naw? Even I'll never work that one out.

FRIDAY 15 JANUARY

Today's headlines – the new Brazilian variant of Covid has arrived in the UK, further heart-breaking Brexit shambles for the Scottish seafood industry and another yellow weather warning for snow and ice.

Time to ramp up the nonsense and bring some fun to this never-ending cycle of doom.

My favourite story of the day revealed linguistic experts have now invented new software they are dubbing 'Google Translate for cows'. Breaking moos, you could say.

Our bovine buddies can apparently chat about food and weather by making their own unique sounds.

Researchers say each cow has its own distinct moo, which gives cues in different situations to express excitement, engagement or even distress. When they are happy discussing topics like food, for example, their moos are high pitched, but when moaning about the weather their moos are markedly lower. It's hoped findings will help farmers improve animal welfare.

Producer Carnage had two separate moo clips lined up and good to go. I introduced Daisy on line one and we heard her moo.

I asked Ewen if he knew what she said. He was clueless. Using my cow interpretation skills, I revealed she'd said: 'Vegetables are lovely, have you ever considered a vegan diet?'

Myrtle on line two was next; after her moo I translated: 'Two cows in a field, which one is on holiday?' Ewen didn't know. 'The one with the wee calf.' Honestly, the old ones are the best.

We take a call from Johnny in Stranraer who says his cows do talk to him. Ewen asks: 'What do they say to you?'

He replies in a comical cow-like accent: 'Hello Johnny and how are you today?'

I'm not sure why this is so funny, it just is.

We are full of hilarity this morning; the Friday feeling is palpable.

Our lovely listeners have chosen the Vengaboys 'We Love to Party!' as our new regular Friday anthem, pipping my choice The Proclaimers 'Life with You' by just one per cent. Didn't wipe the smile off my face though, as the Vengaboys are one of my many guilty pleasures.

Today's Aye or Naw question is a belter too. Carnage came up with this one and I laughed out loud when I saw it.

'The Scottish classic "Ye cannae shove yir granny aff a bus" is based on a nineteenth-century Finnish folk song where you were encouraged NOT to throw your grandmother off a sleigh.'

Fifty-eight per cent said 'naw', which was the correct answer. We totally made this one up. It's loads of fun coming up with these and, just in case anyone was concerned, I would like to put it on record that no Scottish or Finnish grannies were harmed in the making of this feature.

And with that, my first week back on Breakfast was over. To be honest, I never realised how much I needed this in my life. The year 2020 was a long hard slog watching all my live events bookings and theatre work get wiped out month by month. I need laughter. I feel like I've come home.

MONDAY 18 JANUARY

Most of the headlines today are about the roll-out of the Covid vaccine, or more specifically supply flow problems and subsequent delays getting them out to people. The Royal Scots Dragoon Guards have now been recruited to help ease the roll-out.

My dad is eighty-six in a couple of weeks and has been shielding. He's had a double heart valve replacement and also has prostate cancer. He's been told he's very vulnerable to infection with the treatment he gets. Not that you'd know it. In the typical West of Scotland male response to medical issues, he says there's nothing wrong with him, he's fine and keeps asking when he can book his next bus trip to Blackpool.

Every day I check in with him to find out if he's heard anything about his jab, nothing so far. If you think I like to chat, five minutes with my dad and you'll know where that comes from.

This morning we talk to Fiona from Elderslie who'd called in to wish her granny a happy birthday. She'd written a message from her family scattered all over Scotland: to Martha Milne from Beauly who's reached the grand old age of a hundred. You could hear the raw emotion in Fiona's voice who, holding back tears, admitted it was really difficult not to be able to celebrate her granny's big day because of travel restrictions.

I told her they just have to go large and party even harder next year on her 101st! We also promised to send a card and some Freddos. Much better than a swanky telegram surely.

A new survey reveals the top five bad bedtime habits:

1. Streaming a TV show or film in bed
2. Drinking beer or wine
3. Watching videos on YouTube or Instagram
4. Scrolling social media feeds
5. Having a snack in bed

I'm only guilty of number three; on the rare occasion I have my phone with me in bed I do love watching videos of animals being rescued. I think right now it is the perfect tonic, seeing happy endings with scared, scrawny, shivering puppies transformed into bouncing, euphoric dogs finding their forever home.

I never eat in bed although it does remind me of one of the greatest unsolved mysteries in my life. The unexplained midnight feast of 1993.

Back in my crazier days I woke up one morning with an empty plate with a knife and fork on top on the pillow next to me.

To this day I have no idea what I made or what takeaway delights had been decanted onto said plate. I looked forensically for evidence. Stains on the plate, smells, kitchen chaos, empty wrappers. Nothing!

I even checked the bin and there was nothing at all to make my cryptic cuisine any clearer.

I'm now older and wiser but feel the principal I adopted back then should still stand: if you can't remember eating it – the calories don't count...

TUESDAY 19 JANUARY

Today came the news parents were dreading. First Minister Nicola Sturgeon has announced the kids are not going back to school for a while to come.

This was not unexpected, but you can hear collective sighs of despair coming from parents everywhere.

I'm in several WhatsApp chats with pals who are mothers, and the most recurring comment is, 'F****** fractions!'

Scotland remains in tier four lockdown and it's very noticeable to Ewen and me how our show must evolve.

Pre-Covid the majority of people would start to listen from about 6 a.m. onwards; between 7.30 and 8.45 a.m. was the peak time for interaction like calls and texts and it would tail off when people arrived at work at 9 a.m. and the kids were dropped off at school.

Now most people are working from home, the kids don't need a lift and in general most folk are getting up a lot later.

I suggested starting the show at 8 a.m. (yes, I am a chancer) but they were having none of it. Ah well, worth a try.

In today's 'Happy News', Dolly Parton is celebrating her seventy-fifth birthday. She's one of my all-time favourite superstars for her songwriting, voice, musicality and humour. Her philanthropic efforts are incredible too. Her Imagination Library, a book-gifting service to underprivileged kids, has given away over 150 million books. She also gave one million dollars of her own cash to help fund a Covid vaccine research project.

I was lucky enough to catch her in concert in Glasgow. Her stories between songs were a delight and I counted her playing eleven different instruments throughout the gig.

If you've not seen it yet, google 'Dolly Parton in an Irish bar'. It's a fabulous clip of a night in Dublin when Dolly was on holiday and the pub guitarist recognised her. She gets up to sing 'Coat of Many Colours' with him and the place goes wild.

We could all do well to remember some of Dolly's finest quotes. Here's my top three:

1. If you want a rainbow you have to put up with the rain.
2. It costs a lot of money to look this cheap.
3. If you don't like the road you are walking, start paving another one.

We play '9 to 5' and it sounds amazing. Just what we need on another rainy day. Happy birthday Dolly.

My Aye or Naw question is causing quite a stir too: the Scotland men's football team qualified for nine World Cups. Is this true? Aye or naw?

I wish I'd secretly filmed Ewen sitting in the corner of our studio during the two songs between question and answer. He had a full-on conversation with himself and even fell out with himself twice. Producer Carnage and I were almost crying with laughter as he got more and more worked up trying to remember the World Cups we'd been to. He thought we had only been to six. I had to explain there was in fact life before he was born!

This was a tricky one again. The answer is in fact aye. Scotland have qualified for nine World Cups ... but we only played in eight!

Back in 1950, we declined our place! Sounds like madness, but the story is quite fascinating. FIFA offered two places to the winner and runner-up of the British Home Championships, which consisted of Scotland, England, Ireland and Wales. Sounds like a joke.

It was an olive branch to get these countries back into the FIFA fold after a break, since just after the First World War, Scotland thought this seemed unfair to all the other countries in the world, that two out of four teams from this wee tournament would progress, while they all had to compete in rigorous group stages to qualify. Scotland decided before the British Home Championships began that if we finished second, we would not go. It came down to the last game. 133,000 filled Hampden where England won 1–0 and claimed their trip to Brazil.

Scotland did indeed finish second in the group but held their moral sporting high ground. While this sounds massively honourable I reckon it was because EasyJet didn't fly direct to Rio back then ...

WEDNESDAY 20 JANUARY

Today is the end of an era. President Donald Trump leaves the White House to be replaced by Joe Biden and it's fair to say everyone I know is more than delighted with this development.

With Putin, Trump, Kim Jong-un and Boris as our significant world leaders, it feels like we've been living in a bad Bond movie.

In the world of celebrity, Take That singer Gary Barlow is celebrating his fiftieth birthday. He's sold over fifty million records globally and has six Ivor Novello songwriting awards under his belt.

I've seen Take That a couple of times: once in the SEEC, which was a memorable gig for all the right reasons, and once at Hampden, which was not memorable at all and that was nothing to do with the skills of Mr Barlow and his buddies.

The show was arguably one of the finest staging spectaculars of all time; it was the Circus Tour and millions had been spent on stunning pyrotechnics, stage design and choreography.

Unfortunately, my friends and I stood in the wrong place on the pitch at Hampden. My pal Mini-Me (who is a toaty wee thing) found a great space right in front of the stage we could all fit into. She'd picked the spot as an official vendor selling wine out of a giant rucksack contraption with two taps, white and red, and was right in front of us. I decided it was best not to ask which year and region in France the grapes were grown. Between us we enthusiastically drained his stock while the support act was on.

So much so, and I am not proud of this at all, none of us really remember the show.

A few days later another pal who'd been on the following night asked me what I'd thought of the elephant. I had no idea what she was talking about and told her there were definitely no animals during our performance.

Turns out she meant the spectacular giant 26-foot mechanical elephant which was operated by seventeen puppeteers inside.

I was adamant there was no elephant in our performance. Then checked my phone. Every single picture of the girls and I dancing to Take That had that humungous elephant right behind us.

Take That and elephants may never forget – but we certainly did. Pleased to report, these days I'm much more sensible. I now never take photos that can be used as evidence . . .

THURSDAY 21 JANUARY

Bold Age Pensioners! What a brilliant title. News today reveals that grandparents in 2021 are more likely to be into heavy metal bands like Guns N' Roses, Deep Purple and Led Zeppelin than more traditional 'grandparent sounds' like jazz, folk or classical music.

Our Bold Age Pensioners are also tech savvy with seventy-five per cent of them enjoying Facebook. A quarter also have their own Instagram account, although surely that should be Instagran.

My dad has only learned a few things on his iPad after going to lessons at the local library. He bought it in a pawn shop in Clydebank for £30 a couple of years ago, so I'm just delighted it's still working.

While he's now mastered Solitaire, he point-blank refuses to get email as he thinks Vladimir Putin will be delving into his bank account and browsing history. I tried to point out that googling the weather in Rothesay and playing Jimmy Shand tunes probably wouldn't be a priority for Kremlin spies to investigate but he's having none of it.

We play Bon Jovi for all the rocking grannies and grandads out there.

For a bit of light relief this morning I share the news that it's Squirrel Appreciation Day. Live on air, we try and think of some famous squirrels and I mention Tufty, a cartoon squirrel who taught road safety tips.

It took Ewen a while to recall, but when Producer Carnage played a wonderfully crackly advert from the 1970s where Tufty tells us how we must take Mummy with us when visiting the ice cream van, we're thrust back in time.

I remember going to the Tufty Club at the local Scout Hall when I was about four. We learned how to cross a road safely and we got a sticker each week if we completed the lesson. At the end of the season, and only if you had paid enough attention, you were awarded the highly sought-after Tufty Club metal badge.

On Twitter a listener called Jamie Morrison asked me if I had ever reached the dizzy heights of achieving the metal badge. I assured him I had. He replied he'd got one when he was little, but his best pal didn't and continued to be outraged at this all these years down the line. I suggested he bought him one on eBay as a surprise for his next birthday which he promised to do.

It's funny how people are loving nostalgia so much at the moment, probably because it reminds us of simpler and happier times.

A bit of googling later and I find out Tufty was retired from road safety duties in the mid-1980s. I wonder if he lost a square-go to the Green Cross Code man. Nah, that's just nuts.

FRIDAY 22 JANUARY

Have you heard the one about the haggis from outer space? As jokes go this one sounds offal.

Simon Howie, the famous Scottish butcher, sent a haggis into space ahead of Burns Night. The haggis reached the edge of space soaring over twenty miles (107,293 feet) above earth, attached to a weather balloon. We now have special footage of the haggis flying nearly four times the height of Everest and 3.5 times higher than a jumbo jet can go, before landing safely once again in the Scottish borders.

Many people are asking the question: why?

I think Mr Howie, who'll feature in every news bulletin across the country today, knows that answer very well. Great PR and a happy story in tough times. The haggis, a small elusive creature native to the Highlands, is no stranger to heights. A charity Burns supper was once held on the summit of Kilimanjaro in 2010. How everyone got a taxi home half-cut after that one is a mystery.

I wonder if I could fire Ewen into orbit for some good PR for the new show. He's always been a bit out there and a space cadet anyway.

Other news today includes Oasis releasing a twelfth album. Liam Gallagher will not be part of it. Which means it's not really Oasis then is it? I'm utterly convinced they'll get back together soon for a comeback tour. I loved Oasis in the 1990s and anyone who's ever had the pleasure of a party back at my flat over the years – that's more than half of Scotland – will know 'She's Electric' is my signature 3 a.m. piano tune.

I always say it's not about perfection, it's about enthusiasm. An enthusiastic but musically questionable karaoke performance is always much more enjoyable than a sedate but note-perfect rendition.

Talking of parties, my Aye or Naw question today really made me chuckle: Hollywood star Bill Murray once gatecrashed a student party in St Andrews, drank vodka, did their dishes and left. Is this true? Aye or naw?

Eight-seven per cent of you guessed correctly. It was 'aye'. He did. Back in October 2019, while attending the Dunhill Cup, he got talking to some students in a bar, they invited them to their party, he went.

There's video footage of the then seventy-year-old star singing 'Loch Lomond' with a guitar-playing student. Apparently, the police turned up about the noise. One student revealed: 'Bill stood up and just stared at them, they couldn't believe their eyes and just told us to politely turn the noise down a bit and then they left.'

I guess if he once neutralised a giant marshmallow man with a laser gun you're not going to mess, are you?

It was at this point the award-winning actor went to the sink and washed all their dishes before thanking them for a great night and walking back to his hotel. What a legend. I hope he comes to my flat one night too. I've got a right manky soup pot for him to tackle.

MONDAY 25 JANUARY

Happy Burns Night. It feels weird not having any gigs this week. I've spoken or performed in some shape or form at Burns Nights since I was about five years old.

My dad used to run Scottish shows for tourists so carrying in a giant haggis behind a piper was my first paid job. If I recall, the fee was one cheeseburger from the nearest Wimpy and I was beyond chuffed with that.

For the last three years I've performed at the Famous Westsound Burns Supper, one of the biggest and best in the world.

In year one I did the reply from the lassies, in year two I addressed the haggis (complete with full-size sword to dramatically stab it open – I'm nothing if not theatrical) and last year I was invited to do the toast to droothy cronies. I'm pretty sure they made the last one up just to give me a slot but it was great fun, and they allowed me to rewrite some Burns songs giving them a modern twist.

I'd spoken on our Sunday show about picking up my dad a microwave Burns supper for one and felt pleased with myself for remembering.

When I went out to visit him (which I do every Sunday, Tuesday and Thursday for basic caring duties), I had the fear when I arrived at his house and the front door was open. I ran up the stairs in a panic and was mighty relieved to be met with cooking smells and the sound of fiddle music playing from his kitchen.

Always the showman, he was wearing his full Burns supper regalia, black trousers, a dress shirt and his Buchanan tartan waistcoat. A haggis was boiling in a pot and, trusty fiddle in arms, he played me a rousing rendition of 'A Man's a Man for A That'.

Well that certainly put my ping haggis dinner in the shade.

He made me address the haggis with the direction: 'Just do the four verses, Toots, before it cools doon.'

We feasted on haggis, neeps and tatties and shared our tales of Burns suppers past. Lockdown is tough on everybody, but I know it's especially hard for him. He's so used to being out and about, it breaks my heart to see him in the house so much. I cherish these times and know how lucky I am to have the time to enjoy his stories.

As a Scottish fiddler this time of year was always his busiest; one year he did seventeen consecutive Burns suppers. I remember it clearly, as the night he finally rejoined us for a family dinner my mum inexplicably served haggis. He nearly boaked.

Ewen's not a fan of Burns suppers at all. He says it all goes over his head and it isn't for 'his type'. I argue that Burns was a man of the people and his words cross all divides. He's not having it. Sadly, statistics rule in his favour. Only forty-seven per cent of people associate Burns Night with his poetry, fifty-six per cent use it as an excuse just to eat haggis while sixty-three per cent use it to celebrate all things Scottish.

I've a few good topical Aye or Naw questions for today so I rapid-fire my way through them with Ewen: There are more statues dedicated to Robert Burns around the world than any other non-religious figure after Queen Victoria and Christopher Columbus. Is this true? Ewen correctly guesses 'aye'.

Did Robert Burns have an unusually large heid? Again, he correctly answers 'aye'. Burns's skull was measured when he was exhumed to be put in Dumfries Mausoleum and it was found to be much bigger than average.

And finally, the one I put to the listeners: Michael Jackson's hit song 'Thriller' was inspired by his love of Rabbie Burns and the poem 'Tam o' Shanter'. Is this true? Aye or naw?

Eighty-seven per cent voted 'naw' as it does sound ridiculous. However, the correct answer is 'aye'. Jackson was fascinated by the lyrics of Burns and even helped write a musical with his producer pal David Gest, putting contemporary music to Burns's poetry. Gest revealed Jackson had told him 'Thriller' was roughly inspired by the supernatural tale of Tam o' Shanter.

Dad and I tried to recite this poem from memory at our impromptu lunch yesterday. I got to about the end of page two and he managed to keep going.

He then said to me: 'Did you know Rabbie Burns once spent a passionate evening with a gorgeous woman from Russia?'

Surprised, I said: 'I know he liked the ladies, but I've not heard about that one.'

He replied: 'Aye, he didn't understand a word she said, but he fair enjoyed her craic!'

There's no hope for me, is there?

TUESDAY 26 JANUARY

G'day Sports. Happy Australia Day. The country that is also a continent is the focus of our show.

We have songs from Australian artists like Kylie, INXS, Olivia Newton-John and Men at Work.

Producer Michael from our Sunday show, and now our big boss on the Greatest Hits Network, reminds us that our previous boss at Real Radio had a hilarious encounter with the lead singer of the latter.

We get the legend that is Bossman Jay Crawford on the phone, and ever the storyteller, he has us in stitches with details of how he nearly got the recording star arrested after a night on the swally.

It was back in the eighties and Jay was a DJ on Forth 1. Men at Work were number one in the UK and in America. Back then this was an achievement only previously accomplished by the Beatles, the Monkees, Simon and Garfunkel and Rod Stewart.

Colin Hay, the frontman from Men at Work, was born in Saltcoats and moved to Australia with his family at the age of fourteen.

Bossman Jay loves to entertain and giving visitors great memories of Scotland is one of his specialities. So much so, Jay and his new bestie Colin had a wonderful night rampaging through a succession of Edinburgh hostelries and nightclubs including late drinks at Buster Browns and the Mercado.

On their way back to Colin's hotel for a nightcap, they sang and danced their way up George Street. Ewen thought one of them had a cheeky wee toilet stop but that was neither confirmed nor denied by discreet Bossman Jay who will never throw a celebrity friend under the proverbial tour bus.

Jay admitted their boisterous behaviour did result in the local constabulary pulling over and putting him in the back of their police car.

The questioning went as follows:

Polis: Name?

Jay: Jay Crawford.

Polis: Occupation?

Jay: Radio presenter on Forth 1.

Polis: Why are you making so much noise on a Tuesday at 2 a.m.?

Jay: See the guy standing on the pavement there?

Polis: Yes.

Jay: He's just got to number one in the charts on both sides of the Atlantic.

And with that one line, in a simpler world before selfies, the local cops shook hands with a bewildered musician who'd feared a night in the cells, rather than the resultant congratulatory 'on your way boys, now just keep the volume down a bit.'

I adore stories like this. Legendary nights out that were never planned. I can't wait until we are allowed out to play again. I'm going to dance all night and eat chips and cheese at closing time with no guilt whatsoever.

We also manage to squeeze in a call with my childhood friend Rosanne Reid who lives and works in Sydney to find out what celebrations were taking place for Australia Day in Australia.

Rosanne was just back from the pub! Thankfully she'd only had a few drinks so was perfectly chatty. Australia locked down in March 2020 with tough border controls and now Covid rates are extremely low. This means pubs, clubs and restaurants are all open, but with restrictions still in place.

Rosanne revealed it was thirty-eight degrees and she'd spent the morning swimming in the outdoor pool with her daughter before meeting friends for an afternoon of celebrations down her local pub. It honestly seems like a parallel universe.

When all of this is over, I must put it on my travel wish list to visit her. The first single I ever bought – Phil Collins 'You Can't Hurry Love' – was a birthday present for Rosanne when we were in primary school. I remember sitting on the floor next to a plate of white bread banana sandwiches at her party. The young team of today with their fancy nachos, popcorn chicken and Nando's don't know they're born!

In other news, scientists have revealed the benefits of having an afternoon nap include better mental agility and increased awareness of surroundings, verbal fluency and working memory. As long as you don't oversleep, I am a fan of a wee forty winks, and given that it's named after me I think I'll grab one now. So, on doctor's orders, I might try for a wee Cat nap to dream of golden Australian beaches. Purrfect.

WEDNESDAY 27 JANUARY

It's always an interesting dynamic when your friend becomes your boss.

Victoria Easton-Reilly is now head of programming for Bauer in Scotland. Wee Vixen, as I've always called her, is not only my friend, she also used to produce different shows involving both Ewen and me in a previous life at Real Radio.

We were drinking buddies, party pals and raucous roommates on previous work trips to Benidorm and Torremolinos, and it's fair to say we both know way too much to ever fall out!

Victoria was always determined, creative and ambitious, and her commitment and love of radio paid off. She ended up moving to London to produce the Radio 1 Breakfast Show before returning to Scotland to be in charge of pretty much everything.

Today is Mark Owen from Take That's forty-ninth birthday and while that might feel like a massively random fact, it has a very important link to our esteemed leader.

For years I've never quite got to the bottom of the 'Victoria and Mark from Take That' story.

The version I heard involved his pants going missing from a washing line and police involvement.

No better time than now to get the definitive as part of our 'Song with a Story' feature. Today Victoria told us the truth, the whole truth and nothing but the truth (apart from maybe a few bits to keep her in employment).

Back in the early 1990s she was Take That's biggest fan. Mark Owen was her 'one' and she travelled to Oldham with a friend to see if they could find him (I told you she was determined).

On the first trip, she arrived at his mum and dad's house to find about thirty other love-struck teens hanging about outside. His parents regularly dished out tea and biscuits.

No luck on this occasion but she was not put off. Many letters were exchanged with fellow devotees, who had a kind of secret Take That pen pal society. Eventually she was given the address of Mark Owen's new flat, his bachelor pad no less.

On her next trip, she arrived once again to a throng of excited girls all waiting for the diminutive pop star to return with his shopping.

The waiting was too much for Wee Vixen who went for a prowl round his back garden. On seeing a gap in the fence, she slipped through and got as far as his back door for a peek through the glass.

She saw a pair of slippers in the hallway, and that is as exciting as this tale gets. He never returned home that day. She never removed his pants from his washing line and the police never apprehended her for being the phantom celebrity knicker knocker.

Ewen has perpetuated this myth for years and was clearly disappointed to hear the truth. The thing is, much as I love her, I'm not sure I believe her tame version of this yarn, a radio edit you might call it.

We play 'Everything Changes' for her, and know with a degree of joy that nothing really does – she's just as full of mischief and as likely to pinch his pants now as she was back then.

THURSDAY 28 JANUARY

Prime Minister Boris Johnson is visiting a vaccine centre in Castlemilk this morning; First Minister Nicola Sturgeon is asking if it's really an essential journey as travel in and out of Scotland is currently illegal.

Everyone is getting very scunnered of Covid and politics and the increasingly depressing mind-games of Covid-politics.

What we need is a fabulous love story to cheer us up.

Our favourite bendy person, actor and Pilates coach Mori Christian told us a few weeks ago she had a great tale about a song. She wasn't kidding; we phone her up to get the gossip and her 'Song with a Story'.

It's the unlikely tale of how Billy Connolly sent her on the path to true love.

Back in the 1990s, Mori met a hottie at her friend's engagement party. This lad was her friend's soon to be husband's best mate. They dated for a few months before he revealed he was moving to Atlanta, Georgia in the USA with his work. She was gutted. They tried long distance phone calls, but it wasn't working out.

To cheer her up, her pal organised a big weekend night out. Her friend, who worked in the hairdressers at the Hilton in Glasgow, organised drinks at the hotel before they hit the pubs and clubs of Glasgow.

Anyone who has partied hard in Glasgow knows the Hilton has a great late-night residents bar where you can always persuade some random with a room key to buy you and your pals drinks with a twenty-pound note.

After moping about the dancefloors, they returned to the Hilton for a nightcap. I'll let Mori take it away from here as she told the story with such enthusiasm and joy we were spellbound.

She revealed: 'I was drowning my sorrows and I saw an impressive figure sitting alone at the bar. I realised it was one of my all-time heroes Billy Connolly. I've always thought he was very wise so fuelled by Dutch courage, I said hello to him and asked if it was okay to ask him a question.

He was lovely and told me to pull up a seat. I then told him the whole story about meeting my man, how I thought I was in love but that he had moved to America, and it was all a disaster and that my life was ruined.

After listening intently, Billy Connolly just looked at me and said: 'Well, what are you doing here? Go and get him. LET LOVE LIVE.'

It was exactly the advice I needed. I downed my drink, got a taxi home, phoned him in Georgia and drunkenly shouted, 'I'VE JUST MET BILLY CONNOLLY AND I'M COMING TO LIVE WITH YOU IN AMERICA.'

Ewen and I are speechless, laughing and in awe at the same time.

I always need to know the ending to a story so asked: 'So what happened?'

She laughed: 'I went to America and twenty-one years and three kids later we are back in Scotland and still very much together thanks to the Big Yin.'

Amazing! We played her request of Alison Limerick's 'Where Love Lives'.

What a magic story for her weans.

FRIDAY 29 JANUARY

Ewen and I are in the *Scottish Sun*.

Usually, this sentence would strike fear through my heart. What did I do on a night out? Who took the photos? How do I explain this to my wee dad?

Thankfully we are not front page, we are the centre spread with a lovely feature written by Matt Bendoris about how we first got together on air back in the Real Radio days and to share the news that we are back on *Ewen and Cat at Breakfast*.

Ewen retweets the article calling it 'the love story for our time'. He's really not right in the dome.

Every Friday on the show we have 'Free Play Friday' where the listeners get to choose any upbeat songs they fancy.

Our first three calls are from Debbie and Gordon in Gibraltar, Davie in Sweden and Kenneth Hughes in Oban. I often forget that with the modern joys of phone apps and internet listening we can spread our cheery nonsense all over the world.

Debbie and Gordon want 'I'm on My Way' by The Proclaimers as he's originally from Edinburgh; Davie wanted anything from Big Country while Kenneth told us he was listening to the show drinking a pint of milk and smoking a large Panama cigar and fancied some Cher.

I have this vision of him overlooking Oban Bay, with the CalMac ferries slowly leaving the harbour with his milk and cigar, the perfect picture of calm.

It's always fascinating getting a glimpse into other people's lives. Kenneth and his slightly unusual breakfast ritual really made us think. Ewen decides that when we finally get round to putting on our Edinburgh Fringe show, he wants to call it 'A pint of milk and a Panama cigar'. I'll make sure Kenneth gets some freebies.

One of the best things about being back full-time is getting to see people in the morning. George Bowie and Cassi Gillespie are the Breakfast Show presenters on one of our sister stations, Clyde 1.

At one point in our careers Bowie at Breakfast was probably our biggest rival. We all laugh about it now because the truth of the matter is that we all get on brilliantly and always have.

We get to catch up, socially distanced and masked-up of course, in the large empty office after we're all off air.

This morning Toploader 'Dancing in the Moonlight' is blaring through the speakers. I don't know why, but this is one of my most hated songs. It just grates on me. Like Simply Red and 'Fairground'. If anyone ever needs secret information out of me, play that song on a loop and I'll tell you my mother's maiden name, my date of birth and the codes to my offshore bank account in Rothesay.

George shares my irrational Toploader feelings, adding: 'It's almost as annoying as anything by The Lightning Seeds or M People.'

I laugh. He has no idea he has just stepped on a musical grenade for he's inadvertently slagged off two of Ewen's absolute favourites. Predictably, Ewen kicks off by listing every successful single M People have ever released and says to George, 'You clearly haven't a clue what works on a dancefloor.'

This is dynamite. I'm now crying tears of laughter. As George, with his famous GBX mixes and club nights, is one of the most recognised and respected DJs in Scotland.

(I once bumped into George when I was out on a walk with my Polish friend Joanna. She asked who he was, and I said: 'He's like the Scottish Calvin Harris.' Before she pointed out the obvious!)

George and I are both buckled as Ewen tells us how he knows best. He was the DJ in nightclubs in Dubai . . .

Cassi, an absolute gem of a girl who is also a fantastic live DJ and presenter, shocks me to the core by agreeing with Ewen that M People are crowd pleasers.

Ewen decides to prove it by blasting out 'Moving On Up' from his phone and getting Cassi up to dance (four metres apart) in the deserted office.

That's my cue to leave. George and I put on our coats and depart.

I look back through the glass doors and these two bampots are dancing like it's 3 a.m. in Magaluf. It is 10.15 a.m. This really is the best job in the world.

MONDAY 1 FEBRUARY

Another day, another actor tipped to play James Bond. This time it is Scottish *Outlander* hunk Sam Heughan. He's been in the running for a couple of years now and I think he'd be brilliant.

Ewen isn't convinced enough people know who he is. He plays the dashing Jamie Fraser in the worldwide TV smash. His success is global. I remember being cornered by a feisty pensioner from Chile on a boat trip in Cuba who, on hearing I was Scottish, demanded to know if I knew Jamie Fraser.

I didn't have good enough Spanish to say, 'He's not a real person' so I said '*Si*'. For the rest of the trip she took pictures of her hugging me to send to her friends.

Sam is in the news today because he posted a picture of himself in a kilt on the Men in Kilts Instagram page (frantically googles Men in Kilts Instagram page for research purposes). His comments with the picture are: 'The name is Heughan. Sam Heughan.' Clearly a nod to James Bond's famous introduction.

What does he know that he's not telling us? I guess lots, that's why he'd be a great spy!

I've never met him, but he did me a massive favour a few years ago. A friend was working on set in *Outlander* and got him to record a video message for my mate *Pop Idol* winner Michelle McManus. Michelle loves Sam Heughan as Jamie Fraser. We went to Kilkenny in Ireland for her hen do and I managed to get the pub to play the clip through their giant TV screens.

Sam, dressed as Jamie Fraser said in the video: 'Michelle, I can't believe you are getting married. Jeff is a nice guy but really I'm gutted.'

I'm not sure what he said after that as I couldn't hear a word as she was crying so hard and screaming 'JAMIE FRASER' at the telly. Drink had been taken. He may or may not be the next Bond but it's fair to say she was both shaken AND stirred.

My post-show lockdown hike today was with my friend Andrew Agnew. He's a fantastic actor and directed my last play 'One Singer – One Song.' Andrew is known to most people as PC Plum from *Balamory* and, even though it's nearly twenty years since the children's TV favourite filmed in Tobermory was first screened, generations of kids and parents alike still know the programme inside out and its iconic theme tune: 'What's the story in Balamory, wouldn't you like to know?'

I always enjoy watching people spot Andrew walk past and try to work out how they know him. Generally, it will take thirty seconds before someone shouts: 'PC Plum.'

Like my friend Stephen Purdon from *River City* who now answers to his TV character Shellsuit Bob, Andrew is always gracious and grateful for playing such a much-loved character.

It really is a showbiz hike as totally by chance in the park, we bump into our mutual pals Johnny Mac from the Kings Panto and his choreographer and dancer wife Stephanie MacDonald, both of whom have starred in my plays.

Andrew and I then meet Anita Manning from *Antiques Road Trip*, *Bargain Hunt* and *Flog It*. She's a proper character and perches on a socially distanced wall for a chat.

Anita once came to my flat after I'd cleared a relative's house of boxes crammed with ceramics, jewellery and silver (to be clear, she had sadly passed away – I didn't knock it!).

There was so much stuff it filled my kitchen and as I'd once hosted

The Hour on STV with Anita as a guest, I figured we were pals enough to ask her to take a look.

I'll be honest, I thought I was sitting on a fortune. Slowly Anita worked her way through the jewellery, diamond rings, gold bracelets and watches.

I'll never forget what happened next. She put her eye glass down on the worktop and turned to me and said: 'They were not a family from money, were they, Cat?'

And with that one sentence, my five-star holiday to the Caribbean and lobster and champagne lifestyle disappeared into thin air. We still laugh at it now. The silver was all silver plate, the jewellery mostly costume jewellery or the cheapest diamonds and all the ceramics, well, she told me: 'I'm sure somebody will buy them if you give them to your favourite charity shop.'

The entire haul netted me less than two hundred pounds. Which I used to pay for my dad and me to go to Islay for a weekend. His dearly departed cousin would have been delighted.

TUESDAY 2 FEBRUARY

Welcome to Groundhog Day. Welcome to Groundhog Day, welcome to Groundhog Day ... you get the drift.

Made famous by the 1993 Bill Murray film, 2 February is officially Groundhog Day, the day which has come to symbolise twenty-four hours on repeat.

Mostly celebrated in the US and Canada, it derives from the Pennsylvanian Dutch superstition that if a groundhog (a small rodent) emerges from its burrow on this day and sees its shadow due to clear weather, it will retreat to its den and winter will persist for six more weeks. However, if it does not see its shadow because it is cloudy, spring will arrive early.

While the tradition remains popular, extensive scientific surveys and research have shown, according to my good friend Wikipedia, 'there is no significant correlation between a groundhog seeing its shadow and the subsequent arrival of spring-like weather'.

As the film was about a weatherman reliving the same day over and over and over again, we ask the question: 'What day in your life would you like to be your Groundhog Day?'

I opted for Thursday 12 November 2020. A night never to be forgotten.

Serbia versus Scotland, the winner qualifies for the Euros. In typical Scotland style, we are winning 1–0 until the last few seconds of the game when they equalise. Extra-time feels like it lasts a fortnight and the game ends 1–1, meaning penalties.

Ewen and I are on air with Steven Mill doing an alternative fan-based football show. I genuinely can't cope.

I've followed Scotland since I was fourteen years old and have been to over forty away games. I've experienced the occasional highs (James McFadden verus France/beating Sweden in Italia '90) and a plethora of lows, nearly there's and nights of glorious failure.

Truthfully, I expected us to go out. Turns out the 2020 Scotland squad are magnificent at penalties; we score all five and wait nervously for Serbia take their fifth kick. Time stands still. It is almost in slow motion; keeper David Marshall dives the right way and pulls off the save to make history.

I have since heard back the audio of that moment and can only apologise to anyone listening. What a chaotic riot. Ewen and I were all over the place. Twenty-two years since we qualified for anything and the emotion got to us.

There were real tears. Ewen fell to his knees and poor Steven had to commentate on his own as I made a succession of involuntary squealing noises of relief, joy and disbelief.

We play the clip back on the show today and it's much worse than I thought, although there's no hiding the genuine emotion.

Lots of people get in touch with us to describe the day they'd love to be their Groundhog Day.

Sharon Imrie said it was feeding wild kangaroos in Australia, Mandy Scott remembered Killie winning the Scottish Cup and the town going mental, Gary Nielson says finally seeing Bruce Springsteen in concert, while Lesley Ewing summed up a lot of people right now by revealing her ideal Groundhog Day would be the last time she managed to sleep through the night. Covid dreams and insomnia are massive problems at the moment.

This afternoon in the Scottish Parliament, Nicola Sturgeon announces we shall remain in lockdown until at least the end of February; nothing is open apart from essential shops and we can only meet one other person outside.

Groundhog Day? This has been Groundhog year. Bring on that vaccine pronto.

It's been a tough afternoon for me. My dad gets the results of his latest scan back from the Beatson and as I expected, his prostate cancer has now spread to his ribs and is causing him pain.

He is determined not to be ill and tells his consultant he is just fine. We discuss his limited pain management options, and my dad promises the doctor I'll give him a shout-out on the radio for all the great work he's done keeping him alive. Dad is stubborn and determined and brave and scared, and I just have to follow his lead. He's not quite in denial but not far from it. He uses gallows humour to survive.

When I leave his house, I tell him he better not kick the bucket overnight as it's his birthday tomorrow; I've already bought his present and that would be massively inconvenient.

He stands at the doorstep laughing and I know regardless of how difficult this is going to get, I must try and keep laughing too.

WEDNESDAY 3 FEBRUARY

Happy Birthday to my dad Bobby Harvey, eighty-six years young today. This is nothing short of a miracle. It is no secret he was an alcoholic for over twenty years, and, as I previously mentioned, has had a double heart valve replacement surgery and is now battling prostate cancer.

On two separate occasions he was given less than a month to live. Once, when he got sectioned back in his worst drinking days and couldn't even eat solids, the other time before the life-saving heart surgery nine years ago.

He knows he is lucky but his gratitude and joy at being given a second and third chance is beyond humbling. He makes every moment of every single day count.

Without getting overly emotional, once he finally managed to kick the booze in 1983, he's been the best, kindest, funniest dad anyone could ever wish for. I know he's tried way too hard to make up for the lost years, but he has and some. He is my best friend and my hero in one.

Today we let him loose on our 'Song with a Story' feature. Ewen and I are both apprehensive about where this could go.

Dad came on the show and told us this tale: 'I used to run the MAFIA. This is the Milngavie Accordion and Fiddle Instrumentalists Association. After these nights everyone ended up in our house where your mum made up some pieces which were usually chicken or tomato.

'One evening Jimmy Shand was there and she asked him what he would like. Jimmy said he wanted a corned beef sandwich. Your mum had to nip two doors down to get a tin from our neighbour as he was showbiz royalty, and she didn't want to let him down.

'Jimmy was bigger than the Beatles in Scotland and number one at the time. He was an amazing man, so I want to hear Jimmy playing the Bluebell Polka.'

Now Dad knows our playlist does not include traditional Scottish tunes, but we managed to play out a short clip. I'd pre-warned him to have a more suitable song as his 'real' request. I did not expect what happened next.

Me: Come on, Dad, you know we can't play that song – do you have another?

Dad: Yes. I want the Prodigy – 'Firestarter'.

Ewen and I are in hysterics.

Dad: It reminds me of dancing in the Ned tent at T in the Park.

Well, that was the end of me. I have absolutely no idea how he knew about the Prodigy, never mind the slam tent at T in the Park, which he'd somehow renamed the Ned tent.

We are inundated with messages from listeners howling with laughter. For a while #nedtent was trending on Twitter.

Eventually we recover long enough for him to ask for The Proclaimers 'Letter from America'.

A lady called Irene Carruthers emails the show asking: 'Was Cat's dad Scottish Fiddle Champion in 1962? If so, I have his autograph. My dad got it for me when we lived in Bearsden years ago.'

Once again, the auld yin has stolen the show. I may be the one with the full-time radio gig, but he will always be the true entertainer and the one getting the last laugh. Long may this continue.

THURSDAY 4 FEBRUARY

Lots of good news today.

1. Eurovision has been scheduled for May in Rotterdam. It was cancelled last year but plans are afoot to make sure it happens this year within restrictions. We get to play our favourite clips including Brotherhood of Man 'Save All Your Kisses' from 1976 and Bucks Fizz 'Making Your Mind Up' from 1981.

2. The secrets of a happy marriage have been revealed. You need to kiss ten times and say 'I love you' nine times a week. Each month you need to go on three dates, have ten deep and meaningful conversations and pull off three surprise romantic gestures. Having three shared hobbies helps too. Ewen says his wife Teresa doesn't like 'Call of Duty' or 'FIFA' and as a result he has no idea how they're still together. A question our listeners ask from her perspective on a daily basis.

3. The top five motivational tunes of all time are announced: The Beach Boys 'Good Vibrations'; Katrina and the Waves 'Walking on Sunshine'; Bon Jovi 'Living on a Prayer'; Abba 'Dancing Queen'; and the top song by Queen – 'Don't Stop Me Now'. (This will delight my friend Janis as it is her all-time favourite song.)

This morning I also manage to get Ewen with a couple of crackers. We're always winding each other up and are equally likely to fall foul of a prank or some banter.

Today he back announces 'Together in Electric Dreams' by Giorgio Moroder and Phil Oakey. I asked him if he'd heard Phil Oakey's sister sing, Carrie. With perfect, albeit unwitting, comedic timing he questioned: 'Carrie-Oakey?' and then groaned as the name sunk in.

Only an hour later I get him again. We've just played 'Sit Down' by James. He is ranting about how people used to sit on the dancefloor in nightclubs to this song.

Ewen: I just don't get it. Why did they do it?

Me: I think the clue is in the title.

BOOM! Job done. I've peaked so might as well go home. Apart from I don't. I'm recording a series of interviews to be broadcast next month on International Women's Day.

Today I have a Zoom call with Jamie Genevieve; she's an internet sensation with 1.4 million followers on Instagram, nearly a million on her YouTube channel and has just launched her own make-up range, Vieve.

The purpose of the call is to find out how she managed to become such a success and to hear her advice for other young women hoping to follow their dreams to eventually own their own businesses.

Jamie tells me about her unexpected rise to fame from working on the make-up counter at Debenhams to being a celebrity in her own right with her own BBC TV show.

I really like her.

I'm a bit too old for the whole 'influencer' concept (a word she doesn't like anyway), but after our video call I can see why she is so popular with the young ones. She seems like a genuinely lovely, grounded ambitious young woman with a good head on her shoulders, as my granny would say.

I ask her for a thirty-second make-up tip to survive all these dreaded Zoom calls. She suggests an early morning face mask. I think a balaclava might be better. Maybe I should be an influencer after all . . .

FRIDAY 5 FEBRUARY

Want to know the secret to feeling young? I have a list of what the experts suggest.

You need to own the latest iPhone, watch reality TV, beat younger relatives at games, regularly surf the web and catch the eye of someone younger than you.

Do you know what? After reading that, I think I'm okay with continuing to carry on ageing disgracefully.

My other 'Happy News' story today reveals that *Dirty Dancing* has become the number one go-to movie for females during lockdown, beating *Bridget Jones's Diary* and *Pretty Woman* to the top spot.

We play the classic finale track, Bill Medley and Jennifer Warnes singing 'The Time of My Life' and fondly recall the empowering end scene, where Baby and Johnny rock the dancefloor at the Kellermans' end of season revue as a bona fide couple. The iconic lift scene where Jennifer Gray is held powerfully above Patrick Swayze's head has been the downfall of many an inebriated partygoer.

I remember getting a head start at one Real Radio party in Shanghai Shuffle years ago, by firing myself from a standing position on a chair on top of a colleague called Ciaran who, as equally full of cheap cocktails, assured me he could take my weight.

He couldn't. The resultant splat was as dramatic as it was immediate. Thankfully cheap drink can sometimes work as an anaesthetic and we both sprung back up in jig-time vowing never to try professional dance moves ever again.

We've had some cracking 'Song with a Story' callers on this week.

Actor Leah MacRae, who plays Julie in *Gary Tank Commander* and Ellie in *River City* told us: 'I used to make up dance routines with my cousins to put on shows for my mum and my aunties. We always said we would be ten minutes but would emerge four hours later with a fully choreographed piece. Even now when I hear this song, I go into the dance moves. I tell this story in my one-woman show "My Big Fat Diary" and I finally get to perform the entire routing to the audience I wanted all those years ago. My song is the Backstreet Boys and "Everybody".'

Her TV sister, Gayle Telfer Stevens, who plays Caitlin in *River City* and is also one half of the hilarious theatre act, The Dolls, also joined the fun.

She said: 'My song reminds me back to 1992 when I was walking back from school. I'm from a place called the Renton and, when it was warm, we all called it 'Nae Jaikit Weather'. That meant we were allowed to go to school without any coats. We all thought we were the bees' knees with our Benetton jumpers on and would sing this song while trying to impress the cool boys. My song is Arrested Development and "Everyday People".'

Our friend and colleague from Forth 1 Breakfast Show Arlene Stuart is our guest this morning.

She laughed: 'I was in hospital when I was a teenager and when I got home my mum and dad had redecorated my room. It was amazing. Sitting in the middle of it was a brand-new Hitachi sound system. This meant I no longer had to listen to my parents playing Val Doonican. The first album I bought, I played over and over and over again. It was Adam and the Ants, and I had his poster on the wall – that's how I practised snogging.'

Ewen admitted he practised his teenage kissing technique on himself on a mirror 'just to see what it looked like'. Sometimes I think we overshare.

We play 'Prince Charming' for Arlene and I try and think of anything else in the world than the vision of Ewen winching his own face in the mirror. I'm surprised he didn't get a knock back.

MONDAY 8 FEBRUARY

Monday already. Jings, where did the weekend go?

Ah I know, we were on the radio talking tatties; makes a change from mince I suppose.

We had such a laugh yesterday discussing the fact that sales of the humble potato have increased sixty per cent year on year.

No exact reason has been given for this dramatic spud spree, so Ewen assumes it's because everyone's cooking more being stuck at home.

I suggest people might be getting creative and doing potato paintings like we used to do in primary school. He gives me his finest glaikit look.

Thankfully we have a full board of callers all reminiscing about printing with paint and halved potatoes and carving out shapes in them to make fancy patterns.

Ewen genuinely believes everyone is in on a joke to wind him up. Mother and daughter duo Jac and Mia call the show from their car on their way to Asda. Jac explained: 'You've both inspired us. We're off to buy paint and potatoes, as Mia thinks it sounds mental and I used to love it.'

See, we really are influencers. It's only a matter of time before the big brands come sniffing around!

Today the back pages are still all full of our jubilant rugby team: Scotland beat England 11–6 at Twickenham to win the Calcutta Cup on Saturday. It's the first time in thirty-eight years Scotland have won there. I can't help noticing our rugby and football teams both appear to be magnificent when the supporters are not allowed in.

My 'Happy News' today involves avoiding Zoom calls and eating curries for breakfast. Thirty-three per cent of us now try to avoid Zoom meetings. Here are the best three excuses: 1) Loss of internet connection or a dying battery 2) Clashing with another made-up online engagement 3) Being in the middle of making or eating food.

Talking of grub, I am delighted with the latest research which suggests we could all enjoy 'effortless weight loss' by eating leftover dinners rather than sugary cereals for breakfast.

Dr Rangan Chatterjee from BBC's *Doctor in the House* said many conventional breakfasts like sweet cereals or toast and jam play havoc with our blood sugar levels and tucking into a spicy curry would be better for the metabolism.

I have never had a problem with eating any kind of food at any time of day but I'm not sure how much Ewen and Producer Carnage would enjoy my company if I started eating veggie pakora and chicken jalfrezi at 6 a.m. in a studio with no windows. I'm guessing there might be a health and safety issue.

A quirky new social media trend says that whatever song was at number one in the charts when you were seven is how 2021 will pan out for you. It is a wee bit of nonsense, but the theory is the title of the song is going to reflect your year.

My song is Gloria Gaynor 'I Will Survive'. I'm delighted with that as the week before it was The Bee Gees and 'Tragedy'.

Our listeners love these silly wee topics as it is a bit of light relief and another excuse to go back down memory lane. These ones made me laugh.

Caroline Boyde: I've got 'Silver Lady' by David Soul; this year will turn anyone grey.

Stuart Kirkland: 'Red Red Wine' by UB40, how apt!

Darren Paul Lamb: 'Dancing in the Street' by Mick Jagger and David Bowie, aye okay but only once I've got my jag!

Clare McGeogh: I've got 'Killer' by Adamski; I don't know the song but I'd rather not if this is how my 2021 is going to pan out.

Jo Laura: Mine is 'Relax' by Frankie Goes to Hollywood; sums up my lockdown.

And finally, Karen Boyde: My song is David Bowie 'Ashes to Ashes'. I'm pretty certain I don't want this song to define my year. She adds three laughing emojis and we know she's embracing the funny side of it.

Knowing where 'the line' is can be difficult on radio. We try to get the tone right at all times but judging it can be tricky. Yesterday I held back on my best potato joke in case it was too violent for any of the little ones listening. However, given that you lot should all be old enough for this one I'm going to grab my moment.

Do you know what happened to the tattie that had his head chopped off? He was deca-potatoed.

I'll get my jacket (potato).

TUESDAY 9 FEBRUARY

Snowmageddon! Scotland is covered in a deep thick blanket of crisp white snow. As picturesque as it is, brushing six inches of heavy snow off my car is not the easiest start to the day.

Ewen lives in a newish estate built at the top of a hill. Even in summer they're building snowmen in his garden. I'm convinced I'll be flying solo today. However, he has pre-empted the weather and at 11 p.m. last night drove to the hotel nearest the radio station just to make sure he got to work on time. I know he hates me saying this, but he really isn't as daft as he likes to pretend.

Talking of work, eighty per cent of us have experienced an awkward moment there. A list of the most common mistakes made is revealed and Ewen reckons he's guilty of nearly all of them.

Accidentally ending a work call with 'I love you', waving at someone you think you know but don't, dropping your phone down the loo and texting a person you were gossiping about by mistake are all on the list.

My other favourite story of the day is the news that turning eighty is the age we reach our happiest. Something to look forward to in these crazy times.

One brain expert says that despite failing eyesight and creaking joints, most eighty-year-olds are at peace with their lot and seem relatively carefree.

My dad has had a ball in his eighties. I think the fact he never expected to hit his sixties or seventies, never mind his eighties, has put a spring in his step. His ongoing medical battles have not dampened his spirit and this positivity inspires me to keep cheery too. I never let him see me upset with any bad news as his cancer spreads. We keep each other going. A good wee team.

My Aye or Naw question today should fall into the category of that wonderfully Scottish double positive making a negative 'aye right'.

So, the question: There's an old Scottish law stating a Scotsman wearing underwear under his kilt can be fined two cans of beer. Is this true? Aye or naw?

Only twenty-four per cent get the correct answer: aye.

Believe it or not, back in 1935 members of the legal profession made this law, although it is thought it was part of a joke. Many astute listeners wondered when cans of beer were first introduced, and the answer was 1935, the sampling of which I reckon might have played a massive part in the creation of this new law.

Ewen has decided to check into a hotel again tonight as the snow is not going anywhere. I offer to take him on a walk this afternoon as I know he'll hate being left alone in a room in an empty hotel. We walk round the park, go for sweeties from the corner shop, build a snowman and have a snowball fight. I wonder if Piers Morgan and Susanna Reid ever do this.

WEDNESDAY 10 FEBRUARY

'Hi ho, hi ho, it's off to work I go.' I left my flat this morning like Snow White's wee pals with a large shovel and a brush over my shoulder and needed both to dig my car out of the West End Winter Wonderland.

The main roads are clear but getting out of my street is a Siberian driving challenge. I hate driving in ice and snow. I ended up having a really bad headache in one eye yesterday when I got to work. The travel reports from lovely Jo on our show keep reinforcing the 'essential journeys only' message.

I've been told spreading uplifting nonsense to the world is essential, so I am grateful to be allowed out and have a stern word with myself to stop moaning about the weather.

You should never air your dirty laundry in public, so today we do just the opposite. News suggests that millions of us suffer from a syndrome called 'first wash anxiety'. This is the fear of putting new clothes in the washing machine for the first time.

More than three quarters of us feel stressed about ruining clothes in the wash the first time they are cleaned; we also no longer think an item is new if it has been through the wash once.

Ewen, who has a mild form of OCD, takes this story to a new level. He washes T-shirts, pants, socks, jeans and jumpers before ever wearing them, even if they come in a sealed packet.

This seems a bit extreme to me, but he won't wear anything that has not been washed first. He asked me what I do. My reply, 'I just scrape off any crusty bits and skoosh on some Febreze,' probably not the most sensitive retort knowing his phobia.

A lawyer from America is making headlines all over the world today after he activated a comedic Zoom filter by mistake during a live online trial. The filter app turned his head into a talking cartoon cat and the audio is hilarious of the judge trying to help him figure out what he has done wrong.

The best bit is he says with no hint of humour, 'I would like to state that for the record that I am here in person and I am not a cat.'

In a shamelessly tenuous link, we decide to play a Curiosity Killed the Cat song for him.

I have two favourite stories about this famous 1980s band.

1. Back in 1989 they played Strathclyde University Union. Some of my pals managed to squish their way to the front. Eilidh managed to grab a cigarette butt the guitarist stubbed out on the stage and thought it was the best memento in the world. However, my friend Jane went one step further and grabbed the tongue of singer Ben Volpeliere-Pierrot's big white trainer and clung onto him for dear life. I was standing at the back laughing as I watched him sing while visibly trying to boot a lassie off his leg before realising it was one of my gang.

2. I was presenting Retrofest at Culzean Castle in 2007, the line-up included Belinda Carlisle, Kim Wilde and Curiosity Killed the Cat. Ben at the time was famous for liking to party. I met him at the side of the main stage, and he was buzzing. He asked me: 'How did I do, was that okay?' I just smiled before breaking the news: 'You've not been on yet. You're up next.'

In fairness to him, when he did go on, apart from an initial blip when he started singing facing the wrong way, he actually pulled it off. Just goes to show a cat must have nine lives after all.

THURSDAY 11 FEBRUARY

It's quite a showbiz affair today. We have Sharleen Spiteri from Texas on the show and as usual she's hilarious.

We've interviewed her many times and she never disappoints. She's down to earth, sharp, witty and puts Ewen in his place in seconds. We had a boozy night with her and the band years ago at a hotel in Wales where they were playing for a Radio conference.

I remember Ewen trying to steal her chips in the bar and her giving him a look that can only be described as pure Glasgow attitude. He is scared of her and fancies her in equal measure which makes for an interesting dynamic, and I love how she can turn him to mush.

Sharleen's been at home in Wales for lockdown with her husband, daughter and dog and told a brilliant tale about how she's been killing time.

She laughed: 'I'm not sure how it started but I've found myself baking dog biscuits. I threw in some ingredients I thought the dog would like and even tried one as it looked okay. I put a picture of them up on my Instagram and was inundated with people wanting to know the recipe. Between that and making dog cushions I've become quite industrious.'

I suggest it is a whole new line of work for her should the song-writing not work out. My tongue is obviously in my cheek as Texas have been banging out incredible hits for over thirty years. I also suggest she starts her own TV show, *The Great British Bark Off*, where celebrity bakers create cakes for dogs.

Honestly, I can't fathom out why I've never been snapped up to replace Lauren Laverne or Jo Whiley.

Our 'Song with a Story' is another cracker today. I'd expect nothing less from Donald McLeod, gregarious club owner and gig promoter. He could probably fill an entire year with the tales he has from his crazy life.

His story involves the legend that was Prince, a bag of cash and a Glaswegian nightclub.

He explained: 'Back in 1995 Prince was playing the SECC, and Elliot Davies and Tam Coyle, a couple of Scottish promoters, came to me and asked me if I wanted to put him on after the big show in my club, The Garage.

'I thought they were kidding, but they weren't. Prince had fallen out with his record company and needed the money. He wanted £15,000 in cash to play a set. It was a no brainer, I said yes. We had one day to plug the event and still never really knew if he would turn up.

'On the night a massive queue snaked down Sauchiehall Street. The crowd came in and there was no sign of the wee man. I was beginning to get very worried.

'Then all of a sudden, an entourage of about thirty very glamorous Americans rocked up. I was told I must not call him Prince. He was to be called Symbol or the artist formerly known as.

'It was 1 a.m. by now and there were still no instruments on the stage. The crowd were getting restless. One of his security team said he needed paying, so I gave Prince a bag with the £15,000 in it. I asked him if he wanted to count it. He said no, his security team would do that. He sat quietly sipping Stolly vodka and I still had no idea if he was going to perform or not.

'Bit by bit the kit was set up on stage which added to the drama. We waited and waited and then when he decided it was time, he walked down the stairs and performed one of the most memorable sets I've ever seen. He was just so talented. I still look back on that night and wonder if it really happened. So much could have gone wrong, but it didn't and everyone who was there that night knows they were part of something really special.'

So we play Prince and Sheena Easton: 'You've Got the Look.'

I'm gutted I never got to see him in action. Prince that is, not Donald McLeod. I've seen him in action many a time and he's probably just as entertaining.

FRIDAY 12 FEBRUARY

I've got my work cut out this morning. As the self-appointed 'Happy News' correspondent, I've trawled all the papers and online news outlets and find scarce pickings.

Time for a bit of spin!

One of the most interesting stories of the day claims we spend seventeen days of our lives and clock up 2,127 miles, trying to find car parking spaces. Sixty-seven per cent of people list drivers taking up two spaces by parking over the lines as their biggest bugbear.

Twenty-five per cent of us have rowed with a partner over where to park, while twenty per cent have argued with a stranger over a space.

My headline today: 'Great news if you are working from home – no need to stress over finding somewhere to park.' It's all about positive mental attitude.

With Valentine's Day just round the corner, other titbits include a study which reveals more than half of men will wear pants until they fall apart. The biggest turn-offs in the underwear department are worn out knickers and big Bridget Jones pants on women.

Fifty-eight per cent of women say they would like new lingerie as a Valentine's present. I would HATE it. As someone who continues to cut off labels despite being single, the thought of a man knowing my actual size gives me the fear, and yes, I am very aware of how ridiculous this is.

Ewen says men are on a hiding to nothing: 'If I buy it too big, she thinks I think she is fat and if I buy it too wee, she thinks she's enormous and gets upset anyway.'

Apparently in 2021 the most desired Valentine's gift is a new iPad. Aye, and I'd like a fortnight in the Seychelles and speedboat while you're at it.

As it is Free-play Friday we ask for songs with 'love' in the title. I get a Twitter request from George Adam. He has a wee blue tick next to his name meaning he is verified, famous and/or important, so I click on to see who he is.

Turns out he's the MSP for Paisley. He asks for The B-52's and 'Love Shack' for his wife Stacey. He adds that she is a terrible singer and always belts out this song. They are twenty-five years married in June and he says her awful singing still makes him laugh all these years later.

Sounds like a beautifully harmonious relationship to me.

MONDAY 15 FEBRUARY

We play not one but two cracking showbiz 'Song with a Story' features today. I'm loving that the great and the good of the Scottish scene are delighted to join our musical fun.

First up is broadcaster and TV star Kaye Adams from ITV's *Loose Women*. Kaye lives round the corner from me, our paths crossed very briefly at STV in the late 1990s, but now I walk her dog Bea when she needs a dog sitter and pop in for a wee drink when we are allowed. Bea is the best-behaved pooch in town and I'm always delighted when the call comes in.

Kaye revealed: 'Between the ages of seventeen and twenty I was very naff and quite proud of it, I loved cheesy music. I'm taking you back to Grangemouth in the shadow of the gas coolers at the Oxgang House Hotel, that's where we all congregated after a few

Moscow Mules. The pinnacle of the evening was meeting on the dancefloor. We would all sit down in between each other's legs and indulge in some sort of Russian peasant-style floor-slapping ritual while fired up by our Moscow Mules. The song that will take me right back to sitting on that sticky dancefloor is the Gap Band and 'Oops Upside Your Head'.

Next to share their tale is entertainer, comedian and star of the Kings Theatre panto in Glasgow, is Johnny Mac, one of my best pals in the world.

He explained: 'My story happened in lockdown on the night of my wedding anniversary. We'd had a couple of bottles of wine and were loving life. My wife Steph took our dog Betsy out the lane at the back of our flat to do her business and I decided to do what I always do when I'm in the house and have had a wee drink and that's watch a concert from YouTube on the telly. My go-to favourite is Wet Wet Wet at Glasgow Green and I need to play it loud.

'I'm not sure how long they were away as I was singing my head off, but when she came back inside, she was raging. She'd met another dog walker in the lane outside the window who was moaning about "the selfish idiots clearly having a party during lockdown". Steph said: "I know it's terrible isn't it", and had to pretend she didn't live here.

'So, for my lovely wife Steph, who puts up with a lot, I'd love Wet Wet Wet and "East of the River".'

What a song! We are inundated with texts and tweets from listeners who won't get out their cars because they've not heard it for so long.

Later in the show, Ewen mentioned he's struggling with condensation in his car and his brother gave him a very unusual tip to keep the windscreen clear – cat litter in a pair of tights! Neither of us has heard of this before, so we ask if anyone has any experience of this curious technique.

Davey calls in and tells us he has a campervan and uses cat litter in a woolly sock, and it works a treat. I ask him why he uses a sock and not tights and he replied: 'I can never get the tights off the wife.'

Line of the year to Davey. I'll laugh at this one for weeks to come.

TUESDAY 16 FEBRUARY

Happy Pancake Day. I'm far too mature to roll out tossing jokes so I'll get straight to my favourite story of the day.

Television chef and all-round good guy John Quigley was to be our guest today to talk all things pancakes, toppings, how to make the perfect batter, tossing techniques (I'm not laughing, you are) and vegan recipes.

However, his chat is so good we promote him to 'Song with a Story' as we can't think of anyone else in the world who could so effortlessly combine celebrity name-dropping with pancakes.

John runs the Red Onion restaurant in Glasgow and is a 'weel kent' face from the telly. He's been on many daytime TV shows and STV for years.

Every time I meet John, I get him to tell me another story from his colourful past as a touring chef for musicians.

He's cooked for Paul McCartney, Rod Stewart, Morrissey and Whitney Houston. My favourite tale involves Guns N' Roses and a reindeer.

The band were in Norway and singer Axl Rose asked a roadie what the local delicacy was; he was told it was reindeer. Just before the band went on stage Axl asked John to make him reindeer for after the show. With a mobile kitchen set up in the car park of a stadium, John had to source and BBQ a reindeer for the 'Sweet Child O' Mine' star. Apparently, it was lovely. Just don't tell Santa.

However, his pancake story is more topical for today.

He revealed: 'I toured for five years as Bryan Adams' personal chef. He chose me as I've always specialised in vegetarian and vegan cooking before it was trendy.

'One day he asked for vegan pancakes for breakfast and I didn't have a clue how to make them so just invented a recipe with banana, flour and almond milk. This was before you could buy almond milk, so I had to make that myself too. Brian loved them and every single day on tour for the next five years he asked for them. That is a lot of pancakes.'

I asked John which song he would like and he replied, 'I Got the Runs from You' or 'Everything I Chew I Chew it for You'. You can tell he was on that tour for a while.

We play, 'The Only Thing That Looks Good on Me is You'. I'm sure that should be is 'stew'. John missed one!

I get a text in the first twenty minutes of the show from my dad reading: 'Heading to hospital', and I panic. He doesn't have an appointment today. I rush out the studio to call. His consultant has spotted something grim in the latest scan he doesn't like and wants him to get an X-ray for his pelvis and legs. He thinks the cancer is now in his thighs and wants to give him radiotherapy as soon as possible. My brother drives him there and back and I nip over and blitz the bits of his house he doesn't let me near when he is in. He won't notice the difference.

As ever he is in chirpy form when he gets home. Instead of worrying about the new bits of cancer, he is full of praise for the NHS and the speed they got him in and out.

Out of the blue he says: 'Now that I've got you both here, I've got an idea.'

My brother and I catch eyes. This is going to be a chat about funeral plans or his will or something.

Full of dread I ask: 'What is it?'

He replied: 'I think we should get a McDonald's.'

I'm not sure why this is funny, it just is. We were fearing the worst, he just wanted fed. I didn't even know he ate McDonald's. My brother obliges and heads out to get the goods. When my dad gets his cheeseburger and chips, he is buckled with laughter.

Me: 'What is so funny?'

Dad: 'Imagine this is the Last Supper – a bloody McDonald's.'

Despite the strain on all three of us, we can't help but laugh, too. I look at his diminishing frame, now frail and shuffly, as he fires down another McDonald's chip. I am in awe of his positivity, in fact 'I'm Lovin' It!'

WEDNESDAY 17 FEBRUARY

Regrets. 'I've had a few, but then again, too few to mention' – a poignant line from Frank Sinatra's smash hit 'My Way'.

New research out today reveals what our biggest regrets are.

1. Love lives – twenty per cent – (No comment! Face palm emoji!)
2. Family – eighteen per cent – I'm lucky I like mine. I am often asked why I don't have children. The simple answer is I was never with the right person at the right time.
3. Career – sixteen per cent – again, I know how lucky I am to be paid to talk.

4. Finance – fourteen per cent – I've never been a spender, so I've managed okay so far. I'm my mother's daughter. Why pay £100 for a designer jumper when Mountain Warehouse sells fleeces for £6.99?

Not working harder at school is another recurring regret with Ewen, Carnage and I all agreeing we wish we'd stuck in more to learn a language when we were younger. But hey, life is tricky enough at the moment without beating ourselves up about underachieving. We need to focus on the positives, so time for some 'Happy News'.

The pandemic has officially made people kinder. Yey! A third of us believe kindness is infectious so one good deed will lead to another, while forty per cent said an unexpected act of kindness such as a stranger saying hello or a neighbour helping with shopping or taking the bins out will make us feel amazing.

I am very lucky. My next-door neighbour Rod and his wife Penny are so kind to me. Rod has kept some of his external Christmas lights up just so it is bright when I go to my car in the early winter mornings. He's linked a string of lights to the front door of my flat too. This comes off his electricity. I regularly leave him cakes and chocolate on the wall that separates the properties. Since lockdown began, we now refer to it as 'the Trading Wall'. I left two Lindt chocolate bunnies in the snow for him last week and just texted the message 'Trading Wall' for him to retrieve his gift.

Chocolate is another hot topic today (remember Topic chocolate bars?). Twenty-seven per cent of stressed-out home-schooling parents have turned to chocolate in their hours of need, with twenty-five per cent admitting they've chucked any diets or healthy eating regimes to get through the school day.

I don't think anyone will ever utter the phrase: 'Home-schooling days are the best days of your life.' A big gold star to all involved.

THURSDAY 18 FEBRUARY

Who says romance is dead? According to new research, gestures like candlelit dinners and buying flowers are now deemed no more romantic than taking out the bins, making the bed and putting the toilet lid down.

Partners who join in household chores and help with childcare are considered romantic. Surely that should be part of the deal? So, if you want to get in the good books, simply pop the lavvy lid down – way cheaper than a dozen red roses.

Talking of houses, another story making the news today says that children born this week will have to spend £1.2 million to buy their first home with the way inflation and house prices are going. This sounds terrifying. The average age of first-time buyers is now thirty-four and £215,000 is the cost of the average first home which sounds pretty expensive to me.

My dad bought the home he is still in over fifty years ago for £5,000. He tells me at the time that was a fortune. My mum told me that they couldn't afford furniture for the first six months as my dad kept spending their money on equipment for his band.

When I moved into my first flat, I used the cushions from his old VW campervan as my 'couch' for months. The Harveys are not high maintenance, that's for sure.

Our 'Song with a Story' today is another showbiz cracker. Liam Dolan is an entertainer, comedian and star of the Pavilion panto; he also used to work in children's television.

He explained: 'I was working in kids' telly on a show called *Dig It*; I was lucky enough to get to interview Britney Spears just as she was breaking through. We invented a game called Great Britney where she had to guess which accompaniment went with a series of British dishes.

'We had fish and chips on a plate and a side dish of peas and a side dish of beetroot. She had to pick the right one. She guessed peas and won the points.

'I said to her "Go on, have a chip", and all hell broke loose in my earpiece with the Director shouting, "No!"

'I couldn't work out what the fuss was about, so I said again, "Go on, Britney, have a chip." This time she picked up a big chip and ate it.

'We recorded that show on a Tuesday. I later found out that the props department had brought in the fish and chips the previous Thursday, so I nearly wiped out the biggest pop sensation in the world with food poisoning without realising it.'

We play 'Hit Me Baby One More Time'. Something I'm sure Britney might like to do to him if they were to cross paths with fusty fries ever again . . .

FRIDAY 19 FEBRUARY

I've known it all along but today Glasgow is officially crowned the friendliest city in the world according to a new poll conducted on behalf of the Rough Guide series of travel books.

Live entertainment, a warm welcome and the pursuit of equality were some of the criteria the competition was judged on. I make sure I include this celebration of all things 'Weegie' in my 'Happy News' just to wind up my Edinburgh born co-host.

Good news for Inverness today too. Loch Ness has been voted the most beautiful view in the UK beating Lake Windermere and weirdly the London Eye to second and third place.

Ewen reckons Burntisland should have been on the list while I think Luskentyre Beach in Harris, Glencoe and Firhill, home of the mighty Partick Thistle, should be there too.

At 8.10 this morning it is time for my big challenge. On Monday Ewen challenged me to learn the fiddle part of 'Sunshine on Leith' in five days after reading a story that revealed learning a musical instrument is the best way to improve your IQ.

Five days might have been fine, but I had a ten-minute lesson with my dad on Tuesday and that was that.

The plan was to have another half hour yesterday, but he got called into the Beatson for emergency radiotherapy on his spine, hip and thigh. When he came home, he looked done in.

He said: 'If you don't mind, Toots, can we leave the fiddle lesson.'

He went to his bed straight away but is feeling much perkier today.

And so, I went into the performance with genuinely ten minutes' fiddle knowledge, which became obvious if you heard my recital.

I'm not sure if it resembled screaming cats or howling banshees or maybe a mix of the two. To be honest, it was not as horrific as I'd feared. I'd worked out where the notes are but hadn't mastered how to actually play them. That bowing malarkey is very tricky!

Still, everyone got a good laugh and that's what we are here for. Thanks to June, Davie, Jim, Brian and many more who got in touch to say they loved it.

Kelsey phoned in and made me feel better saying she had tried for years to learn the fiddle but it's one of the hardest instruments to master. She added that she'd moved on to the spoons and found her niche, and that my friends, is why I play the kazoo!!

Carnage made me laugh by changing the title on the rolling graphic on DAB radios and the internet streaming sites to 'Sunshine on Leith by The Proclaimers featuring Cat Harvey'. If Craig and

Charlie ever hear this version, they'll be walking five hundred miles to get away from it . . .

MONDAY 22 FEBRUARY

Rod Stewart is the subject of my 'Happy News' today. The multi-millionaire spent £25 on a birthday present his son Liam will never forget – a video message from a Rod Stewart tribute act.

'Rud Stewart', for that is his stage name, is Michael Dean from Yorkshire who was delighted with his commission. He told Liam, 'You're in my heart and you're in my home' before serenading him with a bit of 'Do Ya Think I'm Sexy?' which is funny, if a bit weird.

This week we are celebrating the twenty-fifth anniversary of *Trainspotting*. All week we're asking questions relating to 1996 for the chance to win a retro prize package with everything we could think of that was desirable in 1996. We have a Euro 1996 Scotland top, a Tamagotchi (digital pet), the *Trainspotting* DVD, a bottle of lemon Hooch (not to be used as a mixer for double voddies – I've learned that lesson for you!) a PlayStation 1 and a can of fabric freshener spray Febreze, which first came on the market in 1996.

We have a daily question to reach the final and each day the lucky listener, if correct, will get a Febreze to call their own.

Craigie called in and successfully answered the question: 'Scientists in Scotland successfully cloned a sheep in 1996 and named her after a famous singer who was it?' Dolly the Sheep was named after Dolly Parton. We told Craigie he had won the Febreze (retail value at time of writing – £2.00) and he celebrated like he'd won a Ferrari.

We love it when our listeners embrace our nonsense and his sensationally over the top reaction cracked us up.

Our 'Song with a Story' star today is another lovely listener, the

Reverend Jim Ritchie, a minister in the Church of the Nazarene currently working in a town on the border between Switzerland and Germany.

Ewen asked him why such an educated man listened to our show and he replied: 'I enjoy the banter and I like finding out where my mates back home in Scotland are being stuck in traffic.'

His storytelling is certainly divine. He explained: 'When I was training to be a minister, I used to play in a Christian rock band. I know what you are thinking, all Jesus sandals and Kumbaya, but we weren't like that, we were actually quite cool. We played schools and colleges, but we were always upsetting the religious polis – you know the ones, the people in the Church who are never happy with anything, with our song choices. I wanted to play modern covers from popular bands, but they thought they'd be a bad influence. I managed to convince them that Bon Jovi's 'Livin' on a Prayer' was about religion, and they let us add that to the set and I got to rock out to that one.'

Rev Jim sounds like a brilliant laugh; I bet he's delivered some memorable sermons in his time. When we launched this feature a few weeks ago we didn't expect ministers to be calling us from Europe requesting 1980s soft rock.

God does indeed work in mysterious ways.

TUESDAY 23 FEBRUARY

'How the f*** are you?' I ask this as we are officially a nation of potty mouths. Researchers have discovered that the average adult uses fourteen swear words a day. I would think this has at least quadrupled during home-schooling/lockdown/the pubs being shut.

One in every 1,700 words we use is from the naughty list. Thankfully, Ewen and I have never sworn on air, which is a miracle given that he used to present a very fiery football phone-in.

The closest I've been to an 'incident' was back in my Real Radio days during the Real Radio Renegade competition. This was a competition where clues were given to a specific location, we had a man there who listeners had to find and ask: 'Are you the Real Radio Renegade?' to win the cash bounty.

My favourite winner ever was the homeless man in the Grassmarket who had been sitting minding his own business on a street corner. He'd been asked the question many times, and with no knowledge of the competition, just happened to repeat the question to the actual renegade.

Straight away he was put through to the studio live on a mobile phone to talk to us. Back then when someone won a prize we would say: 'Say those words' and they'd reply: 'I'm a real winner.' The man was quite naturally delighted to be £3,000 richer and when asked to say those words, paused for a moment, and shouted: 'YA F****** DANCER'.

I genuinely hope he enjoyed every penny.

It's emerged today that eighty-eight per cent of us are now embracing the simpler things in life. With tough restrictions still in place, we are finding the most comfort in laughing, spending time with loved ones and, top of the list, comfort food.

It comes as no surprise to me that top of the comfort food list is cheese followed by ice cream. Which pretty much sounds like my dream dinner. Can you tell my healthy eating plan remains a daily struggle?

As it's Tuesday, after the show I head over to my dad's via Graeme the fish van man for a catch-up and a wee tidy of his house. I find it much easier now I have established the routine of three cleaning days a week. He doesn't have quite so long between my visits to cause culinary chaos in his kitchen.

Dad was given emergency radiotherapy last Thursday and has been feeling the effects. I see him wincing in pain when moving in his chair. I hate feeling so helpless. I ask him if there is anything I can do.

He said: 'I've taken my painkillers, but can you rub some Vindaloo on my back.'

I burst out laughing and go and get his Voltarol! He's none the wiser. I'm always trying to keep him happy but even I wouldn't curry favour by doing that.

WEDNESDAY 24 FEBRUARY

Only days after Glasgow was named the friendliest city in the world, we are voted the third-best city in the UK for having a sense of humour.

Once again, I only highlight this to wind up Ewen as Glasgow beat his beloved Edinburgh, which came in eighth. Liverpool topped the chart followed by London.

I've been to Liverpool twice and absolutely loved the city and all the locals we met. I did the Beatles tours, plus explored the history around the docks and took the famous ferry across the Mersey. Perhaps not the best journey, as my wee pal Julie was very hungover and had to battle to keep her breakfast down.

We'd been at Ladies' Day at Aintree the day before. It's an experience. The Liverpool Ladies make quite the effort. So much so hairdressers are open until 2 a.m. the night before and at 5 a.m. on the morning of the big day. Everyone, and I mean everyone, gets a 'curly blow'. Which is a big footballer's wife-style bouncy blowdry. The racecourse is packed with fake-tanned lovelies with eyelashes longer than the horses. The day is one big party, and it makes T in the Park look like a religious festival when it comes to outrageous levels of boozing.

As our taxi driver to the racecourse explained: 'I pick them up like princesses and drop them off like tramps.'

I'm not telling any tales when I say myself, Julie and my other friend Lynsey kept up with the locals. When it comes to partying, we are best of breed and prize fillies all the way.

During our show we have to break the news that Celtic manager Neil Lennon has resigned. It was only matter of time, as his side are so far behind Rangers in the league and the fans, angry at blowing ten in a row, have been shouting for change. I've known Neil through football for years and have always found him to be a nice guy and good company, so I sincerely wish him all the best.

My Aye or Naw question is a cracker today: A tattie-bogle is a Scottish term for a scarecrow. Is this true? Aye or naw?

Ewen and Carnage make me laugh with their reasoning for both choosing naw. Ewen: 'I think it's a Scottish word but it's probably a dish made with potatoes. Carnage: 'Are scarecrows not made of turnips?'

I ask why anyone would make a scarecrow with something birds like to eat, that's like giving them bread arms and donut feet.

Fifty-seven per cent of the listeners correctly say 'aye'. What a great name – a tattie-bogle. The tattie part comes from potatoes, most scarecrows heads are straw-filled potato sacks, while a bogle is a word for a spiritual being or ghost in folk tales. The Berkshire equivalent are hod-me-dods. Who needs home-schooling when you have us? Regular listeners will have an Honours degree in nonsense in no time at all.

THURSDAY 25 FEBRUARY

Trainspotting star Robert Carlyle is in the news today and it's nothing to do with tomorrow's big twenty-fifth anniversary of the launch.

He has emerged as the bookies favourite to play Robbie Williams in a new biopic of the Take That singer's life.

Now I'm no casting director, but Robert Carlyle turns sixty this year and Robbie was just a teenager when he started on his route to fame and fortune.

Whoever is pitching him for the role must have the world's best make-up team in place. Send them my way!

I can't get Carlyle playing his famously psychotic *Trainspotting* character Begbie out my head, and quite frankly, Begbie in a Take That pop video would be well worth seeing.

Others on the list are James Buckley from *The Inbetweeners* and Taron Egerton, who was phenomenal as Elton John in *Rocketman*. Ewen is winding up celebrity chef Gordon Ramsay on Twitter and in the *Scottish Sun* today. The famously foul-mouthed Scot (Ramsay not Ewen) called Falkirk a s***hole on his new quiz show. Ewen, who has lived there for nineteen years, jumped to the town's defence and called Gordon Ramsay a 'b**bag'. Honestly, weans!

The problem was, despite Ewen's gallant attempt to defend Falkirk's honour, most replies on his social media indicated Ramsay may have a point, and the majority of these came from local residents.

I've always enjoyed my outings to Falkirk although they've either been to the football or on a night out to 'Behind the Wall'.

The show flies in today and I stop off at the shops with a long list of messages for my dad. How one wee man can get through so much chocolate is beyond me!

During my visit to Dad, we fondly reminisce about my mum. It's nine years to the day she passed away and it feels like no time at all. We sit round the fire laughing with cups of tea and Maltesers, she would have liked that.

FRIDAY 26 FEBRUARY

Happy twenty-fifth birthday to *Trainspotting* – one of Scotland's most iconic films. Today is the climax of our big 1996 competition and our four finalists have five seconds each to answer a 'nearest to' question. They can't hear any of the other answers, so everybody has the same chance.

The question: 'According to ScotRail, how many train stations are in Scotland?'

The guesses ranged from 120 to 700, the correct answer is 359. Our winner was Charmaine who guessed 178, which is still miles away from the right number.

As a result, she is killing herself laughing when we announce her as our big prize winner. Along with the 1996 Scotland top, PlayStation 1, Tamagotchi and DVDs she gets her second bottle of Febreze of the week.

She screamed: 'I don't care about the rest of the stuff I'm just delighted I'm getting a second bottle.'

Charmaine and her family will now have a beautifully fresh smelling house for months to come.

Our 'Song with a Story' also has a *Trainspotting* theme. We chat to actor and musician Tom Urie, he's mega-talented and a good friend of the show. Tom was cast as the leader of the Orange Order in *Trainspotting 2* where they filmed the iconic scene with Ewen McGregor's Renton having to sing on stage before they pinched everyone's bank cards.

He said: 'I was cast as the leader of an Orange Hall and didn't have a clue about any of that kind of thing. I knew nothing about 1690 as I'm into *Mary Poppins* and the *Sound of Music* so they had to fill me in about the history of these organisations.

'When I was offered the role, I had to sign one of these

non-disclosure agreements not to tell anyone I was in the film or what my scenes were about. They gave me a pound coin at the audition and, by accepting it, that was deemed a legal transaction. They'd bought my silence. It was so difficult not telling my pals about it and they couldn't believe I'd managed to keep it secret when it eventually came out. I'm so lucky to have played even a small part in such a cinematic phenomenon.'

Tom picks Queen and 'Radio Gaga' as this was one of the big songs from the *Trainspotting 2* soundtrack.

Through working in theatre and entertainment, Tom and I share many mutual friends including Lynne Ewart who writes the stars for the *Sunday Mail*. Lynne is one of the kindest ladies you will ever meet and her knowledge and enthusiasm for astrology is second to none.

Whether it's your thing or not, news today reveals more than half of us make big financial decisions based on our horoscopes, a third of us make big life choices based on advice 'in the stars'. We are also more likely to take advice from horoscopes in 2021 than we were before the pandemic.

I'm a Pisces, which means I'm meant to be creative, gentle and a bit of a dreamer and I think that kind of fits. My favourite prediction ever was in a fortune cookie my dad got from his local Chinese on his eighty-fifth birthday. He opened it with trepidation and read out: 'The best years of your life are ahead of you.'

MONDAY 1 MARCH

Overnight we've amassed over 100,000 views on Twitter for a daft moment from our Sunday show. Me doing Ewen like a kipper. He was reading a story from our prep sheet which contains lots of topical stories collated by Producer Michael and me.

Michael had made a very rare mistake (trust me, this never happens). He'd written the Golden Globes were taking place in London instead of LA.

Ewen didn't process this information before reading it out. He then realised what he'd done and claimed it was Michael's fault.

Michael accused Ewen of being *Anchorman* – the hilarious film with Will Ferrell starring as Ron Burgundy the news reader who will read whatever is on his autocue with no thought towards content or context.

Ewen admitted: 'When I was a presenter at STV they used to do this to me. They would write stuff on the autocue and I would just read it out.'

I quickly scribbled a note on a bit of paper, held it up and said: 'read this'.

He instantly obeyed, reading out: 'I love Stevie G' before realising what he'd just done as Michael and I went into hysterics.

Ewen is a Hearts fan and is always being accused of being a Rangers Fan. When Steven Gerrard first joined Rangers, Ewen famously jumped a wall at Ibrox with a cameraman so he could be the first journalist to interview the new boss. The TV pictures have Ewen chatting to the former England and Liverpool captain with what can only be described as the look of love.

He's taken pelters for it ever since and I have not helped. Producer Michael quickly edits the audio and posts it on Twitter. Thankfully fans from both sides of the Old Firm are having a right good laugh at it too. I think I'll try and get Stevie G on the show live one morning, although after our recent encounter with Drivetime presenter Garry Spence and the 'transport links from Bishopbriggs' banter, if I was the Rangers manager, I'd be avoiding my call!

Today's Aye or Naw question gives me the chance to play one

of the jolliest TV theme tunes of all time: *Postman Pat* (I bet you're singing: 'and his black and white cat' in your head right now!).

Seventy-three per cent of listeners correctly said 'aye', the oldest post office in the world is in Dumfries and Galloway. It's on the High Street in Sanquhar and was opened in 1712.

So many people get in touch to say they're swaying and singing the *Postman Pat* tune in their cars and kitchens.

First-class Monday morning smiles delivered all over Scotland. Happy days.

TUESDAY 2 MARCH
Today is the day I am told.

WEDNESDAY 3 MARCH
Yesterday was the day I've dreaded all my life. I was told my dad, my hero and my best friend, is terminally ill and his cancer can no longer be contained or treated.

I'm struggling to process this as he's my constant go-to for everything. We are a team. My sense of anticipatory grief is overwhelming.

I've been included in his last few consultations at the Beatson and due to my knowledge about the spread of his cancer, I was not expecting terribly good news; however, I was not expecting this. Not to Dad. He beats everything. Alcohol, dodgy heart, he overcame them all but at eighty-six his prostate cancer is now advanced and rampaging through his ever-decreasing, broken body.

From where I am sitting in the consultation room, I can see Dr Venugopal's computer screen, my dad can't.

I ask if that is Dad's scan on the screen and the doctor confirms that it is. I ask if the dark patches are the cancer and he confirms it.

I can see dark blobs on his ribs, chest, hip, pelvis, thigh and, most worrying to me, his head. The doctor tells us the cancer has now spread to his spine, lymph nodes and to his skull.

I struggle to remain calm. Dad is as stoic as ever: 'Och, that's not so good but I'd like to thank you for everything you have tried to do for me; here, have a CD.'

At which point, he gives the bemused doctor a copy of his *Welcome to the Party* CD, full of Scottish songs and perfect for Hogmanay. I can tell the doctor thinks my dad is bonkers and in complete denial.

We're told there's a very strong chance of paralysis from bone breakage and that it's maybe time to discuss his end-of-life care plan.

It all seems other-worldly. I ask the right questions. I'm focused and in control, but I can feel a gripping pain in my heart and a ball of anxiety forming in my stomach. I won't cry. I must be strong.

Dad tells the doctor he doesn't want to hear any more bad news so he will wait outside in case I have any other questions I want to ask.

There is only one question.

He will never know the answer. The thought of what lies ahead terrifies me and more than anything I just want him not to be in any pain.

As Dad never heard the doctor's response to the big question, he is in great spirits when I drive him home.

He smiles: 'That went well. I don't have to get any more treatment.'

I'm momentarily stunned. How can he be so happy when my world is crumbling?

I drive on in silence, gripping the steering wheel so tight my fingers hurt while fighting back tears.

I realise this is how he is choosing to deal with this. He even sings the Monty Python song 'Always Look on the Bright Side of Life'.

He tells me that when lockdown is over, he wants us both to go on a Rhine cruise.

As hard as this is, I play his game.

I swallow hard and say: 'So where shall we go and what do you want to see?'

He then goes down memory lane with stories of cruises with my mum and gigging with his accordion player Ivor on the QE2 and sharing a dressing room with forty topless Brazilian dancers, always his favourite story!

My dad has been a professional entertainer all his days. I honestly believe he knows he is on his last performance but wants his audience (i.e., me) to continue enjoying the show until the curtain comes down.

I studied theatre at Glasgow University and I've written and performed plays, but this is going to be the most emotionally and physically demanding role of my career.

There will come a time when we will both know his run is coming to an end, but until then, in true Harvey style, the show must go on.

He would be distraught and probably angry if I stopped writing this book because of him, so as tough as things may get, I shall endeavour to keep you up to date with the fun stuff in the world. Deep down I know it will be good for me to keep going and it will be even better for him to know I am doing so.

I rock myself to sleep with warm tears trickling onto my pillow. I feel empty and scared and despite having the best group of pals in the world, I feel crushed and drained and very alone.

I'm not religious at all but I ask the Universe or whoever is listening to give me the strength to get through this and to make his final fling as full of love and laughter as is humanly possible. Bobby 'two cakes' can now have all the cakes in the world . . .

Ewen and Cat – back making a splash on air.

I've been carrying him for over a decade.

Winning UK Commercial Breakfast Show of the Year, 2012. The night I didn't go home with a Rolling Stone!

Chris Tarrant and the night the world first met CARNAGE!

Causing mischief with Wee Vixen – double trouble.

The Dream Team, with Ewen and Producer Michael.

Radio partner swapsies with our pals
Boogie and Arlene from Forth 1.

The legend that is Bobby Harvey.
Dad playing on his fiddle for the NHS.

Dad and I campaigning to save our
favourite boat, the PS *Waverley*.

Beep the Sheep. Ewen plays a baa-d prank on his wife Teresa.

Rollercoaster Spaghetti. A loopy idea if ever there was one.

Tommy bum drums! Wet Wet Wet drummer Tommy Cunningham proves he can drum anything.

Scotland qualify for the Euros. Could this really be the UK radio moment of the year?

Sharleen Spiteri – always smiling, even when Ewen steals her chips.

Hollywood star James McAvoy thanking me for providing medicinal salt and vinegar square crisps.

Susan Boyle – from ice buckets to kazoos, she's always game for a laugh.

Festival frolics as Ewen joins the Ladyboys of Bangkok.

I'm on my way from misery to happiness with The Proclaimers.

On set with The Proclaimers and Matt Lucas on the 'Spinning Around' video.

Getting cheeky with Olly Murs.

'Too many broken hearts' after this snap with Jason Donovan.

'You're Beautiful' – I'm hoping that's what James Blunt was thinking.

Ewen and his one true love – Rangers boss Steven Gerrard.

My best selfie ever – with Amy MacDonald and the *Still Game* cast.

Have wand will travel – fairy duty in the Pavilion Pantomime.

Where's my panto career? It's behind me since Useless Ewen and Smart Cat starred in *Elfie's Magical Adventures* at the Pavilion.

Fairy Bampot joins forces with *Pop Idol* winner Michelle McManus in her Winter Wonderland show.

Michelle and I arrrrr great pals in real life.

Ewen's courage takes a dive.

Launching the 2013 Partick Thistle strip – my one and only modelling assignment!

Exotic travel adventures – Dad winching a sea lion.

Christmas crackers – a night out with Amy MacDonald – global superstar, great pal and a welcome part of our wee team.

The super-talented cast of my first play – *Love Me Tinder*

First night nerves with the *Love Me Tinder* cast backstage just before we open.

Fabulous fun, feathers, glitter and jazz hands all the way in *One Singer One Song*.

Backstage with my amazing cast from *One Singer One Song*.

Stand back – this haggis is about to get it at the Westsound Burns Supper.

Glad rags on for hosting a Cash for Kids fundraising lunch.

Partick Thistle win promotion and I make sure Dad and I are in with the bricks.

Harley – our new addition to the team. When Cat and dog meet for the first time.

Temptation and Angel Eyes. He is the first and has the latter. My first love, Marti Pellow.

The Euros trophy comes to visit. We have a dream …

The most glamorous Hen Do in Cumnock with former Miss GB Deone Robertson and the panto girls.

I made it! Wembley 2021 for Euro 2020. The best 0–0 of my life.

The happiest man in Scotland. Dad back in Rothesay where his dad was born.

All smiles touring Scotland with Faither.

Life is sweet with my breakfast club – Ewen and Producer Carnage.

THURSDAY 4 MARCH

It's World Book Day today. How apt. Time to start a new chapter in my life and to adjust to the narrative that's unfolding. My main themes must now be positivity and happiness. I am going to do my best to master both of these to make my dad proud.

Today we have lots of book-related content. First up we have the new official list of the best movie adaptions from book to film. 1) The *Harry Potter* franchise 2) *The Shawshank Redemption* 3) *The Lord of the Rings* franchise 4) *Schindler's List* 5) *Forrest Gump*.

I am outraged that *Mary Poppins* by P.L. Travers is not in the top ten. Clearly one of the best films of all time.

My Aye or Naw question is also book-themed. Sixty-eight per cent got it correct today: Ian Rankin who wrote the Edinburgh-based *Rebus* books is from Fife. Ewen got it wrong and is claiming him as an Edinburger, despite the fact he was born in Cardenden.

Over the past twenty-four hours we've been running a Twitter poll to see which book our listeners would like me to read a story from this morning. Their choices were: *The Magic Porridge Pot* (my favourite kids' book), *50 Shades of Grey*, the 1992 Argos catalogue and *Steven Gerrard: My Story*, which we included just to annoy Ewen.

Punters clearly love a wind-up, so Stevie G won hands down. However, I thought it was better to add a twist.

So, I quickly wrote a short story based on Stevie G's experience of meeting Ewen for the first time. We joked it was from the Rangers' manager's soon to be released new book *Stevie G – Ewen and Me*.

Many listeners got in touch before my big moment and asked that I read the story in a Liverpudlian accent. Now I love Liverpool, but this accent is not easy. I gave it my best shot but the text message I got from PR consultant Mickey McMonagle best summed it up: 'Why are you speaking like a Cornish pirate?'

Over the romantic 'Love theme from Romeo and Juliet', in a very dodgy accent I read the following: 'fourth of May, 2018 – one of the best days of my life. I'd captained Liverpool and England but today I was becoming the manager of Glasgow Rangers.

'I was nervous. They'd let supporters and reporters into Ibrox.

'Then I saw him [at this point Carnage drops in the *Psycho* stabbing music]. He looked at me, really looked at me. At first, I thought I was in danger. He looked like a right eejit – I'd only been in Glasgow forty minutes, but I'd already picked up some of the banter.

'Then it happened. He jumped a wall and ran towards me. Then I saw it. I saw it in his eyes. It was LOVE. True love of the purest kind, but I'm from Liverpool, Ewen, and as John, Paul, George and Ringo would say – all you need is love [at this point we go into the Beatles].'

We are all in bits laughing. My cheeks end up hurting as we've giggled so much, and I realise despite everything that is going on 'in my life', the Beatles were right: 'I'll get by with a little help from my friends.'

FRIDAY 5 MARCH

Another new strain of coronavirus discovered in England; Salmond versus Sturgeon and now the Euros at Hampden in jeopardy. Time to crank up the feel-good to overcome the oppressing doom and gloom.

My favourite story of the day is about a couple from Irvine who laid green carpet in their garden instead of AstroTurf by mistake. Pauline didn't have the heart to tell her husband Andy what he'd done, after he thought he'd got the bargain of the century on eBay. I wonder how many times they'll have to hoover their lawn.

Happy News today for fans of McDonald's cheeseburgers (must

tell Dad): a company in America has just released a scented candle which promises to fill your room with the aroma of meat, onions, pickles, ketchup, mustard and cheese. Brings a new meaning to flame-grilled!

Our 'Song with a Story' is from Tam Coyle, a music promoter and DJ most famous for putting on parties for the Tartan Army. I've been mates with Tam for over thirty years and know he could write a book of his many hilarious experiences. His story is about the World Cup in France 1998.

He explained: 'It was the night before the opening match of the World Cup, Scotland versus Brazil, and we were in Paris. A few days before, I'd received a phone call from a guy called Yarrow who wanted me to bring some "real Tartan Army fans" to a party he was organising in the famous Buddha Bar in Paris. I told him I was from Clydebank and used to live near Yarrow's shipyard. He laughed and said: "Yes, that was my dad's."

'He promised me free food and drink if I could sort out some genuine fans to come along to add atmosphere for his corporate guests. I wasn't going to say no to free drink. On the same day I was asked to bring some pals to the recording of the McCoist and MacAulay show at the Eiffel Tower. Ally and Fred were hosting a TV show. The researcher asked me what we were all doing that night and I told her I was part of a party in the Buddha bar. She asked if it would be okay to get Ally and Fred on the guest list. I said I would make a phone call.

'A few hours later she called again to ask if it would be okay to also bring some guests – they were racing driver Jackie Stewart and movie star Ewen McGregor. I sorted them out too. Not long after that I get a call from Ewen McGregor's people asking if it was okay if they brought Sir Sean Connery, who in turn arrived with Sir Alex

Ferguson and Kenny Dalglish. I still ask myself if it really happened or was it all a dream.

'The funniest bit was I ended up in the gents' toilet with Sir Sean Connery. When we'd both finished our business and stepped outside, I managed to get a photo with him. Gary Ralston, a newspaper reporter, saw this happening and asked me if I'd just been to the loo with him and did I have a look? I told him, he's James Bond, of course I had a look . . . and it's the second biggest one I've ever seen.'

We play Carnival De Paris by Dario G and I try not to think of 007's boaby.

MONDAY 8 MARCH

Happy International Women's Day 2021. I've been working on content for this for a few weeks now and clips of my interviews will be played on every radio show across both networks (Hits and Greatest Hits) highlighting successful and influential women throughout the day.

Along with Producer Cat Mullen (yes, two Cats for the price of one), who was the motivational brains behind this mini-series, we recorded seven interviews with women who have succeeded in male-dominated fields and who have lots of pearls of wisdom for helping other young women achieve their dreams.

My magnificent seven are:

Jamie Genevieve: Businesswoman and influencer. With a BBC TV show, over 1.4 million followers on Instagram and her own product range, the former Glasgow Debenhams beauty counter worker proved she's much more than just a pretty face by revealing how she had a meticulously researched business plan all along.

Judy Murray OBE: Tennis coach, Judy Murray Foundation charity campaigner and of course maw to not one but two Olympians, Andy and Jamie. Judy is dynamite. Fearless to call out sexism in sport and strong with her advice and encouragement for women in male-dominated industries. Feisty and fun. I'd love a night out with her.

Dr Katy Stewart: Sports scientist at the Hampden Sports Clinic. Katy also runs the Scottish FA Cardiac Screening programme, co-ordinates the Support in Sport programme for Mental Health in Football and is part of the research group examining the links between football and dementia. I've sat next to Dr Katy and Dr John MacLean from the Hampden Sports Clinic at the PFA dinner. Not only are they experts and lovely people, they also enjoy a glass of Prosecco and gave me a 2 a.m. diagnosis on all my sore and wonky bits without judgement!

Dr Marie Macklin CBE: Entrepreneur and businesswoman Marie is a leading female light in the world of construction. Her Halo Project in Kilmarnock aims to rejuvenate the community with affordable housing, local jobs and all sorts of training and apprenticeships. Marie is a well-known face on the Glasgow social scene, but I never realised how impressive her career path, success and vision were until this interview. Marie came from 'The Scheme' in Kilmarnock and is all about giving people in deprived areas a chance. I must admit I'm now in awe of her drive and ambition.

Dr Punam Krishan: GP, Director for the British Society of Lifestyle Medicine, writer and mum of two. She's always brilliant on air and is keen to remind all the ladies that despite Covid, GPs are very much 'open for business'. She says women, and mums in particular, are often too busy looking after others to take good enough care of themselves. Her words are wise and needed. Ladies, give yourselves a break, get anything dodgy checked out and please don't be afraid to ask for help.

Talat Yaqoob: women's rights and equality campaigner. Talat

shared her in-depth knowledge of fighting for equality in the workplace. A passionate and educated lady, I felt inspired after our chat. I love people who battle hard for others. I guess listening to her I feel a bit guilty – what more can we do as individuals to help? Having these uncomfortable thoughts is good. It's the entire point of these interviews. Knowledge can help us understand how we can all help with inclusivity more on many levels.

I decide to throw in an Aye or Naw question about an inspiring woman in my life. My Granny Harvey. The question has Ewen and Carnage bamboozled: My granny first flew in an aeroplane over Rothesay in the 1920s. Is this true? Aye or naw?

Even though this is now one hundred years ago it is 'aye'. She did. She was working in Rothesay as a farmhand as a teenager. During a fair at Ettrick Bay there was a small airplane giving tours over Bute for anyone brave enough.

She was always game for anything and threw caution to the wind and took to the skies in a First World War plane. She lived to be ninety-six and crammed in plenty more adventures along the way.

Telling this story makes me both happy and proud. Both my grannies and my mum were wonderfully strong, kind, intelligent women. Girl power! If nothing else, I come from good stock!

TUESDAY 9 MARCH

Meghan and Harry are on all the front pages after their controversial interview with Oprah Winfrey was aired on UK television last night. They've certainly opened a regal can of worms and it will be interesting to see how this chapter in history pans out. I can't help but feel sorry for them; who would ever want that level of fame and the restrictions that come with it. The fact people are now actively discussing issues of race and mental health can only be a good thing in general.

Today is a big day for me. It is vaccine day. It feels weird to be excited about getting a jab but I am. It signals the start of the return to whatever normal will be and more than anything it gives me more comfort when I'm in looking after Dad.

My appointment is at NHS Louisa Jordan, the temporary hospital facility they built in the SECC at the start of the pandemic.

My friend Russell Mair worked on the build and I've seen lots of footage on TV, but nothing can prepare you for the vastness of the rows and rows of cubicles.

It's emotional to walk through the empty rows no longer with beds thinking of what might have been. It's overwhelming and feels like it could be a scene from a disaster movie. This hospital was never used for mass scale Covid treatment and recovery and for that I am very glad.

The process itself was flawless; I was in and out in eleven minutes and everyone involved had a reassuring smile on their faces. The fact we have a vaccine before we hit the one year of lockdown milestone is nothing short of remarkable.

I head out to my dad's where we celebrate my brother's birthday on a Zoom call with my niece in her student halls in Edinburgh and Scott with the rest of his family in their house.

The birthday boy arranged a curry to be delivered and again my dad and I share one between us.

He only eats a couple of spoons of sauce and tries to throw his chunk of naan bread in the bin behind him without me noticing. His last few shopping lists have been nothing but soup and creamed rice pudding. I now know he is not eating solids.

However, he's in great form, joins in the silly quiz and gets into the ice cream and jelly also provided.

Jessica in Edinburgh asks us all to grab our props. We have silly glasses, cake and balloons. She takes a screen grab of the scene. Despite the circumstances, once again, this has been a great day . . .

WEDNESDAY 10 MARCH

Piers Morgan has left his morning TV show after an angry backlash from his comments about the big Meghan Markle interview with Oprah. He said he didn't believe her.

Ewen is blocked by Piers on Twitter although for the life of me I can't remember why. I'm honestly at the stage that I try to avoid an excess of negative news. This approach has served me well in the last year. I've been a people pleaser all my life but with age comes wisdom and the ability to say no to stuff and to stop caring about upsetting things you can't change.

I thoroughly recommend the Sarah Knight book: *The Life-Changing Magic of Not Giving a F**k!* It's marvellous. Trust me, you will never pay into a leaving present for someone you barely know ever again.

Our 'Song with a Story' today is a cracker. It's from showbiz journalist Beverley Lyons. Bev has interviewed some of the most famous people in the world so we can't wait to see where she is taking us with this one.

She revealed: 'We are going back to the noughties with my story and trust me they could have been very naughty. Robbie Williams was playing a gig in Glasgow and ended up in a club called Strawberry Fields because it was his birthday. I'd already been told he wasn't giving interviews, so I was just hanging about and talking to a guy called Kevin King who wrote songs for Robbie. At this point Robbie came over and asked us both back to a private birthday party he had just decided to throw at Malmaison. I told him I was a journalist and he thanked me for my honesty and said I was still welcome to come.

'I got to the hotel and Robbie was behind the bar pouring pints. He had gaffer tape on his face for fake sideburns and told me he wanted to be like Justin Currie from Del Amitri. I asked if I could get a photo with him but he said no because he "looked like a state". Then he said: "But I would like a birthday snog." I couldn't believe it! He was one of the biggest celebrities in the world at that point. I was seeing someone at the time so said no. My mum later told me I was an idiot. He said he was going to walk through the door in the corner and that I had to wait a couple of minutes and then follow him. I never followed and he never got a snog.'

Bev then chose Robbie's song 'No Regrets'. I asked if she had any now, all these years later and she laughed: 'Och, I think about it a lot. My mum was right, I was an idiot.'

THURSDAY 11 MARCH

Motherwell, Kilwinning and the Isle of Harris have been named in the top ten UK destinations for a safe staycation. And for the avoidance of doubt, yes, I did say Motherwell and Kilwinning.

A new 'safecation' report looked at the best destinations with social distancing, the availability of contactless payment, free activities and being dog-friendly.

Harris is one of my favourite places on the planet so that makes sense, but Motherwell and Kilwinning are bewildering choices even for the people who live there and love their area.

I've enjoyed the Motherwell panto very much and used to love covering junior football games at Kilwinning Rangers, but I don't think I'd be packing a suitcase for an extended break to either.

One tweet did make me laugh: 'Kilwinning has been just like Disneyland this week with the nightly fireworks displays.' The Ayrshire town is famously a hotbed of Rangers supporters who have been celebrating their title win for days now.

Ewen is outraged at the survey and keeps repeating in shock, 'Motherwell?' Jim calls in and says: 'Motherwell? I wouldn't even take my mother-in-law there'. Seems the North Lanarkshire town has a bit of work to do on its summer vacation marketing plan.

Ewen's chart today is the top three horror films of all time. 1) *The Exorcist* 2) *Saw* and 3) *The Texas Chainsaw Massacre*.

I can't believe *Freddy Krueger* and *Nightmare on Elm Street* are not on the list. Those films terrified me and my friends when we were teenagers. Although I think we were more upset about the super-hot young Johnny Depp meeting such a gruesome end by being sucked into his mattress and kind of exploding. Life is much easier as a pirate.

We are off on so many tangents today. Where do you stand on the three second food rule? Well, scientists are encouraging us to eat food we drop on the floor. Apparently, it will expose the body to a range of germs which could help boost our natural defences and make people more resilient to infections and allergies. As long as it's not hairy, I'm generally okay with quickly retrieved food from a clean floor. The very thought has Ewen squirming. And I've not even got to the main bit of this tale.

The researchers also suggested anyone who has eaten their own bogies will have massively helped their own immune system by doing so. I'm not sure a story about noses and snotters was my best choice of 'Happy News' when people are eating their breakfast.

Maybe I should have picked another.

FRIDAY 12 MARCH

I shall try egg-ceptionally hard to not spoil this story with too many puns. My brain is scrambled thinking of them all.

This morning Ewen and I face a cracking (sorry) challenge. Something we have never done before and are not looking forward to.

A few days ago, while discussing chip shops, we somehow got onto the subject of the big jars of pickled eggs that remain, seemingly untouched, in the corner of the shops for years. I'm sure the same jar was in my local chippy for over twenty years. We don't know anyone who has ever ordered one. Who does? What do they taste like? How long can they last in that jar?

CJ, a listener, got in touch by Twitter and suggested the inevitable: 'You need to taste them live on air.'

Always game for a laugh and new experiences, I agreed. Ewen reluctantly played along. And so this morning I found myself delving into a giant jar brim full of pungent malt vinegar trying to fish out a slippery boiled egg with my fingers. Ewen's idea – no cutlery.

This was trickier than it sounds as they kept slipping out of my grip. Finally, I captured one between thumb and index finger and pulled it from the jar.

Initial reaction. Smelly, squishy like a bouncy ball, but not offensive. I bit in and to be honest it just tasted like a boiled egg covered in vinegar. I like eggs. I like vinegar. No real problems for me. I probably wouldn't rush back but it was fine. I tried one of the black fermented eggs when I was in China and survived that so I knew I would be grand.

Ewen, well Ewen puts the drama into dramatic. He insisted on skooshing the room with Tom Ford aftershave before even opening his jar.

He clicked open the lid and gagged at the smell. He gagged when he reluctantly pulled the egg out the jar (took him a while to catch one!) and he looked petrified with the thought of the next stage.

With Producer Carnage and me now ritualistically chanting 'swallow, swallow, swallow' I can only imagine what anyone just tuning in thought was going on.

He eventually bit into his rubbery treat and tried to chew. He gagged again. Whimpered that he couldn't swallow it before regurgitating the entire lot into his coffee cup.

His reaction was predictable yet hilarious. Carnage hits play on a song, I finish my egg because I'm hungry and quite enjoying it and Ewen disappears out of the studio.

I take a call from Sheila who celebrated her eightieth birthday this week. She can hardly speak for laughing. She said: 'I used to get pickled eggs when I was a wee girl and you've put me in the mood for one right now. That was so much fun to listen to. Thank you for being here with me every morning and making me laugh.'

These calls mean so much to us. Unfortunately, Ewen is not present to chat to Sheila, as he was last spotted running down the corridor towards the gents' toilet and has not returned. It really is beyond a yolk.

MONDAY 15 MARCH

The day after Mother's Day! We had a good laugh talking about this on our Sunday show. It's always a tricky day for us as Producer Michael and I no longer have our mums and Ewen has a complicated relationship with his.

However, we remember the fun times and that's massively important too.

I told the story of the Mother's Day when I was about ten when I bought my mum a goldfish. I'd walked to the shop with my pals and spent my own money (40p if I recall) on her present. We called him Findlay and he loved music as he used to swim in circles anytime I played the piano. In retrospect Findlay didn't have a choice as his bowl was on top of the piano and I now realise it was probably the vibrations and not his love of Bach for beginners.

For a chuckle we asked if anyone could beat a goldfish in the random Mother's Day present chart. We had some very decent contenders.

Mandy in Turriff got new washing poles and a washing line, Liz Lynch received a new toilet seat and shower curtain from her daughter Angela, Lee Cassiday was given a cardboard cut-out of Gerry Butler. She added: 'I've wanted the real one in my bedroom for years, but I suppose this will have to do.'

This made me laugh as my nieces Kirsteen and Jessica ordered my sister-in-law Ann a cardboard Marti Pellow a few years ago. They never checked the size and a 24-inch cardboard Marti arrived. Mini-Marti, as he is now known, is present at every party and in most celebratory photos to this day.

Angela texted in this story: 'A few years ago my son worked in Bookers and he gave me ninety-six toilet rolls as there was a two-for-one offer on at the time. He must have thought I needed them.'

If this had been Mother's Day 2020 Angela would have been sitting on a gold-mine given the value loo roll was soon to have.

Kay also sent in her confession: 'When I was seven, I went to my local graveyard and to the bit behind it where they put all the old flower arrangements. I managed to gather a few real flowers that were still okay and some plastic flowers for a bouquet for my mum. They do say it's the thought that counts, don't they?' She adds the shrugging person emoji and lots of laughing faces.

Our Scottish mums certainly have a sense of humour that's for sure. They, along with relieved dads, are on cloud nine this morning as primary school children are back for the first time, plus some selected secondary pupils. Hopefully things are getting back to normal.

As today is the Ides of March, 15 March, the day Caesar was assassinated in Roman times, my Aye or Naw question has a tenuous link to this: there was a Caesar's Palace in Aberdeen. Is this true? Aye or naw?

After explaining that the Ides of March signified the first full moon of the month and used to indicate a new year, new beginnings and time to celebrate in Ancient Rome, he went off on his usual tangent.

Instead of trying to work out how far north the Romans got in Scotland, he decided that it must be a trick question and that Caesar's Palace could simply be any business 'like a tyre shop, an ice cream van or a Chinese restaurant'.

His brain works in a very mysterious way. I pointed out that any restaurant calling itself Caesar's Palace was more likely to be Italian. However, like fifty-four per cent of people this morning, he was actually right.

Aye – there was a Caesar's Palace in Aberdeen. It was a late-night music venue. We get a lovely email from Sandra Crawthorne: 'I met my husband in Caesar's Palace in 1991. It was a nightclub with a very sticky floor.'

It may have been sticky, but it certainly proved ROMAN-tic! Get yir toga you've pulled.

TUESDAY 16 MARCH

The sun is shining, and it makes everyone feel chirpy. Nicola Sturgeon also unveiled a roadmap out of lockdown which has given everybody a little lift. The thought of being able to go on a day trip to Rothesay in May feels like the most exotic adventure of a lifetime.

Dad has mentioned going 'doon the water' a lot recently. I'm determined to get him at least one more Zavaroni's cone on the Costa del Clyde.

News today reveals on average, people in the UK have not written anything by hand with a pen for over forty-one days. I can't believe this. I'm old-school and love writing notes and lists.

My Granny Symington used to have labels on everything. She'd write her own label saying 'TEABAGS' and stick it on a box from the shops clearly already marked 'TEABAGS'.

I write a small journal every day, just one line to remind me of what has happened and what I have to do the following day. Thirty-three per cent of people have not written anything in over six months. Ewen is one of them. Everything he writes is taken down as a typed note on his phone or on his iPad. He says when he does have to write with a pen, he only uses capital letters. Instantly I accuse him of being a psychopath or murderer (I really need to calm down my consumption of stabby documentaries on Sky Crime). I am convinced I've seen it on TV somewhere that many sociopaths do this.

Thanks to the wonders of Google, I find a handwriting website that confirms people who write only in capitals have the following traits:

1. They don't like sharing.
2. They suppress their feelings.

3. They are narcissists.

4. They are egotistical.

Ewen denies all of the above. Until I get to number:

5. They are set in their ways and think they are always right.

We all laugh. Ewen is ALWAYS right. Even when he is completely wrong. Which is why our Aye or Naw game is becoming so memorable. He never accepts defeat graciously. Like this morning's question: A Scottish cheese was once banned in Italy for being too powerful an aphrodisiac. Is this true? Aye or naw?

He said categorically 'naw'; his reasoning: Italians are famous for being enthusiastic lovers so they would not be holding back. Fifty-six per cent of people voted the other way with 'aye' and they were correct.

Back in the 1960s, Italians banned Islay Dunlop cheese as it was apparently making people too randy. In fact, when the creamery reopened in the 1990s on the Island of Islay there was an unprecedented baby boom.

Ewen claims this story is nonsense. Then sprints out the studio to fill a shopping trolley to the brim with cheese for his wife's dinner. I think she's going to need something stronger than that to melt into his arms.

WEDNESDAY 17 MARCH

Happy St Patrick's Day. I've always envied the Irish for their ability to turn a celebration of a religious patron saint into a full-on giant Guinness hat-wearing knees-up.

In retrospect I should have perhaps researched my Aye or Naw question a bit more thoroughly before asking the nation and popping a poll on Twitter. For the first time ever, the answer could be either.

St Patrick was born in Scotland. Is this true? Aye or naw?

I thought it was a decent topical question. Not realising that historians do NOT have a definitive answer. Yes, he ended up in Ireland, but Wales claim him, some say he was born south of Hadrian's Wall whereas I always thought the answer was 'aye', he was born in Scotland.

The majority of experts reckon he was born in AD 387 in Old Kilpatrick, Dumbarton, in Strathclyde. So far – so Scotland. The only issue is, at this time, it wasn't technically Scotland – it was Britannia under Roman rule. So, is it aye or naw? Ach, who knows, today you can have either! You can imagine Ewen's confusion at this one.

Our 'Song with a Story' guest today is Irish comedian Jason Byrne. Jason has sold more tickets than any other comedian in the entire history of the Edinburgh Festival and Fringe. He is hilarious, talented, energetic and completely bonkers. My favourite kind of person.

In his beautifully melodic Dublin accent, he told us: 'My house was always the party house when I was little. Ireland is like Scotland; our parents love a drink and a party. In the countryside in Ireland all the children stay up to 3 a.m. and were handed a fiddle or a whistle in their jammies and had to play 'deedly deedly dee' music to entertain all the oldies. I grew up in Dublin and we only had a record player.

'I'd be about ten and would say to my mum "can you turn the music down?" as it would be about two in the morning and I would have school the next day, and all her pals would say, "Ooh, listen to him with school in the morning" and laugh at me for being sensible.

My dad was a rubbish singer, but he loved his moment in the

spotlight. So, he'd put Perry Como 'Magic Moments' on, and all my fake aunties and uncles would start swaying like the Muppets.

'The thing is, he never knew any of the words. He would stand in the corner of the room with his fag in one hand and would sing "pa pa pa pa pum, pa pa pa pa pum, pa pa pa pa pum pum". And they'd all say, "Paddy you're an amazing singer. What a great voice" and he wasn't he was sh***. He died last year but I still love this song as it reminds me of his party piece all those years ago.'

It's the first song from the 1950s we've played since I joined *Ewen and Cat at Breakfast*, and it's a magic moment right enough.

THURSDAY 18 MARCH

I arrive at work to find a large parcel from Louis Vuitton waiting for me on my desk. Given that my usual designer names are Primark and Mountain Warehouse, I knew this was either a mistake or a very unexpected gift.

Turns out it is a beautiful bottle of perfume from Amy Macdonald. She is covering for me this Sunday coming and knows things are not great with my dad. This unforeseen slice of kindness makes me teary but in a good way and after a lovely supportive message, she signed off 'I hope it doesn't smell boggin'.' She is honestly one of the nicest women of the world. I text to say thanks and to reassure her it is the opposite of bogging. She replied: 'I actually wrote I hope it doesn't smell like sh*** but the website didn't accept my message.'

Obviously with the headquarters of the luxury brand based in Paris she should have typed '*merde*' instead. Regardless, she's magic.

Truthfully, her wee surprise has given me a massive lift. Times are tricky but I've the best pals in the world.

We all know Ewen loves a chart countdown and the excuse to be a proper DJ, but today he is scraping the barrel: The nation's favourite top five pub snacks. 1) Pork scratchings 2) Salted peanuts 3) Dry roasted peanuts 4) Salt and vinegar crisps 5) Ready salted crisps.

This survey has obviously been done in one pub in London. None of us can ever remember seeing pork scratchings in a pub, never mind eating them.

Ewen says he'd rather opt for a bowl of chips. Carnage was happy with the salted nuts (no Chris Tarrant this time) while I get excited when I see a pub with pickled onion Space Raiders.

There's a posh cocktail bar in Edinburgh called the Voodoo Rooms which used to sell them from a Tupperware tub under the counter. It was always a joy watching the barman look shifty before decanting the Space Raiders into posh bowls. I'm pretty sure they sold the 10p from the corner shop crisps for £1 a bowl but hey, they were worth every penny at 2 a.m.

Scottish actor James McAvoy is in all the papers today for winning *Celebrity Bake Off* last night. He made perfect scones, a dreamy lemon meringue tart and a stunning showstopper cake made with rum-infused buttercream and shaped like a snow leopard. His baking was incredible but all the chat on social media is about his tight T-shirt, muscly arms, piercing blue eyes and his hilarious innuendos.

The clip every radio and TV show in the country is replaying today is him talking seductively about his meringue: 'Oh, my peaks are very stiff.'

Yes, James, mine were too . . .

FRIDAY 19 MARCH

The V&A in Dundee has announced a reopening date with an exhibition on nightclub design. 'Night Fever: Designing Club Culture' will look at the relationship between club culture and design.

I'd love to see this and hopefully when Scotland opens up again at the end of next month I can go for a visit. The concept is a curious one to me as my favourite nightclubs were always blessed with the same design features: sticky carpets and dark and dingy.

I used to love a night out clubbing in the 1990s and in fact despite living in the metropolis that is Glasgow, I went on many weekends to Aberdeen back in the day because they had so many epic dance nights. One of my favourite nightclub stories of all time involves taking *Scotsport* commentator Archie MacPherson to the legendary super-club Amadeus in Aberdeen in 1999. He was probably about sixty-two at the time. Along with STV anchor Jim Delahunt and former England and Rangers star Gary Stevens, we ended up in the VIP bit after a stressful CIS Cup semi-final at Pittodrie. I was the trackside reporter for this game.

Cutting a very long story short, it was Aberdeen versus Rangers in the CIS Cup. The game had been brutal. Nil–nil after ninety mins. During the second half of extra time, ITV Transmission told us they would be cutting to Coronation Street at 9.45 p.m., regardless of what happened in the match. This was horrendous. Imagine watching 120 mins of a 0–0 game only to be met with Bet Lynch in the Rovers instead of penalties.

During the last few minutes, both Jim and Archie threatened to resign off mic. It was beyond fraught. Andy Dow scored in the 118th minute. The final whistle went, 1–0 Aberdeen. Jim could only say bye. No chat, no analysis, no after-match interviews (my big moment!).

Needless to say, when we all got back to our hotel on the beach-front the bar was hit big time.

I'm pretty sure it was my idea to take them all to Amadeus for a laugh. The bouncers couldn't believe their eyes. We all got in for free and were escorted to the VIP area which was basically a velvet rope separating us from 2,000 students all wired to the moon on the Tuesday night special pineapple Bacardi Breezer offer.

In fairness we had a decent enough night and returned at about 3 a.m. to the hotel when Gary asked the night porter what food was on offer. Ten minutes later he was given a plate of the thickest tomato soup I've ever seen.

I asked the porter if he'd just microwaved a jar of Ragu. Truly shocked by my culinary expertise, he replied: 'How did you know?' Good times.

In other news, Monopoly are revamping their community chest cards. All sixteen of the yellow cards will now reward a more modern act like helping the elderly, adopting a puppy or supporting a local business. The game is eighty-six years old and makers Hasbro are always looking for ways to keep this classic relevant. I love all of the local editions that they've released although I'm still waiting for one with Firhill Stadium on it. Surely that would be the Mayfair or Park Lane of the board.

Ewen reveals he always had to choose the top hat counter when playing, Carnage wanted to be the little Scottie Dog while my brother always made me go the wee boot. Until now, I've never questioned his reasoning.

MONDAY 29 MARCH

First day back after a week off.

What have I missed? Nicola Sturgeon's been cleared of knowingly misleading parliament, Alex Salmond's started his own Alba Party, a big container ship is stuck in the Suez Canal causing delivery chaos, Scotland drew 2–2 with Austria then 1–1 with Israel in our World Cup qualifiers, while the Scottish rugby team scored a late try in Paris to beat France in the dying seconds of the match.

What have I done for the past week? I've walked round the park a lot, took Dad to a plethora of hospital appointments and got a big pipe blockage fixed (my bathroom not my dad!).

The clocks changed yesterday but we made our Sunday show in good time. I still phone the speaking clock, as ridiculous as that sounds. I mean, how do you know your devices know to change? Unfortunately, this means my car clock will now be an hour behind for the next six months. Finding the manual would be the easy option but I like knowing I'll never be late for anything.

My Aye or Naw question pushes Ewen over the edge: Was Brora the first place in the north of Scotland to have electricity?

He he, I'm at the wind up. I forgot to mention his team Hearts were put out of the Scottish Cup in the second round last week in a 2–1 win for Brora Rangers.

He goes in a proper wee huff and refuses to play. Our listeners are loving this and several suggest I come up with a question about Dumfries tomorrow. Dumfries is home to Queen of the South who beat Hearts 3–2 at the weekend. He's not chuffed but I see him crack and he reluctantly enjoys the banter.

Ewen's chart today is the top five jobs that kids want. The most desired career is to be a YouTuber. I'm really beginning to feel my age: is this actually a thing? If you're not a Kardashian, is this a viable option? A quick google shows that you earn 0.01p per view from advertisers so you get £1.10 for 1,000 views. I'm now regretting not monetising my dad's NHS doorstep fiddle-playing sessions. He's had over a million views which means we could be living in the Caribbean by now or at least getting a chippy at the weekend.

I'm going to squeeze in a quick Happy Birthday to my good friends Dolina MacFarlane and also Mrs P. I've worked in the media for over twenty-five years and Mrs P has been my biggest, and only, fan. She's loved my columns; she's been to every stage show I've ever been in or written and she's always so positive about my latest crazy endeavours. She's also my friend Debbie's mum, but hey, I'll gratefully take the adoration when it's given. Mrs P not only sends nice texts to the show, but every so often she makes lentil soup, steak pie and chicken chasni for me as well. Bet you Beyoncé doesn't get this!

TUESDAY 30 MARCH

Plenty of talking points to get our teeth into today:

- Cheap wine scores just as highly as expensive wine in blind taste tests. In the study run by psychologists, participants only marked it lower when they knew the price (my policy of never buying Prosecco over £8 has served me well).
- Parents are too scared to call their child Alexa in 2021 because of Amazon's virtual assistant. This is probably just as well, or the poor lassie would grow up her entire life answering questions about the weather and trying to figure out where your stuff is!
- We ignore 337 phone calls a year; these include calls from our partners, workmates, friends and relatives. Sixty-one per cent of people regularly don't pick up the phone when someone rings. Ewen admits he never answers my calls if he's busy on his PlayStation. Big wean.
- Canadian neuroscientists have proven music triggers the brain in the same way chocolate and alcohol does. The scientists focused on the effects of pop music in the brain using magnetic imaging and using transcranial magnetic stimulation and have found communication between the brain's auditory and reward circuit. By that reckoning, listening to the radio with a wee glass of something chilled and a jar of Nutella is pretty much as good as it gets.

CAT'S OUT THE BAG

Our 'Song with a Story' today really is a magical tale. It's from Edinburgh-based magician Kevin Quantum who recently enthralled the judges on BGT with his act.

Kevin revealed: 'Ten years ago, at Christmas time, I landed a gig working in the Spiegeltent in George Street. I needed to find some-body to saw in half every night for fourteen nights. I'd just started dating this lovely Russian girl called Svetlana and I thought I might as well ask her. We'd only been going out for about two weeks, so this was a good test to see if she had a sense of humour or not. I asked her if she was up for taking part and straight away, she said yes, well she actually said '*da*' which is yes in Russian!

'For the next fortnight I sawed her in half every evening in front of a live audience. I was trained by Penn and Teller, so my act is quite out there. We had loads of fake blood and people in the front rows got splattered. I realised at the end of the run that she was pretty special to not be freaked out by my extreme magic behaviour. Ten years later we are married with two children. The song I chopped my wife up to was Frank Sinatra's "Fly me to the Moon".'

We play the song and throw in a chainsaw sound effect at the end. I'm supremely confident that we're the only radio show in the world today mixing the vocals of a legendary crooner with a power tool. Magic!

WEDNESDAY 31 MARCH

Two Scottish tourist attractions have made it to Lonely Planet's new list of lesser-known places to visit in the UK.

Craigievar Castle in Alford and Benmore Botanic Gardens near Dunoon have been selected as hidden gems.

Craigievar is known as the pink castle because, well, it's pink! This is the castle which is said to have inspired Walt Disney to create an almost identical one for Cinderella's castle in Disneyland.

With foreign travel looking to be unlikely this year, I think I've done parents a massive favour by sharing this story. They can tell their kids they are going to see Cinderella's castle and not have to leave Scotland. Disney matters if it's only in Aberdeenshire.

Scotland play the Faroe Islands this evening in another World Cup qualifier. It's a game we should win easily but I've been in the Tartan Army way too long to take anything for granted.

I decided to test Ewen with a topical Aye or Naw question. Many houses in the Faroe Islands use sheep to keep their roofs tidy. Is this true? Aye or naw?

He says I am being ridiculous, and the RSPCA would be involved if sheep were working up on roofs. I did point out that I was not talking about a tenement block or a high-rise, but single-storey cottages, many backing onto hillsides with low, gently sloping roofs. He was still having none of it and incorrectly voted 'naw'.

Carnage thought it was true, revealing: 'I was looking at Torshavn in the Faroe Islands on Google Street View the other day and some of the houses had thatched roofs.'

(If anyone else in the planet had told me this sentence I'd be sending for the wee people in white coats, but Carnage is Carnage. He's missing travelling and virtually wandering round the main town of a remote North Atlantic archipelago is probably a decent Friday night in for him.)

Sixty-two per cent got it correct with 'aye'. Lots of houses in the Faroe Islands still use birch with turf for roofs, in fact it has more turf-roofed houses than anywhere else in the world. The sheep basically jump up on the lowest point and munch their way right over the top and round the chimney pots. It seems like the perfect symbiotic relationship. They get fed; the owners get a tidy roof.

Three listeners, Ross, Margaret Reid and Alan Sedstrem, all ask the same question on Twitter at exactly the same time. Where do I get these crazy questions? The answer is a combination of Google and my own imagination. Does that make me a little bit bonkers? One hundred per cent of you know the answer to this one – 'aye'!

THURSDAY 1 APRIL

What a day for show business news. West Lothian's finest, Lewis Capaldi, is teaming up with queen of pop Beyoncé for a remake of the Grease classic 'Summer Nights'. The Spice Girls have been announced as the headline act for TRNSMT and will be on the bill just after the Chemical Brothers and *Trainspotting 3* has finally been given the green light.

It will be set in Glasgow; Renton will import avocados and run a health food café, Begbie is out of prison and working in the botanic gardens growing plants and Spud has become an influencer.

If you think this is all rather far-fetched then please do take a look at the date. Yes my friends, it's April Fool's Day. A day feared and revered in equal measure in radio stations throughout the land.

A well-executed wind-up will generate massive talkability, a bad one and people just think we're eejits.

Today we are sitting halfway in between. We never reveal everything I say is fabricated nonsense, but we are having enough fun for even the most gullible of listener to know we are up to mischief.

I've been involved in some crackers over the years. My favourites are:

1. The Proclaimers are not related. Yes, we somehow managed to persuade Craig and Charlie Reid, the world's most famous musical twins, to tell us they were a manufactured novelty act,

and management made them wear glasses to look like each other. Both brothers were hilarious as they revealed how traumatic it was living the lie for so many years.

2. The Cumbernauld Space Shuttle landing. The space shuttle was due to fly over Europe at some point this week. We just made up a refuelling stop at Cumbernauld Airport. We told everyone that at 8.30 a.m. it would be making a half hour touch down before taking off again. We did not expect so many excited space fans to fall for it to the extent that tailbacks at Cumbernauld were featured in all the subsequent travel bulletins. Rockets!

3. Ewen's big American adventure. We announced that Ewen had been headhunted to do a prime-time American TV show similar to *The Late Late Show*. He was taking his family and heading over the pond. I think he enjoyed all the listeners phoning in to say he would be missed. The best bit about this story is a few years later Ewen spoke to an events organiser who had failed to book him for one of his regular gigs. He asked why and the man said: 'I'd heard you were off to America, so we had to look elsewhere'. Another day, another dollar.

My Aye or Naw question is also a cracker. Scotland manager Steve Clarke and three players got 'Yes Sir, I can Boogie' tattooed on their backsides after qualifying for the Euros. Is this true? Aye or naw?

Sixteen per cent of our listeners and Ewen said 'aye'. He reasoned that as I'm friends with defender Stephen O'Donnell I must have inside information. I told everyone on air the answer was indeed 'aye'. I mean it's not, but it's April Fool's Day so I'm allowed to be confusing. I get a message from Stephen about three hours later reading: 'You are a spud!' I wonder how many people have asked him what's written on his bottom. As rumours go, it's sMASHing . . .

FRIDAY 2 APRIL

Good Friday and a holiday for many. Not us, we're in bright and early and full of spring joy as we get to launch our big Easter chart – the Hall of Fame Top 200, as voted for by our listeners, which will run through all the shows over the Easter Weekend.

It's billed as the ultimate chart, celebrating the world's most iconic artists. No band or singer can appear more than once.

We all have a guess at who number one on Monday will be. I go for the Beatles, Ewen thinks Queen and Carnage goes for the Rolling Stones (just to remind you – I am innocent!).

One of the best things about working on a big radio station is being involved in massive competitions with prizes that can genuinely change lives. At the moment we're running a competition called 'The £1 Million Cash Register'. You pay two pounds to enter by text or you can enter for free online and each day a large amount of money us up for grabs until we've given away £1 million.

We get the job of setting the daily winner's amount (who am I kidding, we're not responsible enough for that, we simply reveal the daily prize pot). For example, that day you could be playing for £45,678. It is important to remember / write down the exact amount because if Garry Spence calls at 5 p.m. and you answer within five rings you have to tell him how much is up for grabs. Do this and the money is yours tax free and in your bank account by the end of the day.

There have been several occasions when people have simply not answered their phones in time or at all. The worst one was the lady who did answer but didn't know that day's prize amount.

There is no magic secret to winning; it is, like the lottery, just luck as the winner is chosen completely at random by a computer algorithm from all the entries.

This week we've had some amazing winners. Charlie from Arran who works offshore in Aberdeen won £61,000. Fate moves in mysterious ways. Charlie was on his computer filling in a form for a new credit card to pay off some debts when he received his life-changing call. The following day Theresa from Dalgety Bay won £60,000. She wept with joy as she'd not been working for two years and this cash was going to ease her worries.

Hearing how big a difference these prizes can mean to people's lives is genuinely a wonderfully moving experience. I'm a big softy these days and I cried at both of these moments. I hope they enjoy every single penny.

It's been a rough week for Dad. He's had appointments with Oncology, Cardiology and Orthopaedics.

I had to use a wheelchair with him for the first time at the hospital and with the cancer now ravaging his bones he's feeling every bump on the road when I'm driving.

This morning when I was on air, he fell in his bedroom. My brother who lives nearer went to the rescue. He's finally agreed to get an emergency button wristband. When I get to see him, he's shaken, a little childlike, but not badly hurt.

In typically ebullient form he laughs: 'I fell on Easter Friday but wait until you see me, I'll be back on top form by Monday!' Jesus, he's nothing if not topical.

TUESDAY 6 APRIL

Back in the fold after a cheeky wee Easter Monday off. As a result, all three of us don't know if we're coming or going. The roads are so quiet it feels like everyone is still on holiday.

The weather is beyond bizarre, sunshine and snow, clear skies then hailstones again. Basically just Scotland.

Today we play out the first part of our interview with Marti Pellow. Now then, here's how it is. Marti Pellow was my first love. He was the first boy I ever fancied, and I've loved Wet Wet Wet ever since. You can imagine my excitement when I heard he was coming on the show again.

We recorded the interview over Zoom last week and he was in brilliant form. Marti and I have met several times over the years. The first time I met him I think I just stared and dribbled a bit, but I'm much more professional now even if I do still nervously giggle a lot.

I've interviewed him about theatre shows in his dressing room at the Kings (we hugged, I hate hugs, this hug was nice), I've interviewed him about solo stuff, and I've interviewed him with the band. Ewen and I were lucky enough to be the hosts of Wet Wet Wet at Glasgow Green for their twenty-fifth anniversary gig. We had the wonderful job of winding up the crowd and then bringing the band on stage. Truthfully, the stuff of dreams.

Marti knows I fancy him. I know Marti knows I fancy him, and we are all now pretty cool with this until Ewen said: 'Cat, tell Marti what you and your pals did when you tried to find his house?'

I reluctantly have to tell the story of getting the number sixty-nine (yes, really it was) bus from Milngavie to Clydebank. We got off outside the Atlantis Bar on Kilbowie Road and then basically wandered about all the streets hoping to miraculously see Marti casually stoating about Clydebank or sitting in a garden waiting for us. It sounds ridiculous now, but when you are thirteen it seemed like the best idea in the world.

Thankfully he laughed: 'Don't worry Cat, it happened all the time. I would be away doing Top of the Pops or something and when I would get back to my mammie's there would be six girls squashed on the couch drinking tea and eating biscuits. I'd look at my mum and she'd just say: 'But they've come all the way from Pollokshaws, I had to give them something.'

I'm now even more raging we didn't have better intelligence all those years ago. I wonder what the lucky Pollokshaws lassies pinched from his washing basket.

We have some quick-fire questions from listeners and they're hilarious.

Michael Dolan asked: 'Do you remember me fitting your Sky dish back in 1985 when it was my first job as a trainee?' Marti politely said he did.

Ian Kelly asked: 'Do you like a pie in a roll?' Honestly, I love our listeners. Marti replied: 'I have been known to in the past and certain pies lend themselves to a well-fired Morton's roll but now that I have a gazelle-like physique, they're not high up on my menu.'

I've only recently found out that a pie in a roll is also known as a Glasgow Oyster. Makes me so proud of my home city. When you think of the visual, it all kind of makes sense it's like a carb tribute to the seafood delicacy.

Final question of the day goes to James Reid who asked: 'How are you getting on with your arthritis?'

Marti knows what this is about straight away. He jokes: 'Well, I feel it in my fingers, I feel it in my toes.' BOOM! This is of course the opening line to 'Love is All Around' which was at number one for fifteen weeks. Tomorrow we'll play out the interview clips of what happened when we let seven superfans ask Marti a question over Zoom.

Every one of the ladies looked a million dollars and had gone all out to impress. Truthfully, Ewen and I had so much fun watching them interact with their hero and they couldn't believe we'd actually made it happen. Magic, magic, magic!

WEDNESDAY 7 APRIL

'Tonight, Matthew, I'm going to be Axl Rose from Guns N' Roses.'

Without doubt this would have been my introduction if I'd ever appeared on Matthew Kelly's *Stars in Their Eyes* back in the 1990s. The infamous smoke-filled doorway was the gateway to fame for many incredible tribute acts back in the day.

Members of the public would be transformed by the ITV make-over team to resemble their musical heroes whom sometimes they sounded like and sometimes they didn't.

Today in my 'Happy News' I reveal that the show is getting a revamp and will be returning, hosted by Olly Murs. Sheridan Smith, Jason Manford, Adam Lambert and Beverley Knight will make up the judging panel.

We have a good laugh working out who we would be. I am a shoo-in for Axl. It's the only song I sing, and I've never played a bum note on the air guitar yet. I think Ewen would make a good Cher as he likes to wear dresses (remember the Ladyboys story). In fairness, if I had his pins I would too.

He surprises us by revealing he would be David Soul (Hutch from *Starsky & Hutch*) and his song would be 'Silver Lady'. Carnage opts for Sinead O'Connor in tribute to his weekend beer-inspired home haircut.

This morning we play out part one of our listener's questions for Marti Pellow. It's an absolute joy to listen to the excitement in their voices and the former Wet Wet Wet pin-up plays an absolute blinder.

Hannah: Marti, do you remember me, we met at a wedding in Darvel?

Marti: Oh aye, you've sobered up a bit since then and you've not changed a bit.

Elaine: Marti, do you remember playing with Jools Holland at the

SECC years ago and there was a mad woman who kept trying to climb up onto the stage to get to you?

Marti: Aye, that was you, wasn't it? What happened?

Elaine: I got my top half up on the stage then my pal pulled me back down, you were singing a Beatles song. I tried again and got my top half back up on the stage before my pal pulled me back down again.

Marti: Well next time I'm in Glasgow you'll have to try harder!

Elaine: I WILL.

And none of us doubt this!

Diane: Marti, I have loved you since I was ten years old and I only have one question for you.

Marti: Go on.

Diane: Will you marry me?

Marti: I really appreciate the offer, I mean I *really* appreciate the offer, but shall we just leave it there?

Me: Diane, he didn't say no.

Diane: [Overjoyed] No he didn't, Ewen and Cat – GET YIR HATS! Everyone is buckled.

Fair play to Marti, he knows even aged fifty-six, to all these women he is still 'Temptation'. (Not sorry!)

THURSDAY 8 APRIL

My 'Happy News' this morning comes as a sense of relief to anyone with *that* kitchen drawer. You know the one, full to the brim of who knows what. It turns out eighty per cent of us find them useful and experts now say they're a necessary part of a home and are good for us.

I used to have a 'cupboard of death' which was just a much bigger, harder to shut version of the dreaded kitchen drawer. Moving flat twice in ten years helped get rid of the junk although the real reason I tidied it was after an unused mini fitness trampoline fell on my head. Life is indeed full of ups and downs.

The average stash of bits and bobs in the kitchen drawer has been unveiled as: six batteries, three phone chargers, five unspecified cables, four takeaway menus, four mystery keys with no known lock, six pens or pencils and five instruction manuals.

My drawers always have bubble wrap too. Make of that what you will.

Today we play out part two of Marti Pellow talking to some superfans over Zoom. Everyone is loving this feature. Fair play to Ewen and Carnage for setting this up. I was far too starry-eyed to be of any use whatsoever. The questions are brilliant.

Louise: This is a bit personal but what possessed you to grow your hair so long in the 1990s?

Marti: Because I could!

Louise: Seriously Marti, what were you thinking?

Annalisa: I saw you in Newcastle about fifteen years ago. Just before you came on, a stagehand walked across the stage with a brown mac and a brush, he had a hat pulled over his face, but I caught eyes with him and there was a sparkle in his eyes. Was this you?

Marti: You never know, I like to suss out my audience.

Me: Even if that wasn't you, that was the right answer, Marti.

Annalisa is now in heaven, as Mandy takes centre Zoom stage.

Mandy: Are you a tea or coffee man, Marti?

Marti: I love my tea and my coffee.

Mandy: Which do you prefer?

Marti: Coffee, black with no sugar.

Mandy: That's easy to remember ... I'll need to know for the morning after!!

And with that we conclude our Marti party. I'm delighted that my childhood sweetheart has managed to melt so many hearts. I'm not happy with all the competition but with 'Angel Eyes' like his what can I expect. And I promise that's the last one . . .

After the show I pop up to visit Dad. The thing about a terminal diagnosis is that for the person who doesn't know timings, life goes on as normal. For the people who do, everything is different. Small symptoms are enhanced. I'm looking for things that I know don't exist. Time becomes both a luxury and a constraint. The person choosing not to know has limited worries, while the people in the know carry double the burden. It's worth it though.

They started Dad on a new pill last week and he has found his appetite again. Today I go round to clean his house and have a catch-up. By the time I arrive, he's already driven to the supermarket and back for his shopping. I can feel my heart race. I just don't want him to fall.

A few weeks ago, he was barely touching soup. Today he announces we have a fun task planned. I'm thinking take the bins out, maybe clean the fridge, help him with his crossword but no he declares: 'Let's make a prawn Thai curry.'

I should point out we have never ever up until now cooked together. He always cooks for me or vice versa.

Whatever is in these steroids, I want some. And so, side by side, one chopping and one stirring, we make a Thai red curry from a wee kit. He snips the packets. I get the fear he's going to chop off his fingers and bleed out as he's on Warfarin. He hasn't a care in the world. I think he's standing too long, and his legs might cave in. But we keep going. Deep red spicy paste, coconut milk, prawns, herbs, and going off recipe, he flings in some noodles from his cupboard that probably have a sell-by date of 2011.

I'm struck by the absurdity of the situation. Last Friday I was sure he was on his way out, today I am sure he's invincible. There's no way this one's clogs are getting popped any time soon.

I go home and google terminal cancer diagnosis and how accurate timescales are. There are just as many stories of people long outliving their predicted demise as those who go downhill faster. I now know for certain Dad will be the exception to the rule. He's always been a maverick.

I go a walk with my friend Peter and we both end up laughing at how typically 'Bobby Harvey' this all is.

I've now no idea how or when this story will end. I must simply enjoy every day like today and reflect with gratitude on being lucky enough to experience another crazy chapter in my life with Dad. The curry was excellent by the way, we are a good team. My heart physically aches and bursts with joy at the same time. We are not a good team – we are a GREAT team.

FRIDAY 9 APRIL

Boo! How do you like surprises? I love them.

My favourite ever remains my Granny Harvey's ninetieth birthday bash in a wee coffee shop in Milngavie, hired for a late-night bash in 1988. All her pals were there; we'd even splashed out and paid for a full salmon in for the buffet and naturally my dad's full Ceilidh Band were standing by and ready to go.

She walked into the room decked with 'Happy 90th Birthday' balloons and banners and on cue everyone jumped out from behind tables, chairs and walls and shouted: 'SURPRISE!'

She replied: 'Aye it's a big surprise right enough as I'm only eighty-nine this year.' She was right.

New research says the best surprise in life is finding money either in the street or in a forgotten coat pocket. Surprise parties, engagements, pregnancies and puppies are the other four main surprises people enjoy.

Ewen reveals that his youngest son Josh was quite the surprise, although he suspects his wife Teresa wasn't quite so shocked as she'd always wanted three! Drink and French sunshine were apparently to blame, but they're blessed as Josh is a wee delight.

All this week my Aye or Naw questions have been TV-themed. *River City* has now aired more episodes than *Take the High Road* – 'naw'; *Supergran* is massive in Cuba – 'aye'; and *Scotsport* remains the longest running sports show on TV – 'naw', it's *Hockey Night* in Canada.

Today's question is so like something I would come up with it's perfect to bamboozle. I couldn't do a Scottish TV week without *Taggart*. Thirty years of material and sold to over eighty countries all round the world. The question: Before becoming a detective, Jim Taggart dabbled in petty crime by stealing Jimmy Shand records from his local Woolworths. Is this true? Aye or naw?

Ewen is convinced I am at it. He knows my dad loves Jimmy Shand and that I'll use any excuse to drop in a bit of uplifting ceilidh music to proceedings. Carnage, as ever, is quick to help and fires in a blast of 'The Bluebell Polka'.

Ewen is one hundred per cent convinced this is absolute nonsense and he is wrong along with forty-eight per cent of the voters. This is an 'aye'. Glen Chandler who created the series wrote an entire back story for the character and yes, that young scamp Taggart did nick records from Woolies. He also lived on the second floor of a Springburn tenement block and his dad was a tram driver.

As I go to save this diary entry onto my laptop, the sad news breaks from Buckingham Palace that Prince Philip has died at the age of ninety-nine.

I've met him several times while I was presenting at the big Duke of Edinburgh Awards at Holyrood Palace. He once asked me what time I started my radio show and I'd replied 5 a.m.

He then said: 'Who listens at that time?' before adding one of my favourite quotes of all time, 'You must be very popular with truckers!' He said this with a glint in his eye which I knew meant he was being mischievous. This was one of the quotes I used on the back cover of my last book.

I also once had to sit next to him for three hours at a fundraising dinner in Edinburgh Castle. He chatted mostly just to me that night because I was obviously not that fussed about being placed next to a senior royal. He liked that. We talked about chickens, kilts and commercial radio. He said it had too many adverts for his liking before singing the Autoglass Express advert word perfectly to me. I could tell his aides were very worried about our banter and sniggers.

He also had his own stealth-like private butler who kept his personal crystal glass nicely topped up with Martini throughout the evening. 'It's the best way to get through these things,' he confided in me. I didn't have the heart to remind him this was a night for his own charity!

HRH Prince Philip means many things to many people. My dad is still convinced he bumped off Diana! I only have my own encounters to go on and I liked him.

Ewen and I text each other. In the world of radio, being on air when someone important dies is my biggest fear. There's an obituary procedure written and in place, there's an obituary alarm that even flashes in the studio, but are we ever really prepared? Probably not enough.

I wish my pals Greigsy and Fraser Thomson good luck as they are on air right now and will be frantically shuffling local, IRN and Sky news feeds and slow songs with nothing inappropriate in the title or lyrics. As unsympathetic as this may sound, I say a massive thanks to the Universe and the radio gods that we've avoided this one.

MONDAY 12 APRIL

Congratulations to Sir Anthony Hopkins who won best actor last night at the Bafta Film Awards for his role in *The Father*. At eighty years young he's celebrating his big win twenty-seven years after winning his last Bafta. I wonder if he toasted the result with some fava beans and a nice Chianti.

Nomadland starring Frances McDormand picked up four awards including best film, best director and best actress.

It feels weird talking about films when cinemas remain closed. I can't wait for the bustle of a weekend evening blockbuster and the smell of sweet popcorn and tepid hotdogs. Before lockdown I'd only just discovered the joys of the big reclining seats at the cinema. Perfect for relaxing although they do make me nod off.

Talking of sleep, my 'Happy News' today has great advice for anyone living with a snorer. Get them trumpet lessons.

As unorthodox as this might sound, new research shows that playing a trumpet or trombone can help with sleeping disorders. Don't worry, you don't have to blast out Herb Alpert's 'Tijuana Taxi' before bed. People who learn a brass instrument develop muscles in their upper airways that prevent sleep apnoea – the collapse of tissue at the back of the throat that leads to snoring. I think I'll stick to lavender pillow spray. Much less problematic for the downstairs neighbours.

After the TV theme to last week's Aye or Naw questions, I think I will have some fun with Scottish movies.

Today's question: Most of the horses used in the *Braveheart* fight scenes were fake. Is this true? Aye or naw?

Today's question gets an emphatic 'naw' from Ewen. He is a massive *Braveheart* fan and claims his wife's cousin was an extra in the battle scenes and said the horses were terrifying. Fifty-eight per cent said 'aye', which is the right answer.

I said *most*, not *all*. There were of course real horses involved but the majority of the cavalry were on 200lb mechanical contraptions powered by nitrogen cylinders and capable of going at 30 m.p.h. So real were they on film, animal welfare officers famously investigated the production post-release only to discover they were props. Ewen is raging and I'm euphoric. I sometimes forget this is just a silly wee game. I need to rein it in . . .

TUESDAY 13 APRIL

Today is a very good day. First Minister Nicola Sturgeon's announced we're allowed to travel around mainland Scotland from Friday onwards and that we will also be allowed to meet six people from six different households outdoors.

For single people this is massive. I can go and see my pals that live outwith my local area and we can be together in a group again. I've missed them all so much and can't wait to sit in someone's garden in ski wear wrapped in a heavy wool blanket, sipping from a plastic glass clutched between my thermal mittens. I'm not even joking. Right now, after being kept home alone for so long, this sounds like the best night out ever!

My friend Nichola (her of the New Zealand biker bar YMCA karaoke fame) sends me a text saying they'll put up a tent for me in their garden in Dalkeith so I can stay over. I'm too excited at the prospect of socialising to tell her I had to scrape ice off my windscreen this morning and it might be prudent to wait until summer.

I'm definitely out of drinking practice. I will need to be gently broken in again. I'll maybe leave Nichola and Fiona for a few months yet.

Talking of booze, new research out this morning says there is a new regret to add to the list of standards after a night out. Apparently forty per cent of us have had a drink and then bought something online we regret the next day. The most common alcohol-inspired purchases are concert tickets, unsuitable clothing and toys of an adult nature (whatever that means).

My two couches came from a night out. I didn't pinch them. I ordered them at 2 a.m. when I came home full of the joys. My ex thought I had no sense of interior decorating style and said I loved the colour purple too much. In an expensive act of late-night defiance, I bought two purple velvet couches. Thankfully they turned out to be nice.

While working in Spain, Carnage returned to his apartment at 3 a.m. and booked himself a weekend break in Amsterdam to get away from an annoying flatmate.

The flight was at 8 a.m. that morning and he woke up at lunchtime with said flatmate asking him why he'd left a note in the kitchen saying, 'I'm away to Amsterdam, back Monday.'

As ever our listeners have some cracking tales. John Farquhar called in with this story: 'I got a big surprise when a delivery guy knocked on my door one Thursday afternoon and handed me a large triangular shaped parcel. I thought someone must have sent me a gift. When I opened it up it was a ukulele, and something rang a bell. I checked my eBay account and sure enough at 3.30 a.m. on Saturday morning I'd paid £90 for it. I am not musical. I can't play any instruments and as for singing I'm like a goose farting in the wind. I've had it five years and can now almost play the intro to "Hey Soul Sister" by Train.'

At this point John played us the intro and he's got potential.

Ewen: That wasn't too bad.

John: Aye but it's not great either.

Me: You know what you need to buy now?

John: What?

Me: Earplugs.

Next on the phone is Craig Watson, he is out delivering pharmaceutical supplies and pulls into a layby for a chat. He explained: 'I've got a bit of a weird man-crush on Patrick Swayze, my mates always slag me off about it. One night I was in the house having a few beers and I was watching *Ghost*. I was loving that famous scene with Patrick and Demi Moore and just assumed women were all into this kind of thing. I woke up in the morning to an email telling me I'd tried to buy a large potter's wheel. Thankfully my card had been declined at the last bit as I'd changed my bank card on the Amazon account the week before. Just as well really as I moved back to my mum and dad's not long after this, and the last thing they needed was me back and a giant pottery wheel.'

We all now imagine Craig sitting in the layby lovingly caressing his steering wheel like Patrick cuddles Demi in the film. We play 'Unchained Melody' for him.

Some of the drunk-purchasing stories on Facebook have me howling.

Wullie Meikle: 'I tried to pay £3,000 on a 1973 VW Beatle I don't remember and woke up delighted to find out I was outbid. Randomly I did manage to buy ping pong balls and three thousand hand-rolling cigarette tips. I don't even smoke!'

Gary Toner: 'I bought a Ford Focus. Luckily, they let me cancel the next day. I can't even drive!'

Michelle Tait: 'I snapped up a two-week all-inclusive holiday to Turkey.'

Trish Duffy: 'A Tony Soprano shower curtain. Don't ask.'

Lesley Ewing: 'A hot tub.'

Andrea Reid: 'I bought a power washer. Seemed like a good idea at the time but I don't have a hose or an outside tap.'

Suddenly my purple couches don't seem too bad. As far as my swally shopping history goes, sofa so good.

WEDNESDAY 14 APRIL

The sun is shining today and yesterday's news about some of the restrictions lifting has really bolstered spirits in the still-depleted office. We've not seen any of the sales, marketing, admin or commercial production teams in over a year. It's going to be one helluva party when we're allowed to mingle again.

I'm grateful to have been able to come in to work and see people face to face throughout the entire pandemic. The testing isn't pleasant but it's worth it.

A list of the top fifty simple pleasures to enjoy after lockdown has been revealed this morning. Hearing tweeting birds, enjoying a coffee in bed, having dinner made for you, sitting at a roaring fire, getting a cuddle from your kids and sitting in a beer garden with pals all feature. The number one simple pleasure was revealed as feeling sunshine on your face.

I'd combine two and have a sunny beer garden with my mates please. Not long now!

Ewen is delighted to see a story about phones today as he loves slagging me off about my tech ambivalence.

On average we spend £40,000 on tech during our lifetime. This includes twenty-one mobile phones, sixteen games consoles, sixteen laptops or computers, sixteen tablets, thirteen TVs and thirteen cameras. We will also use over one thousand batteries and have 126 charging cables. I think that number of batteries and charging cables are all currently squeezed into my kitchen drawer.

Ewen is gadget daft and always has the latest in everything. I get a new phone when my old one stops working and not before. I am currently using an iPhone 7 (2016) which I thought was pretty modern. I'm still missing playing snake on my old Nokia which lasted decades.

I gave my dad my old iPhone 3 (2008) because he likes sending me selfies of him eating ice cream. I have to guess his location by his iCone.

Bobby 'two cakes' Harvey is also Bobby 'two phones' Harvey, which would imply an element of subterfuge. His other phone is an ancient purple flip phone that takes £10 top-up vouchers from his local corner shop. The only person who calls him on this is my Aunty Jean. I have tried time and time again to assure him that she can input his newer number into her phone but no, he keeps it charged and with credit for her personal hotline.

My Aunty Jean lives with my cousin Karen in Helensburgh. Karen is always so happy to see us, she has Down's syndrome and is the one person I genuinely love a cuddle from. Once the restrictions lift and cafés open, they are our first dining dates. Dad will be delighted. I know in advance he will have a slice of lemon meringue pie from the Craigend Tearoom followed by a cone from Dino's. So much to look forward to.

We finish the show by surprising Anne-Marie Murray. Her husband George phoned in early doors to ask if he could get a shout-out for their thirty-seventh wedding anniversary. Ewen is brilliant at grabbing a fun opportunity and asked for her home number. We call Anne-Marie and she is in shock.

Anne-Marie: I can't believe he's done this to me. I'm going to kill him when he gets home.

Me: But he said he loves you loads and told us lots of wonderful things about you and when you first met on the dancefloor of Tiffany's in Blackpool.

Anne-Marie: That's nice and I love him too – but I'm still going to murder him when he gets through the door.

We play 'Love is All Around' and assume she is joking ...

THURSDAY 15 APRIL

We are guilty of chatting about some right random nonsense on our breakfast show and in my 'Happy News' today I share the tale of Fraser Gilchrist from Stirling who has successfully bred the first-ever Egyptian miniature tortoise in Scotland.

He's been taking part in a captive breeding programme run by conservationists trying to save the breed from extinction. The wee baby tortoise is only the size of a two-pence piece.

Carnage fires in the theme tune of Teenage Mutant Ninja Turtles. Honestly, how am I ever meant to sound like I know what I'm talking about with these bams at the helm?

Ewen asks me: What is the difference between a tortoise and a turtle? In the back of my head, I know the answer. A tortoise is a turtle, but not all turtles are tortoises.

Ewen's face is a picture. I try to explain that tortoises are from the turtle family, but they only live on land. A turtle can swim and live in or out of the water. It gets even weirder when he asks about terrapins. Google helps with this one: a terrapin is also a turtle and in fact the name means mini turtle in Algonquin, a North American Indian language.

Further research informs me the collective noun for tortoises is a creep of tortoises and the oldest on record is Jonathan, who is 187 years old and lives in St Helena. We both agree that while this is fascinating, we should probably leave the natural history lessons to David Attenborough.

During the next song I continue googling the life expectancy of wild sea turtles (three hundred is not uncommon!) while Ewen and Carnage argue over the names of the ninja turtles. We really are quite different. And to save you the bother of checking, they were Donatello, Raphael, Michelangelo and Leonardo, named after Renaissance painters.

We always have the news on screens in the studio just in case anything big breaks. The channels are muted but we can always see the rolling graphics to be alerted to anything major. Ewen lets out a destressed 'No!' while staring wide-eyed at the TV. I assume some big bad world event has just been announced and swivel quickly to see the winner of *MasterChef* 2021, Tom from Newcastle, raising a glass of champagne.

The news item on the winner has just ruined Ewen's day as he was planning on going home to catch up on last night's final after his lunch (KFC popcorn chicken and a double decker – not a trio – of oysters followed by a reverse-seared ribeye topped with beetroot pickled in Japanese seaweed and wasabi leaf like Tom made).

After the show we have a couple of interviews to record; most of our callers come on live but we sometimes have to record interviews to fit people's schedules. This morning's is with comedian Fred MacAuley, who is making his debut on the Greatest Hits Network this Sunday.

This is brilliant news as Fred is not only a hoot, he's also a really nice guy and it would be lovely if he joined the team. There's a certain irony to Ewen and I interviewing Fred for our Breakfast Show because twenty years ago I worked on his show. I used to do the newspaper review on his BBC Radio Scotland programme once every couple of weeks.

I remember being in awe of him as he was properly famous and was so good at ad hoc one-liners. However (and this is a bit telling), the thing I remember most about being part of his show was the incredible breakfast buffet that was laid on every morning for guests.

I mean if you think about it, it's probably my own tax money but back then I was offered fresh juice, herbal teas, piping hot brewed coffee, a substantial and exotic fruit platter and a selection of delectable Danish pastries and patisserie treats from the local artisan bakery (the BBC was in the West End back then, dahlings!). I reminded Fred of this decadence and he laughed: 'We used to get bacon rolls too, those were the days!'

I politely remind him he's joining commercial radio and as such he'd better pack a flask and bring his own biscuit.

Ewen and I will be next door on the Hits Network (the 1's) on Sunday morning at the same time as Fred's show, so just for old time's sake I'm going to bring him in a tangerine and a Yum Yum from the local garage.

FRIDAY 16 APRIL

It's sunny and we can now travel anywhere in mainland Scotland. We can meet six people from six different households and hope springs eternal.

My home city of Glasgow is making the news today by winning a very prestigious title – we are officially the UK's 'most sweary city'. F****** magic! I have no idea how they research this phenomenon but I'm competitive and I'll take any win that's going.

According to research, Glaswegians use 109 profanities per one thousand words, this is almost double Liverpudlians who finished second with sixty-five per one thousand.

Peter Capaldi's famous Malcolm Tucker character in *In the Thick of It*, along with comedians Billy Connolly and Frankie Boyle, are given as prime examples of sweary Weegies.

We have to be very censored on the radio, which has become second nature to both Ewen and me who probably swear more in real life than we ought to. Ewen suggests we should work in Irish or Australian radio where the regulations are not so strict. B******* to that, I'm not leaving. I still happen to think we live in the best wee country in the world.

Gnome is where the heart is! A shockingly tenuous link to my next story. Due to lockdown there's a shortage (no pun intended) of garden gnomes. With many people spending much more time and money on their gardens, the wee dudes have been flying off the shelves. The Suez Canal boat hold-up has impacted manufacturing as the raw materials required have been stuck on container ships.

I get Carnage to fire off a clip of the theme from *The Gnome Mobile*, a Disney film from 1969 about a grandfather who is locked up because he claimed he spotted gnomes in a forest. His grandkids (the same two kids who played Jane and Michael in *Mary Poppins*) and the gnomes hatch an escape plan. Ewen has no recollection of this film and indignantly asks how he is meant to know it when it was out before he was born. I reply: 'You've seen the *Wizard of Oz* haven't you?' (1939).

His stunned silence says it all and I can see it in his eyes – take me Gnome, Toto!

My movie-themed Aye or Naw week has been fun. On Tuesday I could hardly stop laughing at my own question. Terribly imma-ture. In the 1969 film *Ring of Bright Water*, were the tricky scenes featuring Mij the otter filmed using a black pudding with sticky-on eyes? Graeme R. Clark, Maureen Craig and Iain Blackbourn were among many listeners willing this to be true. It wasn't and no black puddings were harmed in the making of this film.

On Wednesday seventy per cent of people voted 'aye' when I asked: The characters Ronnie and Will in the 1985 film *Restless Natives* were originally meant to wear Kermit and Miss Piggy masks but couldn't get permission from the Jim Henson company on time so wore the now iconic clown and wolfman masks instead. Aye or naw? Ha ha, got you! I made this up. It was 'naw'.

Yesterday it was a close one, fifty-three per cent of people saying 'aye' to this: In the 1981 film *Gregory's Girl*, the famous tree which Gregory and Susan lie below and dance under was hit by lightning and no longer grows. Aye or naw? This is true. It's known locally as 'the dead tree' and still stands in Cumbernauld House Park.

Today I ask: The 1983 film *Local Hero* is former US Vice President Al Gore's all-time favourite film. Aye or naw?

When discussing his reasoning Ewen says that me picking Al Gore is far too detailed so it must be true. I casually say I was thinking about making it Bill Clinton but chose Gore and he didn't notice. The listeners do though.

Stu and Tam the painters text in straight away: 'Cat said she nearly made it Clinton so it must be "naw".'

Ewen and Carnage dig out the replay of me saying it and are gutted they didn't cotton on. Unfortunately for all the Miss Marples and Hercule Poirots out there, I'm on form and it was a double bluff.

Clinton was the red herring. It IS Al Gore's all-time favourite film, he told Oprah Winfrey in an interview.

Ewen stares at me in awe. 'Who are you? You lie so easily. You are some kind of spy mastermind.'

Stu and Tam the painters get back in touch: 'Roll on Monday, we are on to you.'

I can't believe people are now looking forward to a daft wee question three days away. Does this make me happy? Very much aye.

MONDAY 19 APRIL

The day parents all over Scotland have been waiting for. The Easter holidays are officially over and all children in primary and secondary schools can return full-time to back in the classroom learning.

I am in awe of how the kids, parents and teachers have somehow made this work. I know from listening to my friends just how testing a time it's been.

'We're ramping up the feel-good music today and every day from now on with a wonderfully cheesy bit of fun entitled 'Ewen and Cat's musical balls'. This is a simple game we've invented to play random number one hits from 1970–1999.

We have three glass bowls containing numbered ping pong balls. In bowl one there are three balls – 1970s, 1980s, 1990s. We pick one to decide the decade.

In bowl two there are ten balls – 0 to 9: we pick one to decide the year in that decade, and in bowl three there are the number of number one songs that year. For example, there were twenty-seven number ones in 1997 so we would put twenty-seven balls in and pull out a number.

Whatever that song is, no matter how horrendous, brilliant, gimmicky or iconic, we MUST play it. Today in our first-ever attempt at the game I picked out the 1990s, year two, and lastly three, meaning the third number one of that year. We were given Right Said Fred 'Deeply Dippy' which is a fantastic song. Ewen points out that we could one day end up with 'Mr Blobby' or 'The Teletubbies' or the St Winifred's School Choir 'There's No One Quite Like Grandma'.

We will just have to accept the melodic fate of our musical balls!

'Song with a Story' returns today with *River City* (Alex Murdoch) and *Scot Squad* (PC Jack McLaren) hunk Jordan Young. He's flying high with this tale.

He revealed: 'I'm taking you back to 1988 when I was eight. My two pals and I thought we were the coolest kids in school. We were obsessed with *Top Gun* and wanted fighter jets but as nobody seemed to have one handy, we made do with our BMX bikes and pretended they were planes.

'We all had Hawaiian shirts with the half sleeves and as a treat for the ladies we never did up any of the top buttons. I'd spike up my hair and smother myself in my dad's aftershave. We'd zoom about the back streets in Fife thinking we were the most amazing kids ever.'

Before he reveals his chosen track Ewen starts singing/murdering 'You've Lost That Lovin' Feelin''. Jordon, replicating the famous Tom Cruise scene where Maverick and Goose woo the girls, takes alternate lines proving one of the two of them can sing. He chooses Kenny Loggins 'Danger Zone' as his song.

He might be missing the fighter jet, but Jordan (the coolest kid in Fife) can at least be proud that his TV career has really taken off.

TUESDAY 20 APRIL

Ewen is excited this morning as the estate of David Prowse, the actor who played Darth Vader, is auctioning off some of his most prized memorabilia. You can bid for a piece of the Millennium Falcon or his original script from *The Empire Strikes Back*. He was also the Green Cross Code man back in the 1970s and this outfit is up for grabs as well.

I remember he came to our primary school as part of a road safety campaign when I was in P2. We got to line up and meet him in the canteen and he was ginormous. I guess when you are six any person who is a six-foot-six bodybuilder is going to look gigantic, but I vividly remember being transfixed by his hands. They were so vast, like shovels. He had a real presence and not one child who met him did not 'stop, look and listen' when crossing the road after his visit.

Today Nicola Sturgeon has announced from Monday we will be able to travel freely round the UK, lateral flow tests will be made available for all and from 17 May we are allowed visitors indoors. Instantly my pals are on the WhatsApp group chat working out when we can resurrect 'Ferryfest', our name for an overnight yeeha at my pal Rhona's who lives in South Queensferry. She fires her husband Gary and sons Gus and Robbie away camping, and we will get to enjoy a pub crawl, drink far too much and inevitably end up dancing to 1980s cheese and 1990s rave in our pyjamas round her living room. Bring. It. On.

I pop to the local pharmacist for Dad's prescriptions in the afternoon. Iain the pharmacist grew up a few doors down from us; it's funny to think the boy I played kick the can and kerbie with is in charge of keeping people alive. I think it must be because I talk for a living (and assume I'll be found out soon) that I'm always in awe of friends who hold down proper jobs.

He asks how Dad is doing and I have to laugh. That new steroid has really perked him up. The last time I spoke to Iain I explained he had no appetite, and the weight was just falling off him, now I go into his house and he'll be face deep in a steak pie.

He gave me a bit of a fright on Friday night. I called him at 6 p.m. – no answer. The same at 6.10, 6.15 and 6.20 p.m. I was about to call my brother to pop in to check he was okay when he sent me a text.

I opened it nervously fearing the worst, and there he was bold as brass, a selfie up at the local chippy. He'd driven there by himself (his surgeon did say it was still okay to drive as he has an automatic car and it's his left side that's bad) and looked happiness personified.

I sent back a stern: 'Phone me when you get home.' Total role reversals here. When he did, he was full of the deep-fried joys; he asked why he had four missed calls from me on his home phone before laughing: 'I was getting a fish supper and I bet you thought I was lying deid on the floor.'

Cod, give me strength . . .

WEDNESDAY 21 APRIL

A wee Scottish mammy has become an overnight internet sensation after her daughter Demi Cuthbertson filmed her chatting on the phone to someone in a call centre.

The person on the other end of the call was obviously struggling with her accent and she was spelling out words using the NATO phonetic alphabet, you know the 'Alpha, Beta, Charlie' one used so often in police dramas.

The only problem was Demi's mum, like most of us, didn't know the full alphabet and ended up using her own words as examples.

The clip has her mum slowly enunciating 'S for sugar' then 'O for Onion' then 'N for . . .' she pauses to think before coming up with 'N for Niagara Falls'.

You can hear the call handler say, 'Niagara Falls?' to which she replies, 'Aye Niagara Falls – it's in Canada.'

The film then cuts to Demi lying on the couch in absolute tatters laughing at her mum and her international language attempt.

Demi's mum can hold her head up high as she's certainly not alone when it comes to improvising; our listeners had some brilliant examples.

James Patterson – 'Best I heard was N for knowledge.'

Jill Miller – 'I was once told U for Europe.'

Paula Munday – 'I've been told Q for cucumber.'

Will Little – 'The best one I've heard was L for elephant.' Surely that should be herd?

While our favourite global superstar pal Amy Macdonald revealed: 'My mum always says K for Kit-Kat.'

We have some funny postcode definitions too. Philip Heller messaged in to say: 'We live in the DB postcode and always say it stands for dead bodies,' while John Parkinson says his wife told someone on the phone, 'We live in KY1, aye KY, like the jelly!'

Ewen is in a brilliant mood this morning as Boy George has launched an international search for an actor to play him in a new biographical film about his life entitled *Karma Chameleon*. The 59-year-old singer made the announcement on his Instagram last night and said *Line of Duty*'s Daniel Mays is linked to play his father and suggested that Keanu Reeves is rumoured to be popping in. In the interests of decency, I'm not going to make any jokes about speed.

I must message my friend Rosanne in Australia. She was head over heels in love with Boy George and had a bedroom wall covered in pictures of him from *Smash Hits*. She was about nine and would learn in time that he wasn't destined to be her one. My friend Debbie was similarly distraught over Limahl, while I suffered heartache over Robin Cousins the ice-skater, Ricky Martin and Duncan from Blue. Although I did end up meeting the latter when I was a guest judge at the live show of *Dancing on Ice* at Braehead Arena years ago. I remember thinking he was a bit up himself and regretted living five years of my life with a cardboard cut-out replica of him in my living room (it was a comedy gift, honestly). So scunnered was I by this encounter, the very next day I gave cardboard Duncan away on air. That's show business!

THURSDAY 22 APRIL

Heatwave. Glorious sunshine for all of Scotland and highs of seventeen degrees forecast. Thursday is beginning to feel like a Friday.

Brilliant news for the Tartan Army this morning. Plans have been submitted to the council in Glasgow for a month-long giant fan zone in Glasgow Green for the Euros.

Glasgow Life – the agency which operates the city's leisure facilities – is behind the application for a large event base for the summer.

This is fantastic news. It lets us all hope that there will be some form of party. I hear on the grapevine that talks are underway in every city in Scotland for similar ventures. Outdoor spaces where people can gather safely to presumably celebrate Scotland's unexpected 1–0 away win at Wembley in June (if this ends up being correct, I'm going to kick myself for not sticking on a tenner!).

I'm not sure yet what my role in our coverage is going to be. I'm a massive Scotland fan and I'm torn between the buzz of working at the games in some shape or form or going totally tonto with my Tartan Army pals. I need to work out a plan in which I can do both. Fan's correspondent or something. Although I'm not sure I would trust me in this role.

Ewen and I found out last night that we've been nominated for the Arias, the radio equivalent of the Oscars.

Along with our friend and colleague Steven Mill, the three of us presented live coverage of the Serbia game which turned David Marshall into a hero and, well, you'll have already read about what happened that night! Before we all got carried away, we presented a four-hour live show. It was a riot, great fun, lots of stories and memories and then we qualified, and we partied the way you would after twenty-three years of missing out.

The audio is very funny and somehow it's been nominated in the category 'Radio Times Award for Moment of the Year'.

While it is very nice to be nominated, we are up against coverage of Black Lives Matter on BBC Radio 1, Absolute Radio marks seventy-fifth anniversary of VE Day and Laura Whitmore's emotional tribute following the death of her friend Caroline Flack, among others.

This is the only category where listeners get to vote for the best moment. How do you even ask for votes for covering a football match against these topics?

Ewen, Steven and I all know we have no chance of winning this and we're more than okay with that. It's an honour to be included.

After the show, I take Dad to Helensburgh as promised. The drive down is glorious as the Clyde sparkles in the sunshine. It has been so long since he's been out of his local area he's beaming from ear to ear.

First port of call as always is Dino's on the front for an ice cream. It doesn't matter that it's only 11 a.m., it is cone o'clock to us. We wander down the pier and find a bench. It is a moment of perfect happiness. We take a cone selfie. 'First of the season,' he observes.

I have the wheelchair in the back of the car and know he doesn't want to use it. He can still toddle along fine with his stick, but I can tell his back and knee hurt.

I manage to persuade him to give it a go and he insists on wearing his mask so nobody recognises him. This is nothing more than battered pride and not wanting to accept his fragile body is letting his razor-sharp mind down. He will get over this. This is all new to him and not the direction he wants to be going in.

I keep him chatting the whole way along the prom to the point and back. I reverse him into a lovely wee sun trap on the front and nip off for a small fish supper which we share. It's a really good one and it's so pleasing to see him scoff it down with relish. Well, it was brown sauce, but you know what I mean.

After this we visit my Auntie Jean and my cousin Karen. We've only seen them once in a year and it feels incredible to sit in their garden for a cup of tea. My cousin David's wife, Linda, pops in too and brings my other cousin Colin's new puppy, Skye. We have a wonderful hour catching up and laughing at the bouncy inquisitive little red Labrador who would melt the iciest of hearts.

My Aunty Jean looks and talks so much like my mum sometimes, I get shivers. I know it might sound silly but I wore her engagement ring today just so she could be with us on our day out.

Fun, fish suppers and family. It really has been the perfect day and one I know I will remember fondly when times get tougher.

On the way home Dad sings, word perfectly, songs from the *Pirates of Penzance* by Gilbert and Sullivan which he performed in the BB in 1949.

This curtain is not coming down anytime soon . . .

FRIDAY 23 APRIL

Sad news filling the papers this morning. Bay City Rollers frontman Les McKeown has passed away aged sixty-five.

In the 1970s the iconic tartan-clad band were almost as big as the Beatles in their heyday and in 2015 and 2016 they enjoyed an unexpected but massively well received comeback tour.

Ewen hosted the press conference where they announced their shock return and was also the DJ in the Usher Hall playing the party tunes ahead of their gigs. I went to one of those nights with my friend Trish and loved it. The BCR, who sold over 120 million records, were a bit before my time but everyone sitting near us told me stories of why they loved them so much.

It was like a lovely tartan cult. We ended up sitting next to Jacqui Johnston, Lynn Jamieson and Arlene Roberts from Musselburgh. As a fifteen-year-old in 1974 Jacqui skived school with a pal to follow the band down south. They slept overnight in a public toilet, each one telling their respective parents they were having a sleepover at the others. They did get caught on their return, but I'll never forget how proud and happy Jacqui was when she smiled: 'It was worth it!'

Ann from Edinburgh who was sitting behind me shouted: 'This was our school winching song' when they started to perform 'Please Stay'.

After the gig I bumped into Kimi Aono and her friends Ayumi, Kimiko and Yachiyo who had flown over from Japan just for the gig.

They'd been fans since the early 1970s and were dressed head to toe in immaculate tartan replicas of the band's famous stage outfits. They first saw the boys in 1973 in Tokyo. Kimi explained: 'We follow them because we belong. It is like one big family. We are always made to feel so welcome and we love being part of it.' It was an honour to witness so many ladies of a certain vintage taking a trip down memory lane.

While the gig surpassed all my expectations, my favourite Bay City Rollers memory was at the *Sunday Mail* Great Scot Awards dinner in the Hilton in Glasgow. I think it must have been that same year, 2015.

The band were the headline act, Les was in dazzling form and everyone rushed onto the dancefloor to party to 'Bye Bye Baby' and the rest of the set. When they finished with 'Shang-a-lang', I remember being next to former Scotland star Gordon Strachan who was dancing with his wife and giving it laldy. At this point Paolo

Nutini, who it would be fair to say had maybe had a sherry or two, gatecrashed the stage and grabbed the mic.

Les was delighted with this celebrity intervention, the two cuddled and swayed on stage and enthusiastically belted out the rest of the song. It's the duet I never knew I needed.

I vividly remember thinking can you get any more Scottish than this? Gordon Strachan dancing to Paolo and the Bay City Rollers. Fantastic night and happy memories of a real character. So many people have wonderful memories of his performances and the gift of spreading joy is a fitting legacy for any artist. We play 'Shang-a-lang' and remember the good times.

Another band making the news today is Abba. Bjorn has announced that a big screen film of the band will never be made while they are all still alive. He says he just doesn't want to see an actor play him and reckons all his other bandmates would feel the same way.

Ewen wonders who would play him in a film. I think he looks a bit like Stanley Tucci but he said: 'People always say I look like Tom Cruise or Sylvester Stallone.' A million one-line answers spring into my head none of which are suitable for broadcast. My brain filter has to work fast but all I manage is: 'No they don't.'

Both Ewen and Carnage burst out laughing as it's so wonderfully dismissive even though I really didn't mean it to be.

I suggest Carnage would be played by the character of Alan from *The Hangover*. The thought of letting Carnage loose in Vegas could be the best reality TV show ever filmed.

And so, we head into the weekend in good spirits. The weather is meant to be lovely on Saturday and Sunday with rain returning on Monday just in time for the reopening of beer gardens. Ach, it's Scotland, what did you expect? If pubs don't market a pint and a poncho deal, they're missing a trick.

MONDAY 26 APRIL

Do you fancy going shopping? Would you rather meet me in a beer garden? What about a trip to a museum, an overnight stay in a hotel or a meal out? Well today is the day that Scotland finally reopens after four months of lockdown.

There's an uplifting tone to the show as listeners up and down the country call in to share their joy at this little step towards normality.

Live radio is an incredibly intimate and important medium; we genuinely feel like you're our friends and vice versa. We share our experiences so honestly and openly (sometimes too much) that we've pretty much nothing to hide. I think this works for us because when our lovely listeners phone in they are very rarely nervous. It sounds like they're calling up their mates. This is everything and makes me think we must be doing something right.

At the moment, Bauer, our parent company, have some of the best breakfast teams in UK radio. Boogie and Arlene are brilliant on Forth 1. They have talent in abundance, ideas and passion and they just get it. George and Cassi on Clyde 1 are a superb team too. There are many more across the country smashing it too, but these are the shows I know the best and the presenters who have propped up bars with me the most when we really should know better. We are curious creatures, breakfast presenters. Obsessed with sleep (or lack of it) and what time we go to bed.

Streaming hours have never been higher for radio, which shows us people really need uplifting music and good company.

Today is about celebrating the lifting of restrictions and we want to hear from anyone preparing to get back to business.

Jackie from Stirling is our first caller just after 7 a.m. She works at the café in M&S and has all her early-shift colleagues listening in the background. She said: 'We are so excited to be back at work.

We can't wait to welcome customers back to the café. It has been a long, hard four months and the doors are opening soon. We're all excited and nervous and raring to go. We've been cleaning the place, preparing the food and dancing to the music you pair have been playing all morning. We open at 8.30 a.m. Ahhhhhh!'

You can hear the joy in her voice. We get a big jubilant cheer from all her team and the offer of a free coffee and all-day breakfast if we are ever passing. I'm pretty certain Ewen will get in his car and drive there directly after the show for a bacon roll.

Next to call in is Nicky Cornet, the head chef at the Craigie Hotel in Penicuik. He said: 'We've had the team in for the last few days working on the new menu, training and getting everything into place. It feels amazing. We've had a real struggle sourcing everything because everybody is opening up at the same time. It's been a challenge, but we are buzzing. We've not worked in months, but today we've got 160 covers booked in. It's going to be quite a day.'

We wish him and his team well. I sit back and enjoy the following exchange.

Ewen: What is on the menu today?

Nicky: Some beautiful fresh scallops and langoustine.

Ewen: I don't like fancy food, what sides do you have?

Nicky: We do chunky chips drizzled with truffle oil or zucchini fries.

Ewen: Do you have any chicken nuggets?

Nicky: We have chicken goujons.

Ewen: They are the same thing.

Nicky: Enjoy your day at KFC.

We also drop the hint that we hope to take our show on the road soon with a 'World Tour of Scotland'. We've done this a couple of times before in a campervan with Real Radio and had a ball. Ewen asks for suggestions of places for us to visit and it's nice to see people from Stranraer to Thurso get in touch. Suggestions include places to stay, eat, drink, visit and broadcast from. Jacqui Sibbald who works for Dumbarton Football Club calls in with an offer.

She said, 'I'm the safety officer at the club and we would welcome you here if you wanted to do a live broadcast. There are beautiful views of the Clyde, we've got the rock and the castle behind us and there are lovely walks along the coast. We will also make everyone a roll and square sausage.'

This is the football hospitality we would all love.

Jacqui continues, 'As I am the safety officer, I would make sure everything is safe and secure for you and I could manage any crowds.'

I can't help myself. I have to know the story about the ladders from last week.

'Jacqui, is it true Partick Thistle fans brought ladders to lean against the wall to watch the game against Dumbarton last week?'

'Yes, it is true,' she confirms. 'Some Dumbarton fans had them too.'

'As the safety officer, how did you deal with this?'

'As it was outside the ground, I could only advise them.'

'What did you say?'

'You are on ladders. Watch you don't fall off.'

This is Scottish football at its finest. Another example of great Scottish football moments shuffles through our studio door at 9.40 a.m. It's a bedraggled Fraser Thompson. His side, St Johnstone, qualified for the semi-final of the Scottish Cup last night beating Rangers on penalties. The Roy of the Rovers moment goes to Saints goalkeeper Xander Clark who came up from his end and helped with the equalising goal in the dying seconds of extra time to take the game to penalties which made him a hero again.

Fraz is emotionally drained. I think he may have had a wee celebration last night, and who can blame him. He posts a picture of the perfect pint of Guinness from a beer garden after his show and I know it's a photo of historical importance. It's his first pint post-lockdown and the straightener he arguably needed this morning. In fairness he was a million times better than Steven Mill and I after the Serbia game. We both would have needed oxygen and a defibrillator to have had any chance of making it on air. It's been some day. Cheers to you all!

TUESDAY 27 APRIL

How are you with timekeeping? I hate being late. Today a new report says sixty-seven per cent of people feel the same. We start to feel stressed if we are seven minutes late for a social event or appointment, while just sixty seconds later at the eight-minute mark is when we perceive ourselves to be LATE. Nearly half of us always plan to be early, with twenty-five per cent admitting to being obsessed with punctuality. This new research has concluded that being early is now the new being on time!

I know I drive Ewen nuts by always being early. This is genuinely a causal effect of working on radio where everything is determined by time. I never used to be so fussy about time, but if I want to make a cup of tea or nip to the loo at work, I'm told a specific amount of time before needing to be back on air again. This is never 'Oh, you have fifteen minutes'; it will be a 'two minute forty-five second song' or a 'three minute ad break'. As a result, I'm a ninja in the kitchen, a blurry vision in the corridors and I pee fast.

Also, in my job you simply can't be late for work. It's too obvious. I've only ever slept in for breakfast radio once in my life but that was nothing to do with tiredness and everything to do with ill-advised mid-week tequila shots. I've grown up a lot since then.

Yesterday's Aye or Naw question is still annoying Ewen: The rowing machine is the most popular machine in the gym? Is this true? Aye or naw? The answer according to Google was aye, with forty-seven per cent, while treadmills only had a thirty-nine per cent rating. I didn't really believe this myself but as the game is a wee bit of fun with no prize other than honour, one bit of research is enough and it was the top answer out of 749,000,000 similar searches. I mean, come on!

Ewen is raging and said he was going to call his friend Duncan Bannatyne to get a definitive.

I am pretty sure Ewen has never even met the entrepreneur, owner of sixty-six gyms and former star of *Dragon's Den* worth over £280 million. He insists we give him a call. He gives Producer Carnage a number and we wait. I'm expecting his personal secretary to answer, not Margaret from reception at Bannatyne's gym in Falkirk.

Ewen: Hiya, can I speak to Duncan?

Margaret: NAW.

Ewen: How no?

Margaret: He's not in today.

Ewen asks Margaret what is the most popular machine in the gym? She replies: 'the treadmill'. Cammy from the fitness team walks past and he asks her too. She replies: 'the treadmill' and with that a chuffed Ewen has all the answers he needs. We say goodbye and tell Margaret to tell Duncan we were asking for him.

Given that I actually believe treadmill to be the correct answer too, we agree to render that Aye or Naw question null and void. Maybe I should have a third option for 'mibbaes'.

I have an exciting Zoom call with Emma and Debbie from Cash

for Kids today. I've known for weeks that this book project is going to happen because Black & White Publishing are now fully on board. We've agreed terms and the best ways to get maximum money for the charity. All profits from sales will go to Cash for Kids. I won't earn a single penny from the book, but this is my decision and it's the right one. It wouldn't be right to cash in on a book in which the principal theme is slagging off Ewen.

Seriously though, I've felt for a long time that I need to give something back. I signed up with two volunteer agencies during lockdown and neither of them used me (I guess being able to talk mince is not as useful as being able to fix things or medical, teaching or social care skills). I like to write and share stories. I hope that spreading some of these fun tales can put a smile on a few faces and raise money and awareness for CFK.

Producer Michael welcomes me onto the Zoom call and I can see the girls have no idea why I'm there. I then pitch my own book to them before revealing the relevant angle – all the profits are for the charity. Emma looks stunned: 'Seriously? That's a lot of work.'

I smile graciously and accept that yes, it is. (Once again, I've possibly bitten off more than I can chew but I like a challenge. I've had to put in holidays for next week off the radio to write the intro and fill in the missing fifteen years, but I'll get there. I have to!) Debbie is just delighted. She thinks it's a great idea and says she's looking forward to helping promote and distribute it in any way she can.

The hours and dedication these women put in for the charity is inspiring. Yes, it is their jobs, but they add so much passion because they really believe in the projects they work across and simply want to make life better for as many families as possible.

I come off the call fired up and determined to make this work. As requested, they've confirmed that all the money raised will stay in Scotland to help our local children with Christmas presents, winter coats, emergency grants, food and poverty issues. I need to make this a success and thanks to you for reading this, the life of some little person probably staying not too far from you just got that little bit better.

WEDNESDAY 28 APRIL

It's world superhero day and a new top twenty of the nation's favourites has been revealed. Kapow! Topping the poll is Batman, followed by Superman, Spiderman, Wonder Woman then the Incredible Hulk. The research suggests that despite his top billing, Batman would be skelped by Superman in a fight.

Hand in hand with superheroes comes their special superpowers and we also have a new top five of powers that we would love to have. Topping this list is invisibility followed by flying, time travel, teleportation and healing abilities.

I'd also like to be able to eat as much chocolate as my body constantly (like all the time) craves without my jeans hurting me again.

With a bank holiday weekend approaching, Ewen and I discuss our weekend plans. We have our big day out on Friday and Producer Vic has invited us back to her garden for some drinks after lunch. We are notoriously dangerous together and I pose a serious question to the boys: 'Am I allowed to camp in a tent in her back garden?'

I would be outside and in a tent by myself, posing no Covid threat to others. I can't see why it wouldn't be allowed but why has nobody else mentioned this before as an option? Ewen and Carnage are both stumped. Ewen decides to text Professor Jason Leitch, the clinical director for Scotland. I am sure he's delighted with this at 7.09 a.m. on a Wednesday morning. However, he's awake and promptly replies: 'This is not allowed. Overnight stays have to be in a controlled environment.'

Meh. I'll just have to get a taxi home after all. He assures us that things will change soon and by this we think we will be allowed into our friends' homes next month. We shall all just bide our time and err on the side of caution.

Ewen thanks him for his hasty reply and asks why he is awake so early. He says he's currently on a Zoom call into an important medical conference in Australia. I'm sure he was delighted to be interrupted from that to be asked if I could crash out in my mate's garden after a night on the sauce. He's certainly keen to keep us all on the straight and narrow.

My Aye or Naw question today even got a celebrity playing along on Twitter: In Scotland it is illegal to be drunk in charge of a donkey? Is this true? Aye or naw?

TV presenter Gail Porter is one of the first to reply. She said: 'Naw, but it is illegal to be drunk in charge of a cow.' This is actually the correct answer.

According to the Licensing Act 1872, it is an offence to be drunk in charge of a horse, a cow, a carriage and a steam engine. A guilty charge could carry fifty-one weeks in jail or a fine of £300.

While it is not to be encouraged, if you are mad-with-it walking to your local Tesco with your donkey for a bag of carrots you will probably just be given a stern ticking off.

Final word to listener Joe Carson on Twitter who asks: 'What does a Blackpool donkey get for his lunch? Half an hour just like everyone else.'

Brilliant! I bet he-aww he-aww he-aww-lways tells that joke.

THURSDAY 29 APRIL

If you've had a cappuccino and a wee peek at Facebook recently then you're now officially an old fart. Sorry, I should maybe have broken that news a little more gently but yes, I'm afraid you are now past it. Game Over. Get the knitting out!

That is the harsh opinion of the young. What do they know? According to the under-30s, only 'ancient people' order cappuccinos. With TikTok and Insta ruling the social media roost, they also think Facebook is now for their mums and dads.

In this new poll, other signs that you are getting on a bit include asking for milk and two sugars in your tea, buying your pants from M&S and becoming obsessed with bin day.

I drink my tea black, my pants are from George (not Clooney, the clothing bit in Asda), and I have no idea which bin goes out when, proving my long-held self-opinion that I am but a spring chicken.

We are never allowed to discuss politics on our show. Ewen and I are both surprisingly well versed on this subject but it's for the best. We are a safe place to escape the real world, to revel in nostalgia and to avoid serious discussions. There's enough misery in the world. Come to us for a break.

We are also currently in purdah, which is the period of time in the media before an election where reporting restrictions are in place and when your bum really will be oot the windae if you mention anything to do with politics, any leader or a specific party.

We will not be in purdah when this book comes out, so I can write this today even though I can't say it. Sleaze is currently oozing out of Number 10 with Boris Johnson accused of doing up his gaff with Tory Party donors' money to the tune of £58,000. A £9,000 couch and wallpaper at £840 a roll? Eejit. And that's the end of my political discourse for this book.

Our show has a bit of everything this morning. We have a clip of Onion the Edinburgh Parrot who is a TikTok star because he sounds like Mrs Doubtfire (see, much more fun than Boris chat). We find out that eighty-seven per cent of photos on your phone will never be looked at again and it takes the average person six hours to spring-clean their digital baggage.

Ewen says he has 480 photos on his phone and deletes regularly. I know what's coming. He just gives me an accusatory look and says, 'CAT?' At last look I have 15,763 photos on my phone. Most of them are my dad eating ice cream. I'm not deleting them.

My Aye or Naw question today is possibly my favourite of them all. Only female midges have teeth. Is this true? Aye or naw?

Ewen and Carnage are both in hysterics at the absurdity of the question. Ewen's reasoning is emphatic: 'Evolution would not make females have teeth and males not, they both need to feed. Do they actually have teeth? How tiny must their teeth be? How do we know they have teeth?'

I reply: 'From research gathered by a wee midgie dentist.' We are descending into chaos. Our Twitter pals are loving this one.

Caroline McGill: No way! Come on the wee lady midgies, get biting those blokes :)

Karen Rennie: Aye – only females bite: this is the one bit of useless information I've somehow known since I was a kid.

Alan: This is by far the funniest question yet.

Michelle McFarlane: Aye – we are the sharper species.

Michael Dickson: The female has sharp teeth? No surprise really!

Ewen and Carnage both opt for 'naw'. Ewen thinks both must have teeth, while Carnage reckons midges sting and don't have teeth at all. Forty-five per cent voted 'aye', which is the correct answer. Only female midges have teeth, which means they are the only ones which bite you. Male midges just suck on sugars from plants.

If you really want to know, the mouthparts are well developed, with cutting teeth on elongated mandibles on the proboscis adapted for blood sucking in the females. There are over 180,750 trillion midges between May and September in Scotland and I think every one of them will find me at some point. Ah well, I've always been a girls' girl!

FRIDAY 30 APRIL

What a magnificent day! I am buzzing and dressed head to toe in Partick Thistle clobber including a ridiculous red and yellow Viking hat with fake wool pigtails.

Last night the Jags won promotion back to the Championship with a stunning 5–0 win over Falkirk.

I caught the tail end of the game with my dad, which was a wonderful moment, as he lifted me over the turnstile at Firhill for years when I was a wee girl. At twenty-six I told him to stop as he'd hurt his back.

Yesterday evening I was in my flat refusing to watch the game on my laptop. This might sound ridiculous, but football fans can work themselves up into silly rituals about luck and winning. Basically, since I stopped watching the games or checking in on the live scores, Thistle have been winning. Four wins and a draw being the last five results. In my head I think it's because I've not been watching. So last night, we had to beat Falkirk to win the league, there was no way I was messing up this vibe.

Predictably, my phone started pinging from jubilant Jaggy pals. 1–0 Thistle, 2–0 Thistle, 3–0 Thistle at half-time.

I sat on my couch in my pyjamas nervy and not sure what to do for the next forty-five minutes. I'd bleached the kitchen and the toilet during the first half. I needed something to occupy my mind.

And then I made my snap decision. My dad and I have been through so much with Thistle. He should see this. Our club getting promoted after the injustice of being relegated when they stopped the league and we were two points behind the second-bottom-placed club with a game in hand and nine left to play.

At 3–0 up we would surely not lose 4–3. Even me tuning in couldn't affect this outcome, could it?

I sprung up from the couch. Threw on some joggy bottoms and a hoodie over my pyjama top, no bra and a pair of trainers, laptop in a bag and was in my car with a bag of Thistle scarves and hats within two minutes.

I called my dad from the car. Get the kettle on, I'll be round in fifteen minutes. He said, 'Yir aff yir heid,' but I could tell he was delighted.

Typically, I struggled to log on. My friend Craig who was one of the match sponsors with his flooring company had sent a code for us, but the computer was having none of it. I happily paid the tenner just in time for goal number four to hit the back of the net. I made us both Bovril for the authentic match day experience and we sat enthralled as Thistle slammed home a fifth and celebrated promotion at the final whistle.

We really had come full circle. My dad introducing me to football all those years ago and me bringing him promotion on a laptop all those years later. Another golden moment I shall cherish forever.

It was even his suggestion: 'Let's get a selfie, Toots.' We were beaming from ear to ear and wearing our scarves. I fired it up on Twitter and 130,000 people shared our joy. I think he's enjoying his internet sensation status.

Today on the show Ewen has a great idea. He knows the mother of one of the players, James Penrice, who won man of the match last night, and thinks we should give them a call.

I wonder how it has come to pass that we now know the parents of players rather than the players themselves.

Theresa answers on three rings and sounds as rough as a badger's. We ask how she's feeling, and she replies 'happy' in a voice so rough and like the Rev IM Jolly we are all in bits laughing. Apparently, a lot of wine was consumed in the Penrice home but the man of the moment, who still lives at home as he's only twenty-two, rocked in VERY late. He is up though and sounds every bit as 'sleepy' as his mum.

He croaked: 'We didn't expect to celebrate quite so much last night. It was just brilliant to get promotion.'

Ewen asks if he remembers getting home. He replies: 'I think so. I've left my car in Glasgow somewhere. I think a lot of cars were left in Glasgow last night.'

This is definitely true as Amy Macdonald messaged me to say that her husband Foz needed a lift home as he'd had a wee celebratory sherry as well. She also asked if I wanted Foz to FaceTime my dad from the dressing room. This would have been so cool, but Dad went straight to bed after the final whistle. Celebrating can be exhausting.

I have a wonderful time winding up Falkirk fan John McInally who produces George Bowie and Cassi on Clyde 1. George wants to film me doing this, so I sneak into their studio and then sing a Jags' song at him. He's groaning and his head is in his hands, but I know he'd do the same thing to me. Banter. It's football banter.

Today is also our long-awaited day out. We've lunch booked at Mharsanta in the Merchant City with Producers Carnage, Michael and Vic.

It feels amazing to be out with friends and to see life in the city centre again with shops, cafés and restaurants all buzzing.

They all slag me off for having a rucksack with a big red tartan blanket in it. One hour sitting at a table on freezing cold Glasgow pavement and everyone wants a shot of it.

I take a photo of Ewen mid rant wrapped in my blanket and post it on Twitter. With his baseball cap and thick glasses there is more than a passing resemblance to Liverpool boss Jurgen Klopp. Comments include: 'He looks like a Poundland Jurgen Klopp' and 'That's what Jurgen Klopp would look like if you ordered him from Wish.' I christen Ewen Papa Klopp as he's like a wee grandad version of himself and it sticks. He hates it but this makes it funnier.

He says under 'no circumstances' are we to tell Steven Mill this. They present *The Big Saturday Football Show* together and are always trying to get one over on each other. I reluctantly agree but can see Producer Vic typing away furiously under the table and sending a message to Steven on her phone entitled PAPA KLOPP.

I can't express how much I am loving working with friends. It is a privilege and a joy and I'm genuinely excited about the future of *Ewen and Cat at Breakfast*. I also realise now that the Prosecco must be kicking in.

Ewen, Michael and Carnage go for their trains at 6 p.m. We are all nicely squiffy but totally frozen. Vixen has a fire pit in her back garden. Predictably it ends up just the two of us playing Wet Wet Wet songs full pelt and dancing round her patio. I'm sure her neighbours must have thought we were auditioning for *Macbeth*. If only we'd known a spell to prevent the hangovers we were going to feel tomorrow. It has been quite a day!

MONDAY 10 MAY

Back after a week 'off'. I've never worked so hard on a so-called holiday in my life. Basically, I needed to write the introduction to this book and fill in the missing fifteen years. I had two whiteboards full of notes, headings and scribbles, but I'd been avoiding writing it up for weeks, like a schoolchild puts off homework.

To be honest, it was all a bit overwhelming. What to put in, what to leave out. However, the idea of collating all of my tales into some form of readable shape was more daunting than the reality.

Once I got started, I had great fun remembering all the enjoyable stories and knocking them into shape.

Aside from the writing, last week I managed to take Dad to Oakwood Garden Centre for our first sit-down soup in months. It sounds so insignificant, but it felt so momentous.

The SNP romped to a Scottish Election victory winning sixty-four seats, I put on four pounds (meh!), I took lots of cardboard to the dump, oh and I also filmed a BBC documentary discussing the best Scotland football songs of all time.

This was a lot of fun because they'd uncovered some belters I'd not even heard before. Did you know Midge Ure and Dumbarton FC recorded a Scotland song? Or that the Krankies sang the official 1982 song including this chorus line: 'We're going to Spain – on an aero-plane.' Seriously, Bernie Taupin would weep at the exquisite-ness of these lyrics.

Primal Scream also had a collaboration with Irvine Welsh for Euro '96 called 'The big man and the scream team meet the barmy army uptown'. Yes really!

Other forgotten gems included Fish, Donnie Munro and the Scotland Squad with 'Say it with Pride'. This was for Italia '90 and included the line 'Say it with pride – the lion will roar in the sun.' (It didn't. We are Scottish. We burn in the sun and get red and sore.) Andy Cameron's smash 'Ally's Tartan Army' was high up the list and also 'We Have a Dream' featuring BA Robertson, John Gordon Sinclair and the 1982 World Cup squad. This remains my favourite.

It's always a bit odd being a 'talking head' on one of these TV clips shows. They film about an hour's worth of material and you could be chopped to a single twenty second soundbite. My fear is they'll pick the bit where you say the daftest thing. I work with Ewen every day; I'll probably have said worse on many an occasion.

The thing I don't miss about being on telly is having to think about my clothes, hair and face. I popped in to see my pal Mags at Taylor Ferguson for a blow dry, slapped on full make-up (which felt weird after a year of barefaced cheeks) and arrived with a bag of props for the production team to choose an outfit. I had six Scotland tops, a tartan shirt and a blue jumper. They chose the blue jumper with a Royal Stewart tartan scarf. The camera adds 10lb. I blame my incurable addiction to Freddos for the rest! The show will be screened next month. Hopefully by then I'll have that Krankies song out of my head. It's catchy, I'll give them that!

Today is a momentous day on air. I finally reveal that I'm writing this tome. Feedback is really encouraging except for Ewen who wonders if he'll need to consult a lawyer prior to publication. He's got nothing to worry about. I will never expose his secret Sky betting account or share the stimulating photos of his shopping trip to Amsterdam.

He's an open book so there shouldn't be anything in these pages he's not revealed before.

To try and explain what the book is about, I read a couple of paragraphs from the intro and Carnage adds some sound effects which make me laugh.

'Why did I throw water over Susan Boyle [big splash]? Why did James McAvoy need salt and vinegar crisps [crunching noises]? Why did we end up in Olly Murs' dressing room with a kazoo [kazoo tooting]? And why does Ewen Cameron love Steven Gerrard so much [clip of 'Je t'aime']?

By making it official, I now must complete this project. I've not announced that I'm giving all the money to Cash for Kids yet, we shall save that big news for next week. Like every thrilling adventure, we need to take our time, throw in some twists and turns and tease a bit before we get to the happy ending!

TUESDAY 11 MAY

Happy Gothenburg Day. Aberdeen fans will know about this one. It is thirty-eight years to the day that Aberdeen FC beat Real Madrid to win the European Cup Winners' Cup in the Swedish city.

I know all about this as my brother Scott wasn't allowed to go as he had to sit his O-grade English. Weirdly he is a Dons fan, despite being born in Glasgow and raised in a Partick Thistle family. Santa is to blame. He left him a red strip under the tree when he was about four and that was it. Still, he had a great time in the 1980s as Aberdeen seemed to be at Hampden all the time winning Cup finals.

There's a great story in the papers today about Sir Alex Ferguson who was manager at the time.

He sent a memo to the footballer's wives ahead of the game saying there was not enough accommodation, and they'd have to bring their own sleeping bags, tin cups and cutlery. He said he'd sourced a nearby army camp for them to use their dormitories. The wives went tonto and Fergie had to reveal he was at the wind-up all along and that their rooms in a nice hotel were already booked.

I remember interviewing him in a portacabin next to Braehead

Shopping Centre in 1999. He'd just finished cutting the ribbon or fitting the final roof bolt or something and I'd persuaded him to do an interview about a forthcoming Champions League semi-final with Manchester United for Scotsport (they went on to win the tournament).

I hastily arranged two plant pots beside a plain white wall to make it a bit more scenic. I'm sure he could sense how nervous I was. At first, he was quite frosty towards me, but after I'd proven my knowledge by filling him in with the name of a Juventus full-back he was trying to remember, his mood totally changed. He realised I knew what I was talking about and gave me a brilliant exclusive. That happened a lot when I covered football. The need to prove myself, ironically mostly with my peers, not the players or managers. I learned everything I could about every team I was covering so I was never caught out. Now I can barely remember who plays for Scotland.

In my 'Happy News' today I reveal that *Toy Story* performed with a live orchestra will be coming to Glasgow and Edinburgh next year. The movie will be shown on large screens and the score will be played live. I think this sounds fabulous. I manage to persuade Carnage to play the full version of Randy Newman's 'You've Got a Friend in Me' from the soundtrack. My favourite Disney song of all time is 'Under the Sea' from *The Little Mermaid*. Somehow, I am going to try and shoehorn that in this week too. I need to look for happy marine life stories or tales of joy from the *Angling Times*. Fishy business right enough.

Aye or Naw is really getting on Ewen's nerves this week. He's been wrong on both days.

Monday's question was 'Mice can't burp. Is this true? Aye or naw?' I love throwing in a double negative to play with his head. Basically, aye means they can't and naw means they can. He got into such a muddle it was hilarious. He said 'naw' as he thought they could, but they can't. It is to do with the anatomy of their stomach. So never feed your pet mouse Irn-Bru.

Today I ask: Humans are the only animals to blush. Is this true? Aye or naw? He said 'naw' as he claims he once owned a hamster that blushed. Carnage thought monkeys might blush and that we just can't see them do this because of their fur. But the answer was 'aye'. Humans are the only animals to blush.

Ewen in a strop bleated: 'According to whom? Name one person who says this is true.'

I replied, cool as you like: 'Charles Darwin.' Thanks Google, once again you've saved the day.

Ewen aggressively hit play on the next song with his face all red and flustered, proving that humans do indeed blush. A beamer, a riddie, a brass neck, whatever your regional variation, he had a cracker!

WEDNESDAY 12 MAY

We're all in a magnificent mood this morning. Probably because Nicola Sturgeon's announced the lifting of many restrictions, moving the country down from level three to level two from Monday.

This means we can go to the pub and drink indoors, visit our pals in their homes and even stay over. Last night I had about five different WhatsApp chats going on trying to plan dates. I can't wait to have friends over to mine for a catch-up. I've missed sharing my home with others.

Living alone through lockdown has made the days and weeks seem so long. I've seen people at work and met pals every day for a walk, but the evenings in particular do seem to drag. I guess for years I've been used to having someone in the flat with me. I can't even get my head round how that would feel again. Mr Right will just have to wait a bit longer. I'm not in the mood!

I am over the moon at my 'Happy News' today. Joyce Falconer is returning to *River City* to play Roisin after a break of thirteen years. Joyce and I have shared many scenes in numerous pantos together and she is truly a one-off. This is a compliment of the highest order, she's a cracking lass. She is usually the bad witch to my good witch or fairy. She's got a gloriously deep earthy voice with a thick Doric accent and is always looking after people.

Every year in panto she would open 'Joyce's Juices'. She'd bring her juicer into the crew room at the theatre and during each interval in the evening show, would fire in fruit and veg and who knows what else into the mix, so we all had enough vitamins to keep colds at bay. She gave all the cast a glass of her juice every night. Some were lovely; some were, well, unusual.

I remember Shellsuit Bob, wee Stephen Purdon, once asking: 'Why do you make us drink this?'

Joyce with her authoritative gruff tones replied, 'It's full o' guid stuff and it makes ye s**** like a camel.' A very moving answer indeed.

In other showbiz news Elton John and Olly Alexander from *Years and Years* are the toast of the Brits for their sensation duet performance of 'It's a Sin' last night. Olly starred in the emotional TV series of the same name, and all profits will go to the Elton John AIDS Foundation.

Carnage proved he's a producing genius by managing to find me a topical, not tropical, fish story for today on the back of yesterday's challenge.

A company in Japan have invented a fish tank handbag so you can take your pet goldfish out for a walk if you fancy. While this seems like a ridiculous idea, it is tenuous enough to let us play 'Under the Sea' from *The Little Mermaid*. I adore this song and so many of you do too, we had so many messages from people singing along at home.

'Ewen and Cat's musical balls' also caused this to happen this morning. I picked out the 1970s and ball number seven making it 1977, and number sixteen, the sixteenth number one of that year.

The musical balls gave us Baccara's 'Yes, Sir, I Can Boogie'. It is a sign. It is the new Scotland favourite and clearly a message from the Universe that we are going to do well in the Euros.

The song sold over 18 million copies worldwide making it the best-selling single of all time from a female group. Yes, even more than the Spice Girls!

Sinclair and Anne-Marie Duffie send a video into our show Facebook page. They're in a car in Dubai singing every single word and bopping along. I love the fact that through the app and internet listening, our musical balls can make people shake their bodies with their finest dance moves nearly 5,000 miles away.

THURSDAY 13 MAY

I wonder if you are tucked up nice and warm and reading this in your bed. If so – stay there. New research out today says that we are most likely to come up with our best ideas while lying in bed.

Some of our inspirational thoughts occur before dozing off, some will happen during the night when we are sleeping and some spring to mind just when we wake up. That pretty much covers your entire sleep cycle, meaning bed is good for you. I'd like you to retain this little gem of information for the next time someone in your life tells you to 'get up'. Simply stretch, wrap the duvet round you and say no – you are working on some new ideas.

Other places which cultivate our creativeness include the bath and behind the wheel of a car. Listening to music and going for a walk are also recommended.

All the plot twists for my two plays were thought up in the bath with Herman. Herman is, of course, my German lederhosen-wearing rubber duck from Pfaffenhofen. I think that name itself inspires me. I'm not really a bath person but with the help of some classical music and a lot of Radox muscle soak, I let my imagination run riot and came up with the story threads for the plays. Just thinking about them gives me goosebumps. I can't wait to get them back out there although I think I'm going to be very anxious being on stage again. It has been so long.

The Isle of Skye is the best place to see rainbows in the world. Is this true? Aye or naw. This is the fourth question of the week Ewen gets wrong. He hates me right now. Sixty-nine per cent of people including Ewen and Carnage said 'aye'. It is 'naw'.

According to scientists Hawaii is the best place to see rainbows. This is due to the remoteness of the islands which means the air is exceptionally clean and free of pollution. There is limited dust and pollen which contributes to the numerous bright rainbows with a full spectrum of glorious colours.

Amanda Dow on Twitter sends in a glorious picture of a rainbow in Skye from 2019, while Philip points out, 'You need sunshine for a rainbow so I'm saying "naw".'

I've not been to Skye for a few years but as a McLeod (my middle name, and granny's maiden name), it's my ancestral home and I always feel a sense of belonging when I do go.

Talking of families, I'm trying not to write too much about Dad at the moment as it is playing with my head a lot, but he had a consultation with his orthopaedic surgeon Mr Kelly today. According to his scan he should be in agony. The doctor asked him how much pain he is in and what he's taking for it. My dad told him he was fine, still just taking the co-codamol, thanked him for phoning and jumped in his car to the local garden centre for a wander. I am beginning to think he is either superhuman or his insides are pickled from his drinking years and with internal organs like sauerkraut, he's not feeling what he should be feeling. Either way it's brilliant.

I arrived for a catch-up and to clean his house this morning after the show and he'd made macaroni with a special treat for pudding. He'd bought a Baklava from the frozen aisle in the supermarket as it reminded him of Scotland! He used to meet his pal Bob in the southside and go for a Greek meal before home games at Hampden. His positivity is certainly helping his overall well-being but how and why is he still feeling so perky? It's all Greek to me.

FRIDAY 14 MAY

It's the news *Friends* fans have been waiting for. HBO Max have announced the long-awaited *Friends* reunion special will be available to stream from 27 May.

All of the original cast – Jennifer Aniston, Courtney Cox, Lisa Kudrow, Matt Le Blanc, Matthew Perry and David Schwimmer – are involved.

Friends is my go-to TV show to have on in the background if my brain isn't in the mood for thinking. Even though a lot of it feels a bit dated now it was certainly of its time and still cheers me up.

I ask the boys which character I am most like and they say simultaneously 'Phoebe'. I happen to agree with them. Monica would have a fit if she saw the amount of clutter I have, while Rachel would need something stronger than a coffee from Central Perk to cope with my unfashionable but comfy wardrobe.

I ask Ewen who he thinks he's like. Straight away he says Joey. Bless. In his head he is still a nightclub DJ from Dubai, a taut, tanned babe magnet fighting them off with a big stick. I just smile and say okay. We ALL know he's Chandler. Carnage thinks he would be Ross and I concur. Gorgeously geeky is cool these days. He seems chuffed with my analysis.

It's Cash for Kids day today and we've put a fun prize up for grabs. A VIP trip to Party at the Palace in Linlithgow with Ewen and me as your hosts.

Not only will the winners get to see Del Amitri, Hue and Cry, the Brand New Heavies, Pete and Diesel and the Silencers from the side of the stage, they'll get a tour of the backstage area too. Peter Ferguson, the event organiser, calls the show to fill us in with all the details and it sounds epic.

One part of the prize includes dining backstage in the artists' area with dinner cooked by the festival's executive chef. At this point Peter reveals: 'This is my mum.' Even better. Stars don't want caviar, they want lentil soup and mince and tatties. I'm sure of it.

Peter tells us about the venue, the line-up and all the red tape they have to get through to make the event Covid-safe and secure for everyone. Before he goes, I tell him I have one diva-like demand for my backstage rider: 'Does your mammy make rhubarb crumble?'

Apparently, Mama Ferguson makes a mean crumble, and I can't wait to see if she comes up with the goods.

The texts selected at random by the computer gave us Ian Dewar, Stevie Esslemont and David Hay as our winners. All of them also join us on our Cash for Kids party show this evening for some banter and to pick some of their favourite party tunes.

I know we are lucky, as our listeners are a great bunch and this lot sound like they'll be a hoot on a night out.

David dedicated his final song to his partner Leah and his four kids Dakota, Deacon, Piper and Paisley. I needed to find out the story behind these spectacular showbiz names.

David revealed: 'Dakota was named after the Stereophonics song, Deacon because we like Deacon Blue, Piper because my daughter likes Highland dancing and Paisley because the receptionist in the TV show *Tattoo Fixers* had the name and we loved it.'

And here's me thinking she was conceived in a Renfrewshire Travel Lodge.

MONDAY 17 MAY

Most of the good people of Scotland are able to hug again as new restrictions kick in, with the majority of the country dropping to tier two.

The Islands are going to tier one, with only Moray and Glasgow City remaining in tier three. I live in Glasgow and therefore I'm more restricted today than I was yesterday. Going backwards does not feel good.

Yesterday I could freely travel to Inverness or Edinburgh as we were all in the same tier; now I have to stay within my own level, which means not leaving Glasgow City.

Ewen (Falkirk) and Carnage (Clydebank) can now both hug pals, welcome friends into their homes and enjoy a pint indoors in a pub. I can't. I live three miles from Carnage. It feels weird and I get the feeling it will be for much longer than the extra week they've told us we need.

I ramp up the 'Happy News' today. I've found new research claiming to reveal the secret to a happy life. Are you ready for this? You need six hours' sleep, work for seven hours a day, enjoy five home cooked meals a week, go out with your pals once a week, play with the kids for two hours a day, watch three episodes of your favourite soap a week and exercise four times in that exceptionally packed seven days. Got that? Easy.

I say borrow a dog, walk with your pals and don't deny yourself a Freddo at the end of a long day. Oh, and elastic-waist trousers are always your friend.

Yesterday, on our Sunday show, Ewen revealed that I do not currently have a title for this book (true). It is a kind of belated sequel to *The Cat's Whispers* from 2006. He asked our lovely listeners if they had any suggestions and we were inundated. This is exactly how I got my title the last time. Thanks, you guys!

There are hundreds of suggestions. The most popular ones are 'Life through Cat's Eyes', 'The Cat That Got the Cream' and 'Cat's Tails/Tales'.

We had some belters from Twitter. 'Cat-A Tonic' from Michele Gray, 'I'm Radio Mental' from John Millar, 'Aye or Naw' from LinzJ, 'Cat Whispers Again' from Stefan Jurman in Austria, 'Hair of the Cat' Alex Airnes, 'Radio Blah Blah' from Helen, 'Cat-astrophe and other tails' Lesley McGregor, 'The Cat's Meow' Tammy McCreadie, and 'Letting the Cat Out the Bag' Leigh Kirsop, Kenny Munro and Yvonne Laird.

Scotty called the show to say he'd call it 'The Tat Fae Cat', while many messages suggested 'Cat and the T**t' which rhymes beautifully but would get me taken off air. I also liked 'Chitty Chitty Cat Chat', 'Ewan-truiged' and 'Ewen – Be Nervous!'

On texts we had Barry with 'Fifty Shades of Cat', Sharon with 'Harvey Wallbanger', Suzanne wanted 'Catty Comments' while John from Corby suggested 'Cat's Tails of the Unexpected'.

I'm going to have a tough job narrowing it down, I think I'll pick four and then put it to a vote. Ultimately, I'm having the final say, but I'd quite like to gauge opinion. Kind of like the contestants do on *Who Wants to Be a Millionaire?* when they ask the audience. I could maybe get Chris Tarrant on to find out what he thinks. I'll get Carnage to sort it. Oh, wait a minute, maybe not . . . and that's my final answer!

TUESDAY 18 MAY

Fans of the *Mr Men* books, which are celebrating their fiftieth anniversary, have voted for two new characters. The 2021 additions to the family announced this morning are *Mr Calm* and *Little Miss Brave*.

We are told Mr Calm is very peaceful with an easy-going outlook on life, he practices yoga, he rock-climbs and has a very tolerant personality. I imagine he has a hipster beard and an addiction to smashed avocado on homemade sourdough. Good on him. He'd be a lovely neighbour. He'd be great at recycling and putting my bins out.

Little Miss Brave stands up for what she believes in. She is fearless when championing something close to her heart.

I think after the year we've had there should be a Mr Box Set and Little Miss Banana Bread.

'Ewen and Cat's musical balls' are becoming quite an attraction. Sonia De Rosa, a bubbly hairdresser, tells us she had to tell a client to be quiet until she heard what song the balls had chosen. I love this. Our musical balls are loved. I'm like a proud mother.

Today they gave us the second number one from 1979 – Ian Dury and the Blockheads 'Hit Me with Your Rhythm Stick'.

A lovely lady called Jennifer calls the show during the next song. We record calls in case they want to go on air. She said: 'What a blast from the past. I used to work at the blind school in Edinburgh. This was the pupils' favourite song. They used to change the lyrics to "hit me with your mobility stick, hit me, hit me". They found it hilarious. Thanks for playing this; it has brought back so many happy memories.'

As charming a call as this is, I know we are all thinking, 'Is this okay?' In today's cancel culture world with everything being so 'woke' (a word I hate by the way), there is always a precarious line between having fun with a subject and someone being offended. We all agree that as it was the blind children themselves who made up the lyrics and found it funny nobody should be upset. We know how sensitive some issues can be. On this occasion it was simply Jennifer sharing a heart-warming story of happy times. I love that our musical balls can do that, although I'm still dreading the first Christmas song that comes up in the middle of summer.

I've been on a roll with my Aye or Naw questions of late. Recent ones include: Was the man who invented the Pringles tube buried in a Pringles tube? – Aye. Dr Frederic Baur asked for his ashes to be buried in one of his tubes. Can a bumblebee fly higher than Mount Everest? – Aye (special mention to Michelle on Twitter who pointed out 'Mount Everest can't fly'). And is pink the most popular colour of toilet paper in France? – also Aye. To prove our show has international appeal I make this one a '*Oui* or *Non*' question, and Jim McLearly on Twitter asks 'Should it not be oui oui or non?'

There is no obvious cultural reason as to why the French love pink toilet roll other than they just do. I like this about the French. Nonchalant, colourful, artistic, bohemian and not scared to love a pink loo roll. This reminds me of a story from one of my Tartan Army trips years ago. Scotland were playing in Portugal in 1993. The day before the game a group of us took a train from Lisbon to Estoril for the day. Many were hungover from the night before. Our pal Shanksy had a dodgy tummy and needed to stock up on toilet paper for the journey. In the supermarket he was bending over with cramps. He needed a fast purchase. He shouted, 'Toilet paper please.' The elderly Portuguese lady behind the till was keen to help. 'What colour would you like?' she asked in perfect English. Shanksy's brain could not compute this offer of an array of colours and he replied desperately and without a hint of humour 'anything that goes with brown!'. You can imagine the reaction from the rest of us. He paid for four white rolls and ran out the shop.

I'm sorry for lowering the tone but this is my only funny story about loo roll. I'm wiped out after that one . . .

WEDNESDAY 19 MAY

It's a beautiful sunny day right across the country and once again everyone just seems that little bit more positive and up for nonsense.

Book titles continue to flood in on social media and I'm drawn to 'Cat and the Giant Man-child' texted in by an anonymous person (ALWAYS put your name on texts please) and 'In Cahoots with Toots' from Esther Milligan. My dad would love that one.

He's been in great form this week. He made a roast chicken dinner, spaghetti Bolognese and chicken soup. His kitchen floor resembled a battle scene painted by Picasso but he's happy!

Today's survey is a list of the most loved pet names to call your other half. The best ones are 1) Darling 2) Sweetie and 3) Babe. The worst are 1) Sausage 2) Doll and 3) Bird.

We have a right giggle shouting sausage at each other as we can't quite grasp the word being used in a romantic context. I've been a silly sausage and a wee sausage but never just sausage.

Linda calls the show, and she can hardly speak for laughing. She explains through her giggles: 'I have a spaniel called JJ but I call him my wee sausage. He now answers to sausage but usually only to me.

He's been going nuts running round the living room because you lot keeps saying sausage. Honestly it is hilarious, his face is a picture. Thanks for making my day.'

During the next song we all agree that Linda was so bubbly she sounds like she'd be great fun on a night out.

'Not aggressive at all,' says Carnage and we laugh.

This is definitely one of our never to be mentioned on air behind the scenes in-jokes. However, Ewen did say I'd spill the beans in this book so here's a wee sneaky peak into previous bad behaviour.

Back in the olden days before GDPR, in radio there was a call system called PhoneBOX where you could type details associated with a number. For example, it could say John Smith, Stirling, funny caller.

There was no sinister reason for this (it was not for competitions, a computer algorithm picked winners), it was merely a tool to help the on-air talent. Occasionally producers would add information that was a little more descriptive like 'nutjob', 'avoid' and 'total psycho'. They would also change some names to famous people just to give presenters a laugh. Oh, I know this is very non-PC and it would not be allowed in 2021, but it happened.

We had some very colourful names on PhoneBOX. One morning I recall seeing Monica Lewinsky and Princess Margaret all waiting on the lines to chat about the best chip shop in Scotland. Other classics were Nostradamus – predicts you won't answer; Alexander Graham Bell – testing his invention; Isaac Newton wants a shout out for his Granny Smith and Vincent van Gogh – using his good ear.

Carnage is guilty of probably the best/worst example of this. To this day he still regrets his actions, but this story has its own place in the annals of classic radio misdemeanours (note to self: this could be a bestseller).

Let me tell you about 'Aggressive Linda'. Linda used to call Real Radio a lot. I mean every hour of every day. She was very angry most of the time and complained about, well, pretty much everything.

One morning after taking an ear-bashing from Linda, Carnage decided to upgrade her name on the PhoneBOX system from Linda to 'aggressive Linda'. It was probably so he didn't have to answer her call again (remember this does NOT happen now).

A couple of years passed, and Linda seemed to call less. Then it happened. One of the worst – or best – things I've ever heard in radio.

Our great friend Paul Harper was on air and his show was a takeover by the girl group of the moment, The Saturdays. The concept being the band chose the tunes and answered the calls, with Paul overseeing it all.

I remember this as clear as day. I was driving on the M8 just passing the Glasgow Royal Infirmary in the sunshine.

Rochelle Hume from the Saturdays: Let's go to line three ... and it's Aggressive Linda.

Aggressive Linda: EH?

Mollie from the Saturdays: Aggressive Linda, why are you aggressive?

Aggressive Linda (in a voice that would turn you to stone): *WHIT?*

Frankie from the Saturdays: It says here you're called Aggressive Linda.

Aggressive Linda (in chillingly threatening tone): I'M NO' AGGRESSIVE.

Well, Paul Harper saved the day and professionally said there must have been a mistake with the computer et cetera, et cetera. Me? I was trying not to crash my car with tears of laughter streaming down my face.

My phone was going nuts from every other presenter on Real. Poor Carnage was so worried he was about to be sacked. Bossman Jay was fair as always. He gave Carnage a telling off with a wry grin and from that day onwards all descriptive names were banned.

Carnage should have known better. On a previous occasion, about a year before Aggressive Linda made her debut, Carnage was nearly taken out by special branch, who were in watching over then Prime Minister Gordon Brown. The armed men in black, speaking into their sleeves, were positioned outside the studio. Carnage and Michael were both taking calls; Gordon Brown could see the names on a screen. What a time for 'Saddam Hussein – is he insane?' to call. Michael and Carnage both jumped for the computer mouse to hang-up this call, but it went flying and they both lunged to catch it. The sudden movement alerted the security guards outside who rushed in to find the Prime Minister totally fine and two talented young producers with bottoms making buttons.

But time goes on and we are all a bit more mature now. I'm sure Aggressive Linda has mellowed, and that Princess Margaret would have recommended the Anstruther Fish Bar. As for Carnage, well, he's earned his name, hasn't he?

THURSDAY 20 MAY

Cat loves dogs! It's official. Ewen brings Harley the puppy into the studios and within seconds I'm head over paws in love.

She is a two-month-old Rottweiler pup and pretty much the cutest thing you will ever see. She's like a little bear cub but with such a soft playful nature, not at all what I was expecting. Her fur is as soft as exquisite velvet while the little crinkles on her button nose are utterly adorable.

We set up a makeshift pen in the corner of the studio with her bed and bowls, but she wants out to play as everything is so new and exciting.

Harley loves chewing her pink flamingo toy, getting her tummy tickled, sleeping and snuggles. Harley doesn't like the bottom of Carnage's frayed jeans but enjoys trying to eat them.

As you can imagine, the show is pretty chaotic, with all three of us trying to entertain a nation while ensuring the pup doesn't take us off air by chewing an important wire or pooing on the carpet.

She never barked once but whined loudly during our competition talk-ups. Harley either prefers music or has no interest in winning the Cash Register's £50,000 tax-free prize. Crazy, think of the treats and squeaky balls she could buy with that!

At 8.10 a.m. she falls asleep on the floor. Out for the count, just in time for 'Ewen and Cat's musical balls'. We end up whispering our link and very slowly and gently swirling the ping pong balls in the bowls so as not to disturb her. The balls chose the eighth number one from 1982, Paul McCartney and Stevie Wonder 'Ebony and Ivory'; it's a beautiful song which works a treat as she remained conked out for over an hour.

Call of the day comes from Jimmy who is driving to work. He is in fits laughing. He says, 'I can't believe I've just turned my radio down so as not to wake the puppy.'

Johnny from Dumfries is on next. 'My wife used to put the radio on and hoover round the weans. You need to let them get used to noise.' Ewen jokingly tells him to be quiet to which Johnny shouts, and I mean shouts: 'COME ON DUG – WAKE UP!'

Honestly, I love this show so much.

Today is also a very special birthday for one of our favourite superstars, Cher, who is seventy-five. We celebrate by putting four of her biggest songs to a poll, playing the winner. I was blown away by her performance in her 'Here We Go Again' tour at the Hydro in 2019. Ironically that was the last time I was in the Hydro until tonight.

My big return is not for a big night out dancing to a superstar or band. I'm getting my second Covid jab. Songs I heard on my last visit included 'If I Could Turn Back Time' (today's winner), 'Strong Enough' and 'Believe'. Do you think she knew what was coming?

FRIDAY 21 MAY

The UK's most tranquil towns have been revealed and Scotland has three in the top ten. They are Dunkeld in Perthshire, Melrose in the Borders and claiming top spot in the entire poll, North Berwick in East Lothian.

I've visited all three and can see why they scored so highly. The competition is judged on the town's peaceful location and lack of nightlife or crime.

I've had many a night out with Bossman Jay and his wife Dawn in his hometown of North Berwick and I can tell you we shattered the peace, made our own nightlife and our patter was criminal.

Ewen is going Eurovision daft on the show with a full half hour dedicated to his favourite song competition which takes place tomorrow night. We play Bucks Fizz, Katrina and the Waves, Brotherhood of Man, Abba and Gina G.

There is only one person who can match his enthusiasm: our vivacious *Drivetime* presenter Micky Gavin. What he doesn't know about Eurovision is not worth knowing. I love Micky. We share the same sense of nonsense and our dedication to being the last person standing at any event is well known. Micky and I have covered Breakfast many times together in the past twenty years and it's always a delight. We're a bad influence on each other and it's probably for the best that we've never been paired up on a more permanent basis. I couldn't last the pace!

Back to Eurovision, Micky is the only person I know who has booked holidays to go the live events. He's been to the finals in Norway and Sweden so clearly knows his stuff. He describes it lovingly as 'The World Cup for gays'. He had tickets for the live final in Dusseldorf one year, but he ended up getting blootered in Berlin, missing his train and having to watch it on TV in a Russian karaoke bar in the Friedrichshain instead.

Micky's love of this competition is so great he even booked Nicki French, the UK's entrant from 2000, to sing at his wedding to his husband Brian. She sang 'Don't Play That Song Again' which finished sixteenth, the UK's lowest-ever ranking at the time.

In fairness, she was brilliant, as was his wedding, which was one of the best nights out in the history of radio. I'll not share too many of the sordid details, but particular highlights were Steven Mill lying on his back on the dancefloor like an upended turtle lolling from side to side but quite unable to get up and our normally super-in-control biggest boss Graham Bryce suggesting it was time for tequila shots. For the purposes of retaining friendships, I will never say what Carnage did to Producer Michael's couch that night.

We get Micky on for a chat and you can tell he is already buzzing. His predictions are Malta, represented by Destiny, who according to Micky was previously a winner of the junior title (did you know this existed? No, me neither), and possibly San Marino.

Ewen suggests a Zoom call between them during the event. I decline on the grounds that I have a life.

I'm just teasing of course; the world needs fabulous, camp, high energy and positivity right now more than ever. That's Ewen summed up to a tee...

MONDAY 24 MAY

Happy Monday once more. We are all remarkably chirpy today and I can't pinpoint why. Maybe it's because it was Ewen's birthday yesterday and our famous Sunday buffet was world class.

Maybe it's because Carnage has sneaked Strawberry Switchblade and Simple Minds onto the playlist or maybe we're just lucky enough to genuinely love what we do.

I'm still laughing at the best revelation from our Sunday show – Ewen admitting he likes to 'sit on a bottle red wine like a chicken' to get it up to room temperature. I thought just leaving it out in a room would seem like the sensible option; other listeners admitted to putting bottles on the radiator, while three separate ladies said they liked to stick it down their cleavage until it was at the perfect temperature. The things that go on behind closed doors!

Our 'Song with a Story' this morning is from Chris Judge, who is the lead singer with The Red Hot Chilli Pipers. He is also Susan Boyle's vocal coach and tours the world working in the music industry.

He said: 'A couple of years ago the Chilli Pipers were invited to Japan to perform in a festival called Fuji Rocks. We were treated like stars and were asked to go on a popular daytime TV show to talk about the band and our music. Everyone at the production loved our kilts. There was an interpreter present for the interview. Before we went on set, we were told one of the presenters had announced her pregnancy and everyone had been celebrating that morning. I'm not sure why I did it, but during the live piano intro to our song I turned to the main presenter, congratulated her and wished her all the best with the new baby. The interpreter relayed what I'd said and the main presenter I'd delivered my message to was furious. We had no idea what was going on. Turns out I'd got the wrong presenter. The pregnant one was behind another desk with the big bump masked. We had to sing "Don't Stop Believing" by Journey and every time I hear that song, I think of that poor woman's totally raging face.'

I asked if they ever got to make amends. Chris replied quite candidly: 'We were never asked back.'

It is a mistake you make once. I remember a taxi driver stopping for me in Edinburgh years ago. I got in and he said: 'I had to stop for you in your condition.' I assumed he was just universally kind to hungover people. I realised within minutes he thought I was pregnant. What a bad mother-to-be I would have been. Reeking of last night's booze and eating pickled onion Monster Munch. I learned a harsh life lesson that morning: smock tops when viewed from the side are NOT flattering.

Fraser comes in for our daily handover between shows with a smile as wide as the Tay. His team St Johnstone won the Scottish Cup on Saturday, achieving a quite remarkable cup double, winning the League Cup earlier in the season.

Fraz has bruised ribs and a sore tummy and thinks he may have tried to emulate the hilarious video of manager Callum Davidson sliding headfirst on his tummy, topless and across the floor of the champagne-soaked Hampden dressing room. Fraz celebrated in his own kitchen with cider from the Spar but I love that he'd felt inspired.

Altogether now: 'Oh when the Saints go sliding in, oh when the Saints go sliding in.'

TUESDAY 25 MAY

CAT'S OUT THE BAG! We have a title. Woo hoo! Not only was it the most suggested title for this book on Twitter, email, texts and Facebook, when I narrowed it down to my four favourite suggestions and put up a poll, this won with sixty-seven per cent of the vote. A landslide.

Carnage collates all the entries and his computer randomly selects Laura Seenan from Aberdeen as our winner. She suggested the title by text on our Sunday show nine days ago so as you can imagine was completely bamboozled when we called her at her work on a Tuesday morning.

Laura seemed shocked to speak to us. She thought we'd maybe called her about the £100,000 cash register competition she'd also entered. I can't help feeling that a signed book and a possible trip to a launch party were maybe not the prize she was hoping for. Regardless, she played the game well and said she was stunned and delighted her suggestion would make the front cover. Laura works in the Met Office and with her sunny disposition she sounds like she'll be great fun at the party.

Talking of parties, tickets for the Euro 2020 Fan Zone in Glasgow Green are released today. There will be two sessions a day with 3,000 fans allowed in each one. Given that Glasgow is currently the only area in Scotland still in tier three, there are more than a few concerned factions.

I'm still not sure yet what my official on-air role will be for the Euros; I know I'm meant to be working with Ewen and Steven again on *The Big Football Show*, but I don't know how to break it to them that I'm going to go to Wembley.

I can't not be there. I want to paddle in the fountain in Trafalgar Square draped in a saltire like I did in 1996, just to prove that I've not aged and can still make it up onto the ledge and into the water without assistance. So many plans still to fix. After avoiding crowds for so long, it still feels a bit surreal to be working out how to join one.

Today is a very strange day for me. Tuesday 25 May is three months to the day I was told in a sparse windowless office in the Beatson that my dad's cancer was incurable. Today I took him out for coffee and a date slice, and he told me all about the bus trip he's going to go on to Liverpool in October. His spirits are high. I truly believe that if he'd stayed in the room and heard his full prognosis, psychologically he'd be very different, and his body would have started slowing down. I'm witnessing first-hand the power of positive thinking. He's actually getting better!

Bobby 'two cakes' is clearly not going anywhere soon. And don't worry; to keep up his fearsome reputation, I bought him an almond slice as a takeaway.

WEDNESDAY 26 MAY

My 'Happy News' makes me smile from ear to ear. It's the tantalising tale of the Tunnock's Caravan Wafer!

Yes, you read that correctly, a Tunnock's CARAVAN wafer. Ewen can't get his head round this concept and jumps in before I even get the chance to explain.

He says: 'How can you stay in a wafer, I mean, how big a biscuit does it have to be?'

Carnage and I are most amused. I suggest they gouge a massive hole in the giant biscuit big enough to fit in the bed and furniture but advise not turning the heating on as that would be disastrous. Ewen just stares at me with his glaikit look. He really has perfected this. Sometimes I do wonder if my surreal imagination can be a bit too much.

When he lets me speak I explain the caravan wafer.

Basically, Tunnock's have teamed up with Argyll Holidays to design and create this caravan. The 38-foot three-bedroom caravan will be wrapped in Tunnock's iconic gold and red striped foil at Drimsynie Estate Holiday Village in Argyll. It has been designed to look like a giant caramel wafer.

The interior of this unique holiday home is packed with biscuit-themed accessories including teacake cushions, caramel-wafer-wrapping striped tableware, ornaments and biscuit artwork. I'm guessing this is paintings of teacakes and not paintings made from artistically arranged biscuit crumbs. (I did once visit a toast art museum in Florida, where every picture was made with bits of burnt toast, so nothing is impossible.)

I think this sounds like brilliant fun and a genius piece of marketing from both companies. Who doesn't want to live in a giant caravan wafer? Just don't wake up munching your pillow.

I'm writing this diary entry at 1 p.m. today as we've all been invited back into the radio station tonight to watch the Arias live from the socially distanced canteen. As I've mentioned, the Arias are the UK radio equivalent of the Oscars, and Ewen, Steven and I are nominated for one of the most prestigious awards – 'The Radio Times – Radio Moment of the Year'.

I don't think we have a chance as we're up against so many famous names and strong important issues, but I like pizza so I'm happy to go along.

Clyde 1 and Forth 1 have both been nominated for Station of the Year; our Sunday Show goes out on both simultaneously so Ewen and I have double the chance of being part of a winning set-up. I'm more than happy to shamelessly jump on any bandwagon for the chance of a wee glass of fizz. I've made life-long pals on each station so the dream would be gold and silver in any order.

Boogie and Arlene from Forth 1 are up for two awards; I genu-inely hope they win something. There's a proper team of talented people here, the best of the best and I'm loving being a small part of it.

I hope for Producer Michael and Producer Victoria there's at least something to celebrate. The work they put in behind the scenes on a daily basis is breathtaking.

I'm going to try and squeeze in a short afternoon nap now as I have a sneaky feeling that, regardless of the outcome of the awards tonight, I might not make my 9.30 p.m. bedtime curfew. I fully intend to be home by 10 p.m. but I'll pack my toothbrush, a sleeping bag and a spare pair of pants just in case. I'll see you on the other side.

THURSDAY 27 MAY

According to my Fitbit I've had two hours and eight minutes sleep. I slept on the studio floor. I'm wearing the same clothes as yesterday although the pre-packed clean pants and toothbrush have proven to be a stroke of genius. Unbelievably we won the Silver Aria for the UK's best radio moment of the year. I'll tell you about it tomorrow. My brain is simply not functioning. Dad wants a trip to the garden centre, and I've had to say no. Forgive me, Father, for I have binged . . .

FRIDAY 28 MAY

It's Friday and I'm feeling human again! So where do I start? Today's news? Or what really happened on Wednesday night?

Let's begin with that. We were allowed a small socially distanced gathering at work to watch the Arias.

Boogie and Arlene won bronze in the Breakfast Show category, so we had a wee celebration for that. Clyde 1 won silver for Station of the Year, so we had a wee celebration for that. Lisa and Lynn, who work on commercial partnerships, picked up bronze for an initiative involving the Scottish Government and Scottish Autistic Media Radio, so we had a wee celebration for that. You can see where this night is heading!

Our category was twenty-fifth out of twenty-five awards! We were up against so many worthy causes I genuinely didn't think we were in the running, but when event hosts Jordan and Perri from Diversity and Kiss FM announced we had won silver, the room erupted. Not quite as loud as our actual entry when Scotland qualified for the Euros but not a bad effort.

Gold went to Jordan and Perri who talked so emotionally about their controversial BGT dance for Black Lives Matter on their show.

To be honest, I would have felt a bit uncomfortable winning gold over a subject so important. It's essential we learn and educate ourselves on this topic and Jordan and Perri were worthy winners by wearing their hearts so obviously on their sleeves.

With Producer Vic and Michael in charge of supplies we had a great night. I had such fun catching up with people I've not seen in months like Louise Douglas, who is big boss Graham's incredible PA (and as such had the power to magically produce more Prosecco just when we thought it was finished), and Producer Cat, and Diane from reception, who is as lovely smiley as you would expect.

I'm not sure if it was the joy of winning such a big award or the fact I'm not match-fit when it comes to drink anymore but by midnight, I could feel myself turning into a pumpkin.

I fired two slices of pizza into an empty box, grabbed a large bottle of water and sneaked off into the darkness of our studio. Despite not being able to sleep much, stopping at the right time and having cheesy carbs for breakfast meant I was totally fine on air at 6 a.m. if a little stale, bedraggled and croaky.

I don't want to tell tales (who am I kidding – this is the content you're all after), but there were still people in the canteen when we started our show. Grant Thomson and Meg McHugh (AKA the young team), take a bow my friends. I've taught them well and they taught me something too – I'll always remember this evening for winning silver and being the first night I learned that Deliveroo drop off bevvy!

So that's Wednesday dealt with. Today everyone is talking about the big *Friends – The Reunion* show which was on Sky last night.

I watched it, I loved it and I cried. I adore seeing behind the scenes footage of shows like this and the early clips of Jennifer Aniston and David Schwimmer flirting were just adorable. They apparently never got together but fancied each other through all of season one. Their first kiss was therefore on screen and in the now iconic Central Perk coffee shop. Knowing these wee gems makes you see the scene differently and you can feel their chemistry.

Lady Gaga joined 'Phoebe' to sing 'Smelly Cat' (this could have been a good book title for me) and Justin Bieber dressed as a potato. All quite amusing, but I just wanted to see the six actors being friends and sharing their tales.

I wonder if Ewen, Carnage and I should set a date in about twenty years' time for a big reunion to look back on this episode in our lives.

I guess 2014 to 2021 could be classed as our Ross and Rachel years – WE WERE ON A BREAK.

TUESDAY 1 JUNE

Another bank holiday weekend and the luxury of a cheeky wee Monday off. Due to glorious sunshine at the weekend, I can only assume Ewen's been sitting outside since I last saw him leaving our Sunday Show studio. He's like a big daud of well-polished mahogany.

He reveals he's fake-tanned his face to show Cassi from Clyde 1 and Bex from West FM how skilled he is at applying it. His neck to face colour change resembles a human chocolate digestive but he seems happy.

I have no idea how and when this conversation first occurred, but he's clearly very proud of his facial blending techniques and the fact the sachet was only a pound from Superdrug. I've never met a man quite so comfortably in touch with his feminine side. Well, I have, but he was a professional drag queen.

Much excitement in the depleted office today. We get a visit from the Euro 2020 trophy complete with a cheerful PR team and bouncers, or handlers as they call themselves. There's one strapping big 'don't mess' lad keeping an eye on everyone, and he is the only person allowed to touch the trophy.

Having once been photographed with the World Cup (one of them), I asked how many of these cups were out doing the rounds. Oooft. A death stare from a gloved giant wearing a face mask is not fun at 7 a.m.

So, it is the real one. The new trophy. The Henri Delaunay Cup. I want to touch it. To lift it. To cuddle it and pretend I'm Andy Robertson at the final. It's based on the original trophy, but to move with modern times it's bigger and better now standing at 60 centimetres and weighing in at eight kilos of sterling silver. It was first lifted up by Iker Casillas, the Spanish goalkeeping legend, in 2008. I've always fancied him and reluctantly realise this is as close to him as I'll ever be.

Snapping back from fantasyland, we dutifully pose behind the gleaming trophy and pull silly excited faces. I'm trying to control my jazz hands when Jeff Holmes the photographer suggests we all punch the air. Yes! A snapper who finally understands my inability to pose for a sensible photo. We get individual shots, then shots with Ewen and me, and then shots with Ewen and Steven Mill for the (now award winning!!) *Big Scotland Football Show* coming your way for coverage of the Euros. I've still not told anyone I've booked my train ticket to Wembley yet. They still think I'm going to be with them in a studio. Aye, like that could happen. Do they not know me at all? I'm going! I've served my time at Scotland friendlies and random away games. This is the big one. It's happening.

I send a sneaky pic of the cup to my Pitlochry Tartan Army pals on WhatsApp. Cammy tells me I need to scratch 'Scotland' onto it with a kirby or tweezers from my handbag and Ricky tells me if I do so, my induction to the Scotland Hall of Fame will be secured. A further glare from big scary man puts me in my place.

Steven forgot to pack a Scotland top for the picture, so I gave him one of my spares. I am so used to covering for Ewen and bringing props, it's second nature to me to have extra items for photos. It fitted him perfectly. So much so he went home with it.

A few hours later I get a text from Steven: 'Sorry I took your top. I'll wash it and get it back to you. I'm just glad we have the same size tits.'

I'm working with a right pair here.

WEDNESDAY 2 JUNE

With easing of Covid restrictions announced yesterday, meaning even Glaswegians (me) can travel anywhere in the UK from Saturday, there's an interesting list out today revealing the most searched for small towns and villages in Scotland.

I guess Oban, St Andrews and Aviemore will feature much to Ewen's shock as all three are in the top five which reads: 1) Fort William 2) Oban 3) Aviemore 4) St Andrews and 5) Pitlochry.

He forgets I've been a travel reporter for over twenty years with my *Mastermind* specialist subjects either places to visit in Scotland or the history of Freddos (invented by MacRobertsons in Australia in 1930 if you really want to know, before being brought over by Cadbury).

We have an interview with James Arthur this morning immediately after our Breakfast Show for our Sunday show. Ten minutes beforehand we receive an email from his people telling us that under no circumstances are there to be 'any personal questions'.

I google him quickly to see why they are being so strict and read an article from the *Daily Mail* online talking about his big emotional break-up with his on-off girlfriend of ten years just four days ago.

Ewen doesn't like to prepare for a celebrity interview, hoping for a more organic feel. I like to know who we are talking to, what they want to talk about and pretty much every detail I can find out about their lives before we begin. I might not use much of this information, but I like the comfort of knowledge.

Chalk and cheese.

Ewen opens the interview. 'How does it feel to be the most famous man in music with two first names as a name?'

It is so horrendously Alan Partridge we have no choice but to laugh. I point out straight away, 'What about George Michael?' and James adds 'or Chris Martin.'

James won *The X Factor* in 2012 and has gone on to become one of the show's biggest success stories. He's finishing off his fourth album and now has over 30 million plays on Spotify, only beaten in the UK by Sam Smith and Ed Sheeran.

He's chirpy enough and we talk lockdown, BBQs, crisps, the middle aisle at Aldi, his new album, touring, his love of all things Glasgow and his new single called 'September'.

We end our allocated fifteen-minute slot with another game of Aye or Naw. It's a good way to try and get a laugh from fatigued celebrities who are stuck maybe doing up to twenty interviews in a row.

I decided that because his new song is called 'September' that I'd theme some questions around this.

1. Was September originally the seventh month of the year? Both Ewen and James said 'naw'. Both were wrong. Prior to 451BC there was no January or February, so September was the seventh month.
2. Is 'Wake Me Up When September Ends' a song by the Foo Fighters? Ewen said 'aye' James said 'naw'. 1–0 James. It was Green Day.
3. Will Scotland beat England at Wembley? Everyone laughs. I know James will be torn as he is English, but his dad is Glaswegian (see research does come in handy!). He makes a very diplomatic answer saying 'naw', but quickly adds that as he is half and half then he feels like any result is okay for him.

As he's our guest, I award him the overall victory. He's still chuckling as we say our goodbyes and hang up the Zoom call. I like this. It strikes me again that trying to make people smile is really not a bad job at all.

THURSDAY 3 JUNE

Must not get carried away. Must not get carried away. Yaaaas, we're going to win the Euros!

Scotland drew 2–2 with the Netherlands in a friendly last night despite seven players having to miss the game because of a Covid issue. We showed some tasty moves and were unlucky not to win the game. A dodgy late refereeing decision let them equalise with minutes to go. Ewen and I are anticipating the tournament like kids waiting for Christmas. Carnage, who has no interest in football, is pleased for us but looking forward to having next week off to escape our mutual fervour. He's booked a week in Tiree. I think after working with the thunderous whirlwind that is Ewen, secluded beaches and the gentle pace of island life is exactly the tonic required.

We have an extra pair of hands in our socially distanced studio today. Ruairidh Tait from Radio Borders is shadowing Carnage to see what skills he needs to produce our show. Patience, tolerance and a sense of humour would be my guess. My favourite moments in radio are spontaneous nonsense like this one which happened today but could stick with one person a lifetime.

Ewen: We need to address the elephant in the room. We have a trainee producer in the studio watching us.

Me: I can't believe we've just met him, and you've already called him an elephant! (much hilarity) I'm going to call him Nelly. Producer Nelly!

And that is how a nickname can happen in radio folks. Prior to this he was Wee Raunchy Ruairidh!

We get Producer Nelly to help with our musical balls and tell him to pick one out with his trunk. He delights Ewen by picking Jason Donovan 'Too Many Broken Hearts' and because it's a good one I tell him he's going to get an extra bun next week. Carnage has already looked out an elephant sound effect and the joyous chorus to 'Nelly the Elephant' which appears at random every time we talk to him. It's total escapism, it's silly, he's loving it and it turns out it's just what some of our listeners need.

Colleen Butler from Bo'ness calls the show and says, 'I'm a 74-year-old disabled lady who lives alone and I'm calling to thank you for making me laugh every morning. I switch you on and I feel like you are with me in the room. You have no idea how much your show means to me and how much it cheers me up. I think every doctor in Scotland should prescribe your show as it is so good for me and honestly makes my day.'

We're genuinely all touched by this. We never take for granted our position and love that our listeners think of us as friends. We make her day and she's made ours.

It's certainly a baptism of fire for Producer Nelly. A show he won't forget. Well elephants don't, do they?

FRIDAY 4 JUNE

Hen dos in Cumnock, Barry Manilow, German birthdays and Sinitta. It's quite a day!

I'll start at the beginning. It's free play Friday once more and we start with a cracker. Barry Manilow and 'Copacabana' for Josie and Anne who Ewen met in a petrol station yesterday. This happens a lot and I love it, random requests from listeners we meet in shop queues, restaurant or bars.

It's also my friend Angela's fiftieth birthday today and we try to call her to play Altered Images 'Happy Birthday'. Angela lives in Pfaffenhoffen and I'd always hoped to be over with her for her big one.

Instead, we are on the radio in Scotland and she is in Germany doing a spin class in her garage. Covid can get on its bike!

I was also meant to be in the sunshine this week for my friend Deone's hen do. This was booked eighteen months ago. Five days in Ibiza was the original plan and now we have one night in Cumnock! I can't get the 'One Night in Bangkok' song out my head, replacing the Thai capital for the Ayrshire metropolis.

I have no idea why we are going to Cumnock. All I know is that our other pal Lynsey Brown has booked everything and I've to meet them at 1 p.m. on Sunday for our magical mystery tour. Lynsey is bonkers, so really anything could happen.

The highlight of today without doubt is Ewen preparing himself for our Zoom interview with 1980s pop goddess Sinitta. He sprayed on so much aftershave I could taste it. He's like a wee boy when she appears on screen as she is utterly gorgeous. I can't believe she is fifty-seven; hand on heart she could be twenty-seven. I hope he's not going to be disappointed.

Thankfully she is bubbly, engaging, fun and up for a laugh from the get-go. She is on to promote a documentary about her hero Aretha Franklin but ends up singing a selection of Ewen's favourite 1980s songs to him. She belts out some Rick Astley, Belinda Carlisle and Kim Wilde. He's one smitten kitten. Halfway through the interview her mum calls her mobile phone which rings loudly. She picks it up theatrically and says: 'Mum! It's me Ewen and Cat want to talk to, not you!' and hangs up. We all laugh, and I can see it in Ewen's eyes he's thinking: 'SHE KNOWS MY NAME, SINITTA KNOWS MY NAME!' In fairness, when Marti Pellow calls me Cat, I feel the same.

I conclude our interview with this Aye or Naw question based on her biggest hit: 'Sinitta, is Ewen So Macho?' She smoulders seductively down the lens and smiles: 'Oh, absolutely!'

He would love to be her Toyboy that's for sure.

TUESDAY 8 JUNE

Another Monday off! This time it's not for a bank holiday, it is to recover from the now infamous Cumnock hen do.

Turns out Lynsey and Steph booked us a lodge at the Lochside House Hotel and Spa in New Cumnock. I'd never heard of it before and it was an oasis of calm in lush countryside overlooking a loch with a top of the range chalet and giant hot tub. I was genuinely convinced we were going to be staying with someone's aunty in Ayrshire.

We'd all packed enough food and drink for a small army, with added extras like cupcakes, chocolate-dipped strawberries and rose-gold colour co-ordinated balloons, plates, cups and random bridal tat. Quality tat, but tat nonetheless.

As Deone was Miss Great Britain (yes really) and Lynsey, Steph, Stephanie and Lauren are all professional dancers, they were more than happy to pose in swimsuits doing the splits holding Prosecco aloft on the lawn in front of our home for the night.

Funny how Ewen and Michael never usually ask me to send photos if I'm ever away with any of my other friends!

Anyway, Deone – who looked like a supermodel with her wee veil to match her cutaway white swimsuit – loved everything about our night, and as the evening sun slowly slipped away and lit up the sky with a glorious orange-red glow, we all agreed sitting in a hot tub laughing with pals was every bit as good in Cumnock as it would have been in Ibiza.

The lovely waiter who served us our morning-after-the-night-before breakfast said, 'I'm so glad you got your ticket to Wembley, Cat.'

He'd heard me talk about it on our Sunday show. Yes, after years of midweek rainy friendlies at Hampden, treks halfway round the globe, and being in every ballot and UEFA draw possible, my friend Michelle and I finally got confirmation we have Wembley tickets.

It's always weird to be recognised from being a voice on the radio, particularly when you are in dark glasses, a mask and a fragile condition best described as hanging!

Over al fresco toast, poached eggs and iced caramel lattes (the girls are way classier than me, I needed a jug of tap water and PRONTO), we concluded the entire evening was probably the first time things had felt 'normal' in a small group in forever. The wedding is going to be epic.

Producer Nelly is in excellent form on the show this morning and has slotted right into the team. He's quick and keen to learn and has already sussed that Ewen's timekeeping is terrifying, he flies by the seat of his pants and I'm the brains of the operation. He'll go far, this boy.

All this week our 'Song with a Story' will be from Scotland fans remembering either their first match or reliving their favourite moment. Today Christopher Martin took a trip down memory lane to the opening World Cup match Scotland versus Brazil in 1998. 'I remember being allowed home from school early to watch the game. I was eight years old, and my best friend Paul and I ran home in kilts and Scotland tops. When we equalised, we honestly thought we were going to win the World Cup. Then when Tom Boyd scored an own goal we wanted to move to Carlisle and to have nothing to do with football or Scotland ever again. Now we are excited again and I think we will do well.'

Christopher chose 'Carnival de Paris' by Dario G and reckons we'll reach the second round for the first time ever.

Six days and counting. I take Dad out for a baked tattie at the local garden centre. He's in great form and has generously promised, 'I won't kick the bucket until you are back from Wembley.' Now, that would be the best result of them all.

WEDNESDAY 9 JUNE
It's the final of Scotland's *Home of the Year* on the BBC Scotland channel tonight and Anna Campbell-Jones, one of the three judges, joins our show for a chat.

She obviously knows the result as it's not live but she's giving away nothing. Her biggest clue: 'I can tell you it is a house ... and it is in Scotland.'

I find this a lovely relaxing television show and tonight nine stunning homes from all over Scotland will compete for the ultimate title. They are judged on design, style and architecture.

Ewen describes his home: 'I have a feature wall with mustard, black and white painted splodges. I also have black glittery wallpaper in my bedroom and large mirrored wardrobes – what do you think of that?'

Anna replied with perfect acerbic wit: 'It sounds very much like the type of house I'd expect a radio DJ to live in.' Brilliant!

News today reveals a supercomputer has predicted the outcome of the Euros. The Czech Republic will beat Denmark 3–2 in the final. This is according to a simulation played out by football experts using an innovated simulated reality solution. Don't worry; I don't know what that means either. They reckon Denmark will knock out England in the semis. Given that England and the Czech Republic are in our group that does not bode well for Scotland, so we are both choosing to ignore it. Or in techy talk – the supercomputer has been virtually unplugged!

I have a much better idea. We should use Ewen's puppy Harley to predict matches, much like the widely revered Octopus called Paul back in the 2008 Euros and 2010 World Cup. Paul had the choice of two boxes containing food and adorned with the colours of rival countries. The box and country he chose would win. His success rate was astonishingly 85.7 per cent.

Ewen thinks this is a great idea so on Sunday we shall bring Harley back into the studios and get three bowls. One with Scotland, one with Czech Republic and one for a draw. There is utterly no science behind our predicting puppy, but it will be fun.

It's time Scotland got to meet its DUG OF DESTINY.

THURSDAY 10 JUNE

My 'Happy News' this morning is decidedly fruity. A lady in Nevada has managed to break the world record for squashing three water-melons in between her thighs.

I'm not sure how she discovered this particular talent, but she's making headlines all over the world. Kortney Olson took 7.5 seconds to destroy the trio of watermelons, the previous female record was 14.65, and male record was 10.88 seconds.

She is planning on teaching watermelon-crushing in an online class for eager squeezers all over the world.

We have the audio of her breaking the record, but the squishing noise isn't loud enough for my liking, so before Ewen even arrives at the studio, Producer Nelly and I cobble together a spectacularly OTT sound clip consisting of me making ridiculous straining and grunting noises followed by an almighty splatting sound effect we found in our data base.

Ewen thinks we're playing out the original audio until he hears it and cries with laughter at how shamelessly bad/magnificent it is.

It's magic being silly for a living.

Ewen is fascinated by all things outer space and is mega-excited when news breaks during our show that NASA and the US Government have announced the level of unidentifiable radio activity they are receiving is increasing, seriously hinting that there may well be life out there that we just don't understand.

During Donna Summer and 'Hot Stuff', Ewen, Producer Nelly

and I discuss the likelihood of life beyond earth. Somehow in the space of a three-minute-forty-seven-second-long song we also manage to examine the complexities of modern science and the fundamental principles of various world religions.

Once we are back on air the following chat ensues:

Ewen: Cat, do you think THEY are out there?

Me: Yes, and they're trying to send a message.

Ewen: What would that message be?

Me: (in a voice like ET's granny) Scotland will make it to the second round.

Ewen is cross with me.

Ewen: Why can't you just be serious for one minute?

Me: Okay, I'm sorry. Listen, Joe Carson on Twitter has just asked this question. 'What is ET short for?'

Ewen: Extra-terrestrial.

Me: No, coz he's only got little legs!

BOOM. These moments are out of this world!

Today's the day Producer Nelly graduates from trainee to a fully-fledged member of our team. In a few hours the poor lad has had to deal with exploding imaginary watermelons, a serious existential debate and ET's granny. Tomorrow is his final day covering for Carnage. After this week, he'll be spaced out, that's for sure.

FRIDAY 11 JUNE

It might be one full year late, but today is the official kick-off for Euro 2020. Turkey face Italy in Rome and our excitement is palpable.

Clyde Superscoreboard legend Hugh Keevins is in the building so you know things must be getting serious as our shifts never cross paths. Shug is not only an encyclopaedia of football knowledge, he's got a wonderful self-deprecating manner and a unique mastery of droll sarcasm which can be comedic gold.

The Clyde SSB team, as they are known in the building, are preparing for their live broadcast on Monday from the pub at the Drygate Brewery.

Shug tells a great story about the last time he was there: 'We were doing a football Q and A event which was not for the radio. Gordon Duncan introduced me and straight away there was a guy slagging me off a few rows back. He was imitating my voice and generally just being very rude. I just stared at him and said over the microphone: "When I am broadcasting on the radio I work under the confines of OFCOM and a very strict broadcasting code. However, we are not on the radio, I do not like your tone or your obvious attempt to undermine me in public, so I am quite within my rights to tell you to GO F*** YOURSELF." His pals were in hysterics, the man apologised, and we got on with what turned out to be a very good evening.'

Do not mess with the Shugmeister.

I've decided that for the duration of the Euros, my Aye or Naw question will be related to one of the countries taking part each day.

Today I ask: 'More people live in Italy than live in Turkey. Is this true? Aye or naw?'

I've also decided to educate myself by learning new words every day. So, you can answer this one in English, Scottish, Italian (*Si* or *No*) or Turkish (*Evet* or *Hayir*).

Ewen, Producer Nelly and sixty-six per cent of our listeners get it correct. No, naw, no and Hayir! Italy has a population of 60 million while Turkey is over 82 million.

I've got that Friday feeling as I'm meeting up with some of my pals this evening. Alyson, Michelle, Joanna, Ger, Mini-Me, Dolina and I have been invited to Annie's garage. This is not a nightclub. It is my pal Annie's actual garage. Many people have spent a fortune converting their outdoor spaces to resemble a pub, but our Annie has moved a lawnmower to the side near the tins of paint dregs and invested in a row of battery-powered fairy lights.

This evening was first suggested when we learned eight people from eight households could meet outdoors back when restaurants could not sell booze. The fact we are now allowed inside to both eat and drink makes tonight's location both mental and magical. I have to go. With only three more sleeps until Scotland play, I'm now officially in training for the Euros.

MONDAY 14 JUNE

NO MORE SLEEPS. Now's the day and now's the hour . . .

SCOTLAND 0–2 CZECH REPUBLIC

I'm in a huff. I'll tell you about it tomorrow.

TUESDAY 15 JUNE

The morning after the game before. Oh dear. That all too familiar feeling. I should have known better. I've been through all this before. Yet hope springs eternal. We are Scottish. We have a dream. We can still do it.

Yesterday was a crushing disappointment. We presented our show live from the beer garden of the Clockwork Bar near Hampden. Steven Mill, Ewen, former Hibs star Steve Cowan and me. Produced by Michael and Victoria, it was my football dream team in action again.

Edited highlights of the day. My friend Ricky from the Pitlochry Tartan Army's wee girls Eilidh and Eabha (aged five and four) singing Scotland songs on air. One of our best two players Kieran Tierney didn't feature as he was injured in training. We hit the post, their keeper was magnificent, they scored a decent goal and then we lost one of the most ridiculous and spectacular goals you'll ever see. Czech star Schick lobbed David Marshall from the halfway line. Incredible to witness and heart-breaking at the same time. A real Schickener! This is the game we thought we could win. Ah well, only one of the tournament favourites England, the Auld Enemy, at Wembley on Friday. Easy!

Moment of day came courtesy of the taxi driver who picked up Ewen and me from my flat to head to the pub to broadcast. (I'd left my car at work, Ewen was meant to be staying in my spare room and he would drive us both to the studio in the morning. We honestly thought we'd be celebrating. As it was, we came home right after we came off air, he took his bag and drove home. Nobody was in the mood for prolonging the day.)

Anyway, I digress, the taxi driver. I got in the cab and he said, 'Are we just waiting on your husband?' I laughed and said he was not my husband; Ewen gets in the taxi and closes the door and the driver apologies, 'Oh I'm really sorry love, it's your dad.'

He wasn't joking. He thought Ewen was my dad. Ah ha ha ha ha! You can imagine the fun I had with that all day: 'Dad, I need the toilet? Dad, can I have a juice? Daddy, are we nearly there yet?'

Today we are a little bit down but still optimistic. Personally, I think we are going out of the tournament, but I am not saying that on air. What harm is there in spreading positivity?

News today includes the seventh sighting of Nessie in 2021, it's the twenty-fifth anniversary of the Spice Girls' debut single 'Wannabe' and a pub chain in Glasgow and Edinburgh called Signature Group are selling a £4.50 Bovril shot for the football. This is a shot of Bovril with some Highland Park Whisky in it accompanied with a pie.

A few of these and we'd all be going 'zig-a-zig aah'.

WEDNESDAY 16 JUNE

We're all feeling a bit more like ourselves today. Reflection and anticipation. Past and future. Tomorrow I go to Wembley. A draw would keep hopes alive.

Today we focus on simpler matters like my daily 'Happy News', Aye or Naw and Ewen and Cat's musical balls.

Nicola Sturgeon has followed Boris Johnson and announced a pause on restrictions lifting. We all need cheering up.

My favourite story of the day comes from the Clachain Inn, near Mallaig. Owners Yvonne MacPherson and her husband Ross, who have two daughters under the age of five, have created the perfect menu for children. Dishes they can order include 'WHATEVER' (soup and a sandwich), 'I DON'T KNOW' (beefburger), 'I DON'T WANT ANYTHING' (fish and chips) and 'I'M NOT HUNGRY' (cheesy pasta).

The children's menu is in capital letters so you can just imagine a petulant child saying it. A photo of the menu has gone viral, and it appears to have struck a chord with parents all over the world.

Yvonne explained: 'We have two young girls, and this is the usual chat we get anytime we go somewhere for dinner so we thought it would be fun to write it on the menu. Customers are loving it, especially when they have to say it to order.'

It reminds me of the Griffin Bar in Glasgow. For years, the owner Bobsy had a menu with creatively named dishes on it, my favourite being 'Glasgow Salad' which was actually a plate of chips.

Clever creative people and certainly food for thought.

THURSDAY 17 JUNE

Wembley, Wembley, we're the famous Tartan Army and we're off to Wembley. Today I'm back on manoeuvres and taking the train to London ahead of tomorrow's big clash against the Auld Enemy. I'm reporting into fourteen Bauer radio stations throughout my trip so even though it should be fun, it is still work. (Note to self: you have work to do.)

The train down is a hoot. So many of the young team heading to their first Scotland match in an actual tournament, it feels like we are heading off to T in the Park.

They're not in my carriage though, as one is travelling first class dahlings! When one tried to buy one's ticket, there were only three posh seats left on the entire train. I had no choice.

As my mate Michelle and I do not usually travel first class on the train, we had no idea they feed you and serve drink. We arrived with two heaving poly bags and a picnic for twenty, most of which was finished before we left the outskirts of Glasgow.

My evening task was to suss out what the supporters were up to in London. I reckon about 20,000 made the trip.

As usual, the plan was to track down Tam Coyle's famous 'nicht afore party'. This was in a smart underground venue where he'd found out that if he was booking a private function and not an 'event', he could have the bar open another two hours. Genius.

And so we all gathered for Tam's 'birthday party'. In fairness to the staff, they quickly sussed what had gone down but were fine with it as everyone was so well behaved.

It was table service only and you had to wear masks moving between them; everyone seemed to be enjoying themselves and sticking to the rules. They even let people dance, as long as they were only standing at their own tables. Cue a world of dad dancing as nobody could really move their legs!

Among many others, I interviewed my pal Neil Ross and his son Lyle. This was too nice a tale not to share. As Lyle is only twenty-three, this is his first tournament, and for veteran foot soldier Neil, the emotion of having his boy with him at Wembley proved too much. He nearly cried on air with me, which nearly set me off too. This was everything to do with the feeling of pride that he could finally share his passion for Scotland with his son at a tournament and nothing to do with all the red wine they'd scudded prior to chatting to me! I believe him. I really do.

As I am due on six different breakfast shows across Scotland tomorrow, we leave before it gets messy. I'm getting worryingly professional in my old age.

It's a massive day tomorrow and I need to be on my A-game. Here we go, here we go, here we go . . .

FRIDAY 18 JUNE

This day has been circled in red in my diary since we qualified last November. England versus Scotland at Wembley. The Auld Enemy and one of the oldest international rivalries in football.

I open the curtain in our hotel room and the rain is stoating off the pavements. How very Scottish. This could be a very good sign indeed.

I chat to Ewen on our breakfast show, followed by Boogie and Arlene on Forth 1, Bowie and Cassi on Clyde 1, Jeff and Lauren on Northsound 1, Webster on Tay FM, and Dan and Grace on MFR 1. They all remark on how fresh and spritely I'm sounding. I remind them I take my job very seriously and then fill them in with stories about the atmosphere (brilliant), London (weirdly quiet apart from Scottish people in kilts), my last trip to London for the Euros (twenty-five years ago, paddling in the Trafalgar Square fountain which is a fenced-off fan zone) and my prediction for the game. I say I would be happy with 0–0. If only I'd stuck money on that.

Michelle and I grab a bit of breakfast and then venture out. We meet the Tartan Army everywhere. In pubs, on rickshaws, on top of the hop-on hop-off tour bus with flags billowing. The rain may be teeming down but nothing is dampening our spirits.

I interview several English fans who were all lovely. I think they pitied me as they all thought England would win by at least four clear goals. Time to send them homewards to think again!

We have a quick ten minutes back at the hotel to hair-dryer our trousers (we had to – it's now a monsoon) then we head up to the official pre-match party in the Crystal Club next to the stadium. It is enormous. Again, table service, socially distanced fun and then a short walk to the game.

The new Wembley cost £1.2 billion and you can see why. It is stunning. The walkway leading up to it feels iconic, and with only 22,000 in a 90,000-seater there was never a queue at anything.

I had a cider and chips just because we could. Food and alcohol are still not allowed to be sold at Hampden.

Scotland did not get gubbed as so many predicted; it did indeed finish 0–0 after a magnificent gutsy performance. Our mutual pal Stephen O'Donnell was immense, and we managed to find his mum and dad at the end to tell them so.

My new best pal is Pauline who I met in the lavvy. Lovely wee woman wearing a Scotland scarf. Turns out she's our Captain Andy Robertson's mum. I know all the best celebs.

By the time we get back to the centre of London everything is closed. We are knackered anyway, so I go to bed sober as a judge and excited to have a clear head to do some touristy things in the morning. Most unlike Tartan Army behaviour. Don't worry, in the city of Bojo I'm about to find my mojo.

MONDAY 21 JUNE

Where did it all go wrong? Probably that first bottle of fizz on the boat trip. I decided there and then I could not face a trip back up the road on Saturday afternoon on my pal Ricky's Pitlochry supporters' bus.

I am a terrible traveller and a bus with hungover boys and girls smelling of stale booze would not end well for me.

Producer Michael knew this was a possibility, Ewen did not. There were no trains or planes to be had on Saturday so the 3.40 p.m. EasyJet from Gatwick yesterday was my only real option. This meant missing my Sunday show.

What would you have done? Endured the hangover bus or had a long lie, taken a lovely boat-trip to Greenwich and enjoyed some cocktails in Covent Garden? I chose the latter. I just kind of regret letting Ewen know this decision when I was half-cut on a Twitter video from a beer garden later that night. I'm sure the 152,000 plus who saw it that evening enjoyed the content.

Yesterday on Ewen without Cat, he asked the audience if they thought I should be disciplined. Former Scotland Women's Team boss Shelley Kerr called in: 'Cat is a maverick. We need these people in our team. Every now and then they make mistakes, but we have to deal with that to enjoy what else they bring to the team. Also, we should take a moment to appreciate Cat's stamina. This is Sunday and the game was on Friday.'

My favourite was the guy who said: 'If Cat is disciplined – we RIOT!'

Big boss Victoria also calls in this morning and she sounds raging: 'I knew nothing of this. I am furious. Did nobody think about letting me know?'

She honestly sounds like she is going to hammer me.

'Do you know what I am most angry about? The fact you did not take me with you!' BOOM.

Trying to pre-empt my behaviour tomorrow night should we qualify, I tell her I have a doctor's appointment on Wednesday morning. She just laughs and says: 'What a coincidence, I have a dental appointment and won't make it in either.'

There she is. Wee Vixen. Management at its finest.

TUESDAY 22 JUNE

The big one. Croatia versus Scotland at Hampden. Results last night mean that a win will guarantee either side a place in the next round. For Scotland, this would make the players legends as no previous team has ever managed to progress.

Our breakfast show is unashamedly Scottish. Alec and Marty from the Scottish band Skerryvore pop in (after passing their respective Covid tests) for our first blast of live music in nearly a year and a half. I can't tell you how emotional this made us all feel.

The band have a huge and enthusiastic fan base all over the world, so our social media exploded with messages of support for them and the national team.

They play an acoustic version of their hit song 'Take My Hand' then go straight into 'Flower of Scotland' on the bagpipes. Wow. Goosebumps. Absolutely sensational.

For a laugh after their performance, Ewen challenged me to get my kazoo out for a duet. We had a three-minute ad break to rehearse and then, with Marty filming, I ended up on a Facebook Live all over the world playing 'Yes Sir, I Can Boogie' on the kazoo with Alec on guitar and singing. It's the collaboration the world has been waiting for. One listener commented that I sounded like Sweep from 'Sooty and Sweep' with a sore throat.

It's a busy one for me today. Four-hour breakfast show from 6 to 10 a.m. on the Hits Network (Clyde 1/ Forth 1 etc.); with Garry Spence and Steven Mill from the Clockwork Bar next to Hampden between 5 and 6 p.m.; from 6 to 7 p.m. I'm on the Greatest Hits Network (Clyde 2, Forth 2 etc.) with Alan Edwards, Fraser Thomson and Gavin Pearson; then from 7 to 11 p.m. I'm part of the presentation team once again for the Big Scotland Football Show.

I'm a bit twitchy at not being at Hampden, but the bosses let me escape to Wembley and have been very understanding at my later than expected return, so I'm happy to play ball.

The show is hilarious. The banter between Steven Mill, Ewen, Steve Cowan and our reporter Andrew McLean at the match is top notch. Turns out when I was at Wembley, Ewen told everyone that Andrew (also at the match) and I were clearly getting it on! Andrew, who is a strapping young man and at least twenty years younger than me, played up to it.

To make matters worse, Ewen told the audience on his Saturday show with Steven that nobody had seen ex-footballer and TV pundit Rio Ferdinand since the England game and that I had him tied up in my hotel room!

Honestly, Ewen loves stirring. He knows I'll now have to explain all of these rumours to my dad.

What with my scandalous Rolling Stones past, Rio in a room and allegedly entertaining gorgeous young Andrew in London, I'm not sure whether to call my lawyer or post it on social media!

Oh, the game? Croatia captain Luka Modric was world class and taught us a lesson; we lost 3–1 and are out. Still, we have a young team full of ambition, we will only get better and hopefully it won't be another twenty-three years until we get to do it all again.

WEDNESDAY 23 JUNE

Hangover free, clear head, and both Ewen and I make it to the show on time. Scotland's defeat meant an early booze-free night which means I'll now have to cancel my imaginary doctor's appointment!

Our job today is to lift the mood of a nation lamenting what might have been.

During a link about the weather, Ewen goes tonto because the TV screen behind my head that we have on mute has the news graphic: 'ENGLAND CHEERS – SCOTLAND TEARS'.

He asks Carnage to change the channel pronto. He does, and we end up with *Fireman Sam* on some children's channel.

Carnage quickly loads the theme tune and Ewen immediately perks up. I tell Carnage to get me the *Thomas the Tank Engine* theme which he does and suddenly we regress to childhood, to simpler times before we understood the emotional turmoil of following Scotland.

I suggest this is a great way to cheer everyone up: request your favourite kids TV theme to take you back to pre-getting-gubbed-by Croatia-days.

This turns out to be the audio cuddle we all need, and we're inundated with suggestions.

Michael wanted *Bananas in Pyjamas*, Fiona suggested *Tots TV*, Brian from Carnoustie is a big fan of *Rosie and Jim*, while others included *Rainbow*, *Magic Roundabout*, *Dogtanian*, *Super Ted*, *Danger Mouse*, *Balamory* and *The Muppets*.

Andy from Dunfermline phoned in saying the only thing that could cheer him up after the Scotland result was a blast of *Captain Pugwash*. We obliged. While Alan and Gary the painters demanded *Rhubarb and Custard*; I think they meant the cartoon but maybe they were just hungry.

By far the two most popular suggestions were *Fraggle Rock*, which we touched upon just a few weeks ago for Sandra Dunn, Pauline Wilson, Jimmy Hodge and Stacey Walker among others, and *The Banana Splits* for Big Gaz, Linda M, M, Alisa Crone, Andrew Steel, Fiona Tennant, Jane West, Debbie Nielson, Nicola McCulloch and Lisa McInnes. Lisa told us she'd been listening to the show for the last two hours just to hear a clip of this. This is hilarious as I'm sure she could get a YouTube clip on her phone in seconds but it's lovely to have her listening for so long.

This content is certainly not award winning, but it is EXACTLY what Scotland needs right now.

Fraser from Dumfries texts in asking for *Supergran*; if only she'd played up front for Scotland last night, we'd still be in the tournament.

THURSDAY 24 JUNE

The entire nation seems to be struggling to remember what day it is today. With three big Scotland matches in a fortnight that made both last Monday and this Tuesday feel like Fridays, it is safe to say we're all a wee bit confused.

On the news front, which I've shamefully been ignoring as I've been carried away with the Euros, Nicola Sturgeon has announced no change in restrictions for three weeks for all of Scotland but has pencilled in the date of 9 August for the lifting of all restrictions.

Having been socially distanced and cooped up for so long, this seems as exciting as it does unrealistic. With two completed plays sitting in a drawer and two talented casts champing at the bit waiting to go back on the road, I cannot wait for theatres to be allowed to open normally.

One of the highlights of our show today comes randomly out of the blue courtesy of Linda from Leeds. She's called us by mistake; she was trying to get through to our counterpart, Rossie, down south who presents the Greatest Hits Breakfast Show in England.

To start with she is confused and keeps trying to name a snippet of music to win a prize. When she finally realises that she has dialled the wrong number and she is on air in Scotland she stays on for a good chat.

Prior to her call, I'd just shared the story in my 'Happy News' that for the first time ever you can buy one of the original Muppets at auction. Grumpy old men puppets Statler and Waldorf are going to be auctioned in Hollywood and are expected to raise over £45,000 each.

Ewen asks Linda (who remember has not heard a word of this chat) to name her favourite Muppet and she goes off on a long enthusiastic answer about Animal.

She also tells us she's not been watching the football so doesn't want to talk about England's chances against Germany in the next round and that she's had a lovely time on our show and will try and listen to us if she ever comes to Scotland.

I tell her to tell Rossie that I said she should win whatever he was giving away for identifying the song clip. I just hope it wasn't £50,000 and she knows I was kidding!

I take Dad out for lunch today with my good friend PR guru Peter Samson. The two of them share so many outrageous stories my cheeks are sore from laughing. Dad's consultant told me on the phone a few days ago that the only conceivable explanation for him remaining so well is because he is 'nauseatingly positive'. I find this the funniest and best description of the year. My cancer-riddled eighty-six-year-old nauseatingly positive hero demolishes scampi and chips with a large side of morphine painkillers and a smile as wide as the Clyde. On yirsel auld yin . . .

FRIDAY 25 JUNE

I'm off to Drumtochty Castle in beautiful Aberdeenshire for a three-day wedding. I'm getting picked up in an hour and I haven't packed an outfit yet as I forgot to check what still fits, so I'll tell you everything on Monday. Now where did I leave my tweed plus fours?

MONDAY 28 JUNE

Phew. That's been quite a week. Wembley, Croatia versus Scotland and an epic wedding along the way. I'm still totally jiggered when my alarm goes off this morning.

After years of doing the breakfast shift, I've mastered the routine. Alarm rings – get up. No snoozing for ten minutes, that only makes you sleepier.

I do my fourth negative Covid test in seven days before leaving for work. There are reports coming from Tartan Army pals who've been in London about a spike, so I need to make sure I am one hundred per cent clear before going to see my dad.

The sun is shining again with highs of twenty-three degrees, Carnage tweaks the music to add some summer sounds like ELO 'Mr Blue Sky', Katrina and the Waves 'Walking on Sunshine' and Dario G with 'Sunchyme'.

My voice is a wee bit croaky from the festivities of the two-night-three-day wedding in Drumtochty Castle. It was picture perfect and a truly delightful weekend. Deone looked sensational; as a former Miss GB we knew this would be the case, but her dress was fairy-tale perfect, she was glowing with happiness and her handsome husband Ross scrubbed up not too shabbily as well.

Truthfully it was just lovely to be part of a celebration. There's been so much misery and worry over the last year and a half, it felt incredible to be surrounded by so much love and positivity.

Distancing and masks to wander round the castle were in place, but at dinner it felt 'normal' and the silent disco was a hoot. This is where you get your own individual headphones, and you listen to one of two specially created playlists (the bride chose cheesy dance hits, or you could listen to the groom's cool R&B stuff. I chose cheese!). A silent disco is as funny to watch as to be part of, grooving in our chairs will never be a substitute for dancing but it was a hoot.

There were only forty-two people at the wedding which made it an intimate affair; this is lovely as you end up getting to know everyone.

The fact I'd played 'Sweet Child O' Mine' on the white baby grand piano at 2 a.m. to the three random groomsmen doing shots probably added to that camaraderie.

Legend of the trip was former Scotland and Celtic star Craig Beattie who'd packed a Breville toastie maker. His girlfriend Lynsey was wondering why he'd packed three onions, some ham and a block of cheese with his suit carrier.

Beattie's late-night toastie bar was nothing short of genius.

Today is also the official start of Wimbledon. Andy Murray is in action again on Centre Court. I admire his love of competitive sport. It takes a certain steeliness and determination to want to play on after hip surgery. We wish him all the best on the show. This is most timely.

It was love-all at the weekend and my rusty Prosecco-inspired piano skills were quite a racquet.

TUESDAY 29 JUNE

England are playing Germany in the Euros tonight so you can imagine how much hype is surrounding this match. I guess it takes the heat off Health Secretary Matt Hancock who has resigned for breaking his own Covid rules by getting caught snogging the face off his married aide.

I can't work out if the biggest stooshie is about who leaked the CCTV footage, why Hancock appears to have given everyone he's ever met a government contract or how little Boris Johnson seemed to think any of this is an issue. It's like a bad TV script and for my own mental health I'm going to turn this show off.

Some very 'Happy News' today if you enjoy singing along to songs at home or in the car. Scientists have discovered that singing out loud and really belting out a tune can make you look younger.

Singing not only exercises the jaw muscles which stretches the facial skin and keeps it supple, but by doing so for just five minutes a day, you'll get a hit of the feel-good hormone dopamine which helps rejuvenate ageing skin as well.

Boffins (such a good word) reckon that singing along to songs from Queen, Wham! and Kylie Minogue are the best ones to evoke all of the above.

I get Carnage to pop Kylie's 'Step Back In Time' into the playlist. That must be the reason she still looks in her twenties. No, it is not the Botox or fillers (I won't have a bad word said about Kylie), it's singing all her joyful perfect pop tunes!

Producer Michael has cancelled our morning meeting which we have after every show to reflect on that day's show and to plan ahead. I'm taking this as a sign. I was humming and hawing about whether to take my dad to Rothesay today and didn't know if I had enough time to catch the ferry.

The sun is shining, his morphine tablets have kicked in, he's feeling good and I can now leave the studios the minute we come off air. The Isle of Bute stars are aligning.

Dad has been wanting to go back to Rothesay for over fifteen months. His granny and dad came from there and he has so many memories as a child and also playing his fiddle there over the years. I text my brother Scott and he's up for it too. Opportunities become memories. We all must make the first to enjoy the latter and that is exactly what we do.

A lovely big Zavaroni's ice cream cone, here I come.

WEDNESDAY 30 JUNE

I'm beaming from ear to ear today. Despite slathering factor fifty on my face yesterday, I'm radiating a facial glow that make-up artists would describe as 'well skelped'.

Our Rothesay plan worked a treat. We never knew if we'd get on a boat or not as the Wemyss Bay-Rothesay route is not bookable. However, we did, and our day panned out to perfection.

I talk about our adventure 'doon the watter' on the show this morning and the feedback is so heart-warming. I love that my dad having a daytrip and enjoying an ice cream is yet again making so many other people happy.

Over 149,000 have liked my Twitter photo of Dad eating his cone on the Rothesay prom already. I phone to tell him this and he said: 'That's the same as Scotland versus England at Hampden in 1937.'

I google this to check and he is right. Europe's world record crowd of 149,415 squeezed into Hampden for this 3–1 Scottish victory. I really wish I could somehow put all the knowledge and memories in his brain onto a hard drive and store them for eternity.

We sat in the sunshine eating ice creams and watched the CalMac ferry come and go. Dad was in his element with my brother and me as his audience. We visited the street where his granny lived, he showed us the hotel his Aunty Anne managed, and the barber shop his dad worked in. We then went to see his dad's old house, but it had been flattened and is now a supermarket car park. We had to smile when he laughed: 'Oh well, you can't win them all.'

I'd taken the car on the ferry so this meant we could travel a bit further round Bute. As the weather was so glorious, we took a turn round to Ettrick Bay where he swam as a kid, and I paddled and splashed about yesterday as a grown-up. If you recall, this is the same beach that my granny had her first-ever aeroplane flight over one hundred years ago.

As we sailed back to the mainland, I wasn't sad. Dad longed to see Rothesay at least one more time and we did it together as a family. In the car as the ferry pulled away from the pier, he sang the words from the beautiful folk song 'Rothesay Bay':

> *It's a bonnie bay at morning*
> *And it's bonnier at the noon,*
> *But it's bonniest when the sun draps*
> *And red comes up the moon;*
> *When the mist creeps o'er the Cumbraes*
> *And Arran peaks are grey,*
> *And the great black hills*
> *Like Sleeping Kings*
> *Sit grand roon Rothesay Bay.*

In my driver's mirror, I caught eyes with my brother sitting in the back seat of my car and we both smiled. We'll all remember this visit forever, however long that may turn out to be.

P.S. England did pump Germany 2–0 at Wembley last night, but I figured you'd all much rather hear about Bobby Harvey eating a cone.

THURSDAY 1 JULY

Our top guilty pleasures have been revealed today and they include ordering takeaway, watching TV in bed and taking an extra scoop of ice cream.

Others on the list include watching a full box set in one sitting and drinking milk out the carton.

These all seem relatively tame to me. Mine would have to be reading on the loo (I hope you are enjoying this tome on the throne), homemade soup at a good garden centre and staying up past 9 p.m. Turns out I'm not very rock and roll anymore either.

In the sensible news, it would have been Diana, Princess of Wales's, sixtieth birthday today. I met her mum once on the Island of Seil where she lived. She was raising money for a local charity and seemed to be enjoying a very large gin and tonic while doing so. Between Frances Shand Kydd and Prince Philip it turns out I'm properly connected. Lady Catriona of Partick has quite a ring to it.

My Aye or Naw questions this week are still based on teams in the Euros. Today I asked: Switzerland owns a greater percentage of the Alps than any other country. Is this true? Aye or naw?

The answer is naw, *nein* or *non* (they speak a lot of languages in the land of chocolates, watches and mountains).

Austria owns 28.7 per cent, Italy has 27.2 per cent, France claims 21.4 per cent while Switzerland only owns 13.2 per cent but that includes the Matterhorn, which is the big stoatir!

I take Dad to Oakwood Garden Centre in Killearn after the show. This is the location where Bobby 'two cakes' Harvey first came to prominence. I ask him the question as he likes to play along and he replied: 'I'm not sure about that, Toots, maybe Austria, but did I ever tell you about the time my pal shot a donkey in Cyprus?'

I've no idea how the Swiss Alps lead to his donkey story (maybe because they're useful carting stuff up mountains?) but his trips down memory lane are hilarious so I sit back and listen. He knows how much I love animals, so I assume this tale has a happy ending.

'We were in the RAF base in Cyprus, and my pal was on night-watch. The base was always under attack from snipers, so it was a nervy posting when it was dark at night. He heard a rustling in the bushes and shouted "stop" in English and Greek. The rustling kept getting nearer and nearer. He shouted again and again until the rustling was nearly upon him, so he shot into the dark . . . and then heard a whinny! He'd shot a f****** donkey.'

At this point Dad is laughing so hard at the memory his teeth nearly land in his baked tattie. I asked: 'And I assume the donkey was just wounded?'

He replied: 'Naw, it was deid. Poor wee thing. My pal never got put on sentry patrol ever again.'

Not the ending I or the wee donkey envisaged! Dad needs to work on his stable manners with that kind of chat.

FRIDAY 2 JULY

It's Friday! Not sure why we always feel so energetic on a Friday, but we do. Sunshine, holiday season and the chance to play some really brilliant song requests from our lovely listeners.

Ewen decides to 'act out' some scenes from our Friday Flashback movie from 1996. I have to guess the film. He tries to emotionally deliver Bill Pullman's iconic presidential speech from *Independence Day* but sounds more like Forrest Gump after a bottle of Jack Daniels who clearly arrived in America via long residential spells in Ireland and India.

We speak to a lovely lady called Sandra who is getting married to John Small tomorrow in the Caves in Edinburgh. She tells us she is very excited as it's her fifth date!

I can't get my head round this– how can you marry someone you've only been out with four times previously? She must really know he's her 'one'. I ask the question and she laughs: 'No, we've been together for years, it's the fifth date for our wedding – we've had to reschedule it over and over again with the restrictions.'

Oops! Although I do know Shari Low the fabulous fiction writer (who is an absolute sweetheart) got engaged to her husband after knowing him just a week and they are still together over twenty-five years later with a family. No wonder she's had so many best-selling romance novels.

We play Billy Idol 'White Wedding' for Sandra and John and wish them all the best. They are both bikers, so I think that's the perfect song.

We also ask on Facebook to complete the sentence: 'I'm looking forward to the weekend because . . .'

John McLeod replied: 'IT'S COMING HOME!'

He's obviously referring to England playing in the Euros tomorrow and that dreadful song. I've invented a scenario in my head that helps me cope with this painfully annoying and taunting tune. I pretend it is about a missing scruffy family cat called Jimmy who has been lost for a week and finds his way back. 'Furrball's coming home'. Every time I hear people singing it, I think of Jimmy the cat purring by the fire and eating a big bowl of Whiskas. Anyone who's been in the Tartan Army as long as I have will appreciate that regardless of how insane this imaginary narrative sounds, it's a much better scenario than the other option . . . Purrfect!

MONDAY 5 JULY

Normal Scottish summer service has resumed. Torrential rain and floods causing traffic chaos. Oh well, at least it means I'll get all the boring admin work done I've been putting off for weeks.

We get a call from Sandra, our motorbiking bride from Friday's show, with an update. You have no idea how much we appreciate our listeners treating us like friends. It's why this show is so much fun to be part of.

Sandra tells us the wedding was incredible and that she ended up getting a motorbike escort to the venue from biker pals. She then sends us the video and it's brilliant, she's like a proper movie star.

Off the back of this chat, we get an email from Alison; she tells us she's had her worst weekend ever, so we decide to call her to cheer her up.

Alison explained: 'I'm a massive fan of Andy Murray and he got put out of Wimbledon, my second-favourite football team is the Ukraine and they got gubbed by England then I fell when I was helping to push a car and broke a bone in my shoulder.'

England are now playing Denmark in the semi-final so I tell Alison she can come to mine to watch the game with my Aunty Clara from Copenhagen. She replies: 'Well I have always loved A-ha!'

They're from Norway, but we know what she means. It's sporting rivalry banter. To be honest for the first time ever I'm not feeling so bothered about England doing well. They've some phenomenal players and manager Gareth Southgate seems like a thoroughly decent chap. I think I will be okay if they reach the last two. That's far enough though. My Nonno Giuseppe and Papa Jose will demand my support in the final . . .

TUESDAY 6 JULY
Spain play Italy tonight in the semi-final of the Euros. I've thoroughly enjoyed theming my Aye or Naw questions from the different participating countries.

Ewen's been going off his nut more than usual as he's getting so many wrong. Today I ask: Americans eat more pasta per person than Italians. Is this true? Aye or No? *Si e No?*

Full of confidence Ewen claims he knows this. It's the Americans without a doubt. His reasoning? He's been to New York once, they have big portions, there are loads of Italians there and he's seen *Goodfellas* where they cook a lot. Sixty-eight per cent of you agreed with him. Wrong! Very wrong.

Americans eat 15.5 pounds of pasta a year while Italians scoff an incredible 51 pounds per person. Nearly 3.3 times as much. I'm now craving pasta.

Thankfully it's on the menu. I've been taking Dad out for mystery lunches ever since he found his appetite again. He doesn't know the destination or who I've invited along.

Today we go to Massimo's, his local Italian, to meet my friends Lizanne and Stephen Thomson who run the UK Theatre School. They have as many wonderful stories as my dad and keep each other belly-laughing for two hours. It is so heart-warming to see him spring to life when he has a new audience to entertain. The poor Cypriot donkey story came out again, along with further RAF tales from Cyprus, show-biz touring tales and how best to humanely bump off a lobster (a bill is going through Parliament today about not boiling them alive). I'm sure I saw a cooking programme once where the chef helped them do wee headstands and they happily drifted off to the afterlife. Stephen tells us you can also make a shark pass out by hypnotically rubbing its nose, then shows us a video to prove it. We all agree that getting a cheeky wee nose rub is a good way to go.

Other subjects covered included: Why do they use the word 'terminal' for an airport? Why is stuff on a ship called cargo but stuff in a car or van is called a shipment? And, my old favourite, how deep would the sea be if there were no sponges?

Honestly, it was nonsense, but fun nonsense and it really lifted his spirits. I know he's sore again today, but laughter's making him forget.

If this book teaches you anything (aside from the fact Italians eat a lot of pasta), please make time for your oldies. They need it, we need it, their stories should be heard and it's a privilege to listen. Also, when your dad (whose teeth struggle with chewing) offers you the rest of his spaghetti Bolognese which has been sucked up and splattered down on his plate over and over again to take away in a box, politely decline. Blame the Covid or something...

WEDNESDAY 7 JULY

'Seven years ago, this very day, a nation celebrated. We had champagne on ice and were about to witness a moment of history.'

This is the dramatic clue Ewen teased us all with this morning ahead of his big story of the day.

I couldn't guess. Was it football related? A Scottish song at number one? He wouldn't crack until 8.30 a.m. when he theatrically and proudly delivered his big reveal: 'Seven years ago today in 2013 Andy Murray won Wimbledon for the first time. The year before, 2012, he won Olympic gold and the US Open but seven years ago today he won the big one. Wimbledon.'

Apart from he didn't.

As Producer Carnage and I and hundreds if not thousands of listeners pointed out, that was *eight* years ago.

2013 is eight years ago from 2021. His face froze as the realisation kicked in, and then the excuses: 'I've been hearing so much about Euro 2020, I just think it's 2020 and I worked back from there.'

Oh, this is delicious. We sit back and watch him flap. Ewen is never wrong. Apart from nearly all the time. His childlike petulance is as annoying as it is hilarious. Everyone is loving his mistake and attempted cover-up.

It's England versus Denmark in the other Euros semi tonight; the winner will play Italy in the final, they beat Spain 4–2 on penalties after the match ended 1–1.

My Aye or Naw question is about everyone's favourite Danish pop star: Whigfield's number one smash 'Saturday Night' was originally called 'Friday Night' – she recorded a Saturday night version for a laugh, producers loved it and it became a global smash. Is this true? Aye or nee nee na na naw?

I have to confess I laughed out loud at my own spur of the moment genius with this one. Nee nee na na naw, honestly, I feel like the entire six months of this feature has been leading up to this one glorious lyrical moment (if you don't know this song, it's the opening line).

Ewen says one hundred per cent it is 'aye'. He remembers this song from being a nightclub DJ in Dubai. He talked about this quirky fact on the radio in Dubai. He says he's never been so confident, he knows the answer.

Apart from he doesn't. It's 'naw'. I made it up. He's having a belter of a day. Just as well we are on holiday next week. He could do with a few Friday and Saturday nights off!

THURSDAY 8 JULY
Oh oh. It might just be coming home!

A few sleepy heads in the studio this morning as we all stayed up way past our bedtimes to watch England beat Denmark 2–1 with a dodgy penalty decision and an own goal. Aunty Clara from Copenhagen is distraught. The final is on Sunday. I'm probably not going to watch the news until then.

The *Sunday Mail* have asked me to give them quotes as a 'celebrity who doesn't want England to win'.

I don't really like the sound of this as 1) I'm not a celebrity 2) I don't want to sound mean or parochial.

However, I will be supporting Italy on Sunday (forty years of Tartan Army indoctrination) so I try and succinctly give my reasons why.

Football is a sport, sport is about competition and rivalries, England are our oldest and biggest rivals. That's it!

You wouldn't expect America to cheer Europe if they won the Ryder Cup, or Celtic to be delighted if Rangers win a cup final, or Bjorn Borg to be elated if John McEnroe won Wimbledon (showing my age with this one).

Twitter is very funny today. There is a thread all about England manager Gareth Southgate and how nice a man he is. It is mostly women explaining why he is their middle-aged crush.

Answers include: 'He is the kind of man who would make the perfect toast and make sure he spread the butter right to the edges'; 'He would drive you to a colonoscopy appointment and sit in the car waiting for you eating a Scotch egg for as long as it takes with no complaints whatsoever' and 'He looks like the kind of man who could build you a good solid bookcase. This is a good thing; I'd really like a bookcase.'

Ewen asks me to add to this. I reply: 'He is the kind of man who would defrost your car for you in winter to let you have the extra time in bed and he'd also go to the shop for you to buy women's products if you ever needed them.'

Carnage and Ewen are buckled at this. We really are going through a fun period.

FRIDAY 9 JULY

Games, snacks and four hours of feel-good summer songs. It's our last show before our two-week summer holidays and it's like the last day of school.

Graeme from Bannockburn calls in all concerned: 'Who is going to look after Ewen for the next fortnight?' I'm pretty sure his wife Teresa, who has somehow managed to keep him on the straight and narrow for twenty-five years, can handle another fortnight. It's just as well she's blessed with patience and a wicked sense of humour.

My favourite call of the day is from Robert who runs the Taverna Bar in Rothesay. He was working yesterday and heard that the couple sitting in the corner were on their honeymoon. He thought it might be Sandra, our motorbiking bride from Edinburgh, and went to chat to them just in case. Turns out it was – their brief radio moment of fame ended up with Sandra and John showing him their wedding video with all the bikers escorting her to the church.

I adore this about radio. The camaraderie. Storytelling. Making people connect. Robert said they were a lovely couple, and he was delighted he'd met them.

Feeling all warm and fuzzy with such a lovely tale, I ask if he gave them a free drink because they were on their honeymoon to which he replied laughing: 'No way – I'm no' made of money.'

I take Dad to the garden centre for lunch today. His side and back are both hurting but he insists 'I'm fine' and once again perks up when he's allowed out to play.

Today I ask him about his years on the road with the White Heather Club. He was a fiddle solo artist in these iconic touring Scottish shows starring the likes of Andy Stewart, Francie and Josie, Calum Kennedy and Mary Lee. He tells me about playing spots on the stages of Carnegie Hall in New York, the Royal Albert Hall in London and an arena in Sydney, Australia that Frank Sinatra had sold out the night before.

I look at his little bruised and wrinkly hands and think how incredible it is that the talent in his fingers took him on so many adventures. As always, he ends with the line: 'They were all great gigs, but nothing will ever beat sharing a dressing room with forty topless Brazilian dancers on the QE2.'

It's funny how this uplifting story always puts a bounce in his step . . .

MONDAY 26 JULY

Back to work after two weeks of glorious sunshine off. A lot has happened. In the news the Delta variant is rampaging through the country causing a track and trace ping-demic, but Boris wants to unlock everything because, well, quite frankly I now think he's unhinged.

His former pal Dominic Cummings has been squealing like a piglet during a big TV interview and has thrown him under a bus (maybe it was the fantasy '£350 million for the NHS' Brexit one).

Billionaires Richard Branson and Jeff Bezos have both popped up to space for a wee shufty in the ultimate game of My Rocket's Bigger Than Yours.

Scotland is now in level zero but there is talk of needing a vaccine passport for nightclubs when they finally reopen. What about all the under-agers? It's difficult enough sourcing fake ID when you're 16 without having to get a fake vaccine passport too. Poor weans. I do feel for them.

I've been busy too. I've been working on this book and collating photos, not easy when I've now got over 16,000 on my phone and the same again on my computer.

I also tried to help with the cover design.

This was not as straightforward as it sounds. At one point there was a wee white puff of cloud coming out from the vicinity of my bottom in the Tartan Bag.

The lovely people at Black & White Publishing have probably never received an email before entitled, 'Can you please remove the fart?'

I've also had fun keeping Faither entertained and with my brother Scott and me coordinating our schedules, I even managed to squeeze in four nights away with some of my pals.

I visited my mates Fiona and Neil to brush their Highland cows (a moo-ving experience for all) and loved the exhilarating freedom of wild swimming in the Sound of Jura, Gigha, the Atlantic Ocean and an old slate quarry on Easdale Island.

My friend Alyson's yelps of shock at the cold during the Atlantic dook could be heard in Newfoundland.

Dad's been in great form and has enjoyed further jaunts to Helensburgh and Gourock for cones.

Ewen, Teresa and I had a fun night visiting Bossman Jay and his wife Dawn and astonishingly Ewen even managed to stay up past midnight without turning into a pumpkin.

It's lovely to be back on air today and I even remembered my log-in password first time, which felt like an achievement. We're a little distracted by the Olympic Games on our TV screens. It's fun watching the synchronised 10-metre diving, the precision and skill required is just breathtaking. This is nothing to do with the strapping ripped men or the size of their teeny-weeny Speedos. Nope, nothing at all.

Tom Daley and Matty Lee won gold for GB and we had a good laugh remembering Ewen's very brief diving career which plunged into oblivion.

The return of Aye or Naw is welcomed by many on social media and I themed the questions accordingly. In the ancient Olympics they used to compete naked. Is this true? Aye or Naw?

Ewen couldn't get his head round how they would cope with the relay baton change! John Cleghorn tweeted, 'What about the pole vault?' while Stu Murray added, 'I think this is Aye, until they included the hurdles.'

Well, 65 per cent of people were correct this morning: Aye, it is true!

The first record of naked events at the Olympics goes back to 720 BC; apparently the nakedness was intended to intimidate opponents.

The word gymnasium comes from the Greek 'gymnos', which means naked, so the literal translation of gymnasium is 'a school for naked exercise'.

I might consider joining one after all . . .

TUESDAY 27 JULY

Deadline day is fast approaching. No Jim White on Sky Sports or multimillion-pound football signings here; it's much more important, I need to finish the words for this book by Friday — 90,000 of them to be exact. I'm nearly there. I hate to imagine how many times I've boiled the kettle and scoffed a Freddo during this process.

This morning we speak to a charming man called David Gleneagles Waddle. He sent a kind Facebook message yesterday to welcome us both back on air and Ewen wondered if that was really his middle name. It isn't. He volunteered at the Johnnie Walker Championship at Gleneagles years ago and was lucky enough to win a 16-month membership at the course. From then on, his mates called him Gleneagles and it stuck.

Lots of listeners get in touch about their middle names. Anne-Marie Marshall only found out she had a middle name when registering her details for a marriage certificate. Her dad had put her down as Anne Marie, two separate names. Aged 34, she decided to tell her mum and she apparently said: 'He only had one f****** job.'

Cheryl Hamilton was given 'Jean Brodie' as middle names, not after the famous book by Muriel Spark but after her gran. Turns out her mum only found out years later that her gran was Jane not Jean.

Kenny Baird worked in the oil industry and said when he was working in payroll, he had a guy on his books called Dean Matterhorn Snowball. I wonder if his parents were social (mountain) climbers.

Ross Mable revealed his daughter's middle names are Sorcha, Morag, Anne, Sheila, Helen, Elsie and Rose. I can't work out if he was paying tribute to a large family or if he secretly wanted his own netball team.

We have a catch-up with Michael and Victoria after the show to plan for the next few months. As usual we laughed more than we talked and I'm not really sure how much we achieved. Fred MacAulay popped in for a chat and topics ranged from Fringe shows, how a stag smells to whether he could set me up with comedian Danny Bhoy for a date. I think he's lovely!

Ewen, Vixen, Michael and Carnage are all being so nice to me this week it is unsettling. It is amazing the power that comes from having a publishing deal and the aforementioned deadline. They all want to know what stories are going in and what are getting left out.

I leave them guessing with a wry smile, take Dad out for a hurl, clean his house then come home to my office to stroke my large white imaginary cat chortling like a Bond baddie.

I think I've been nice to them, don't you?

WEDNESDAY 28 JULY

Musical highs and lows today. Doune the Rabbit Hole Festival due to take place in Stirlingshire next month has been cancelled. This follows on from Party in the Palace at Linlithgow postponing until 2022 as well.

We are all so desperate to enjoy live music again it seems a shame that confusion over restrictions has impacted on so many people, but as disappointing as this is, I'd always rather be safe than sorry. The musical high today was finding out my 22-year-old niece Kirsteen Harvey is No. 5 in the iTunes singer-songwriter chart with her latest single 'Time Flies By'.

There was also a big feature about her in the *Scottish Sun* proclaiming her songs to be 'the perfect tunes for your summer playlist'.

Very proud Aunty Cat here and I can't wait until I am able to introduce one of her songs on the radio. That will be a very surreal but special moment.

Our 'Musical Balls' gave us a song that was a high for me and a low for Ewen and Producer Carnage – 'Bright Eyes' from Art Garfunkel, No. 1 for six weeks in 1979. They both hate it, while I sang every single word, even though as a former bunny owner (RIP Bouncy and Thumper), I remain traumatised by the film it came from, *Watership Down*.

With time ticking closer to my writing deadline, Ewen has come up with an idea that I love and dread in equal measure.

To ensure I am revealing enough of my own inner secrets and not just telling silly stories about him, he's asked our lovely listeners to 'ask Cat anything'. He will pick out the best ten questions and I must answer them truthfully in the final day of this book.

I suggest 'ask Ewen anything' should also be included and after much debate we agree to select our five favourite questions for each other. So, before you waste a text, I'll tell Ewen, Carnage, my dad and all of you one final time. I NEVER got jiggy with a Rolling Stone. Okay?

THURSDAY 29 JULY

After seventeen years on our screens, Simon Cowell has revealed the *X Factor* will not return to ITV this winter. I guess that makes it the ex-factor.

At the beginning, it was must-watch television, but I can't even name the last three winners.

We've had great fun with the programme, interviewing many of the contestants such as Leona Lewis, Shayne Ward, Alexandra Burke, Little Mix, One Direction, James Arthur, Olly Murs, Nicholas McDonald and Livingston's Leon Jackson who won the show back in 2007.

I helped host a showcase for the *X Factor* cameras for Leon at the Almondvale shopping centre when he reached the semi-finals. It was bonkers. Thousands of screaming schoolgirls, maws and grannies all cheering on their local laddie. I think I still have his mum Wendy's number in my phone. Nice lady.

Questions are flooding in on our socials for 'ask Ewen and Cat anything'. We have to pick five each for tomorrow's show. You are a funny bunch, let me tell you!

For Ewen, examples include:

'Have you ever had a sexy dream about Cat?' from Allandro Cooperelli.

'How come I have never seen you at Tynecastle?' from Jimmy Brown, and:

'If you won the Lottery would you still be on the radio?' from Carly Morris.

Liz Aitchison asked what my first impressions of Ewen were,

which I think I've explained at the beginning of this book, while William McPherson asked: 'If you were both single back then at the right time, would you have been an item?'

This made me LOL, but not as much as the reply TO William from another listener, Teresa Gallagher. Gallantly defending our honour, she informed him: 'No, William. They are the Torvill and Dean of the radio world.'

Carnage plays Ravel's *Boléro* while I'm telling this story. He is skating on thin ice that boy.

FRIDAY 30 JULY

It's the final countdown – *do do do doooo, do do do do dooooo*! Not only did we play that song by Europe for Margaret who is off for a weekend with her sister in Peebles this morning, this is my very last diary entry for this book.

I feel quite emotional. To be honest, I wasn't ever sure there was enough going on in my life to make this a worthwhile project. Hopefully you've enjoyed the ride.

As promised, I am ending this literary challenge with the ten best questions about Ewen and me that you wanted to know the answers to. And we promise these answers are true. We shall start with Ewen, as he always wants to go first!

Q: Who is the most famous person you are prepared to kiss and tell about? From Jean White.

A: I once tried very hard to pull TV star Clare Balding at the Dubai World Cup horse racing. She was working for the BBC at the time. We even had a slow dance together and I gave her my best chat, but she made it quite clear I wasn't her type.

Q: Who is the most talented between you and Cat? From Alan Coote.

A: We are both talented in our own way. We are chalk and cheese, Ant and Dec, Laurel and Hardy, Sooty and Sweep. The perfect double act!

Q: Have you ever been to Dubai and if so, what did you work as? From Hangryhippo.

A: Are you suggesting I mention this too much? Well, if you don't know, I was a nightclub DJ in Dubai. A pin-up and a total catch.

Q: If you had to choose one role model who would it be – and why is it Steven Gerrard? From Ashleigh J. Hanratty.

A: Steven Gerrard is a born winner. I have huge admiration for him and what he has achieved. He is inspiring. My role model growing up was John Robertson of Hearts. He was the epitome of professionalism.

Q: Have you ever fallen out and how long did it take before you spoke to each other again? From Mandy Wilson.

A: Hand on heart, Cat and I have never had an argument. Not once in twenty years. We can disagree on things but then she will realise I am always right.

And now for the five directed towards me.

Q: Where is the strangest place you have ever woken up after a night out? From Norma Hayes.

A: That would have to be my friend Fiona's dog Struan's basket after a uni night out. I was in the basket with Struan and we were sharing his very hairy jaggy blanket. The next day I was rough!

Q: Why did it take you so long to rejoin Ewen on the Breakfast Show? From Ellen Boyd.

A: Truthfully, after twelve years I wanted a break from 4.30 a.m. alarm calls. I also wanted to concentrate on theatre projects, but the pandemic put paid to that. I'm delighted I was kind of forced back, it feels right.

Q: If you had to change one thing about Ewen, what would it be? From Louisa Gaines.

A: Just the one??!! That's tricky. Okay, his timekeeping. He arrives so close to the start of the show it stresses me out.

Q: How come such a nice lady like you is not married yet? From Halinka Rands.

A: Wow! Ouch. First of all, thanks for thinking I am nice; secondly, it's a complicated story. Edited highlights – as an adult child of an alcoholic I've not been great at relationships (this is VERY common; please google as there is SO much to learn about patterns of behaviour and why). I had two lovely boyfriends I just couldn't let in. The one I finally did let in completely broke my heart and now my defensive walls are borderline impenetrable. I hope one day they can come down.

Q: Have you ever had or nearly had a drunken snog with Ewen? From Karen McManus.

A: NO. NEVER. He's like my annoying brother or, as Teresa pointed out yesterday, we are the Torvill and Dean of radio.

We had so much fun answering these questions we've decided, as a cheeky wee bonus, to do some quickfire answers to a few more.

Q: If you had to do it all again, who would you replace the other with? From Kerry Ann Curley.

EWEN: Amy Macdonald.

CAT: Calvin Harris – ooft!

Q: What is the most embarrassing thing you've seen the other do on a night out? From Michelle McFarlane.

EWEN: Cat once couldn't find her mouth with a pizza after an awards do in London. Michael and I watched laughing for twenty minutes as she kept shoving the same cheesy crust into her cheeks.

CAT: Ewen chasing Sky News anchor Kay Burley round the Sony Awards for a selfie was nothing short of hilarious. She kept turning away from him in disgust.

Q: What is the funniest moment you have ever shared? From Anne Dick.

EWEN: The Ronnie Wood story is the story that keeps on giving.

CAT: It's not even true!

Q: What is the most important thing about your friendship? From Elizabeth Baird.

EWEN: Trust and loyalty. Cat is the best friend you could ever wish for.

CAT: He might be a headcase but Ewen always has my back. I could trust him with anything.

Q: What are your party tricks or hidden talents? From Moira Halbert.

EWEN: I sing 'True' by Spandau Ballet better than Tony Hadley.

CAT: I can still kick my height.

And it is only fair Carnage has his say. Andrew Steel asked him this.

Q: Best and worst qualities of Ewen and Cat?

CARNAGE: Ewen is one of the most genuine people you could meet but his timekeeping is atrocious and he is loud. VERY loud. All the time. Cat is one of my favourite people on the planet. She is so kind and caring and like a big sister to me. She also brings me Freddos. The only bad thing about Cat is when she forgets to bring the Freddos.

So, there you go. Like the subtitle on the cover says, you've just learned all about Ewen and Cat – the good, the bad and the nonsense!

Feline Paw-Sitive –
The Purrfect Conclusion

Time flies when you are having fun. It's estimated over that 750,000 people in the UK have written some form of book during the coronavirus pandemic. It's a very busy time for publishers and even though it's only the end of July, to get ahead of the Christmas rush I have reached the official deadline for *Cat's Out the Bag*.

This gives me the Fear. What have I missed? Are there enough stories to keep you entertained? Could I have shared more, or should I have shared less?

The writing process has kept me focused during an unusual year, which has revolved around being back on air six days a week, along with caring for my dad five days a week too.

Ever since we were told back in March his cancer couldn't be cured, I've cherished every moment of family time together.

We have laughed, shared stories and enjoyed more seaside jaunts for ice creams than is good for either of us.

He's actually written 85 per cent of his own book, sharing his show-business memories and, after I've finished this one, I think that shall be my next writing project, helping him knock it into shape. He wants all the money to go to the Beatson and I'd be delighted to help.

We know he's enjoying his last hurrah, but I also know how much I've learned from and been inspired by his 'nauseatingly positive' attitude. No regrets. We shall continue to remember the light in the dark days. Powered by homemade date slices and strong morphine, Bobby 'Two Cakes' Harvey fearlessly fights on.

As much as I've loved our Sunday show, I think the time will be right soon to stop and concentrate fully on our Breakfast Show. I'm a little bit frazzled, not getting any younger and would love to have two consecutive days off again. As Ewen now works every Saturday on the hilarious *Big Saturday Football Show*, it is a decision he agrees with. We will miss it terribly, but please come and join us Monday to Friday from 6 to 10 a.m. on the Greatest Hits Network.

I've now been writing this book every weekday since January. It's been quite a discipline and a lot of effort (as I'm such a talented procrastinator), but hopefully Cash for Kids will reap the benefits.

The Cash for Kids team are so passionate about helping local children and I am delighted I could play a small part in what they are trying to achieve. The money this book generates should help thousands of children right across Scotland.

In 2020, Cash for Kids helped 108,955 children. They supported 48,123 children affected by poverty; supported 7,511 children's health and well-being; they funded 1,056 fun experiences for kids who needed these the most; they supported 11,186 kids to join educational programmes; they helped 3,057 children join in with sports and they provided 38,022 children with gifts and essentials at Christmas time.

The pandemic has increased demand for support. So far in 2021, food poverty remains a massive issue and Cash for Kids have supported more children this year than ever before with food, trips and access to activities over the summer.

I cannot thank you enough for helping us help these kids who need it the most. You really have made a difference. This book may be a wee bit of light-hearted fun, but it will genuinely help families dealing with some very serious issues.

Likewise, many mental health advisory sites recommend journaling and offloading your thoughts by writing them down. I would urge you to give it a go as I feel the benefit for having done so.

With regards to my first six months back full-time on the radio, it has truly been a joy. Some of my personal highlights include:

- WEMBLEY: Scotland back in a tournament for the first time in 23 years and the best 0–0 draw of my life.
- SKERRYVORE: After a year and a half without hearing live music, Alec and Martin sounded sensational in the studio. Bagpipes before a Scotland game. Gallus!
- HARLEY: Every show should have its own puppy.
- CARRIE-OKE: The imaginary singing sister. I still laugh every time we play Phil Oakey.
- SEEING PEOPLE: After months working from home alone, being able to chat to people face to face in the office was incredible. Even a quick catch-up chat with Cassi, ma wee lassie in the ladies' bog, can make my day.
- THE CASH REGISTER: This year we will have given away over £2 million in tax-free cash to over a hundred listeners. Hearing how joyful and surprised the winners are when they answer the call from Garry Spence makes my day.
- MARTI PELLOW: He knows my name. He called me Cat. This means he must love me. It's only a matter of time.
- AMY MACDONALD: Beyond delighted, our musical pal has had so much success this year. She deserves it and more. Let's rock that Hydro.

- SHARLEEN SPITERI'S CHIPSTICKS: It shows you how comfortable the Texas star feels in our Zoom company to tan her crisps mid-interview. Legend.
- DEL AMITRI'S TOUR BUS AROMA: My favourite interview answer of the year.
- FRIENDS. Not the TV reunion. My bosses and colleagues. Victoria, Michael and Carnage. It feels great to be together again. The entire team at Bauer have made me so welcome I can't wait until we can all catch up properly.
- YOU: Without our listeners we are just two numpties talking at each other. Every day you get in touch, share your thoughts and tales and make what we do worthwhile.

Out of interest, I've just read the conclusion to my first book *The Cat's Whispers* from fifteen years ago. It contains the line: 'I remain naively optimistic that by my eighty-fifth birthday I'll be able to tuck a top in.'

Having put on a stone in the last eight weeks (hen dos, Scotland games, weddings and holidays are bad for the waistline), I'm suspecting my original timeline is just about right!

However, I'm back in the zone and looking forward to the fitness challenge. Again.

All that remains to be said is – THANK YOU. A big massive heartfelt *thank you*. To everyone who has bought this book and to all my friends and colleagues who have kept me laughing and enjoying life when it's been challenging.

Rest assured *Ewen and Cat at Breakfast* shall continue with our unique brand of nonsense for as long as we keep getting away with it.

The third part of this book trilogy *CAT-ASTROPHE – Ewen and*

Cat – THE TRUTH will be coming your way in 2036. This is where I shamelessly take down EVERYONE I've ever met with spectacularly titillating stories, videos and photos that couldn't be included in this book for legal reasons because this is a nice fluffy charity edition.

I'm more than willing to discuss film and TV rights to my scandal-packed book three (AKA my pension), and I'm open to Hollywood approaches and exorbitant financial negotiations. My biggest dilemma? Who will I cast to play Ronnie Wood ...

THE END *

* For now ...

The Final Farewell

In the end it was exactly what he wanted. In his own bed at home, with his favourite music gently playing in the background, perfectly content, holding my hand and with nothing left unsaid.

The very day this book went to print, Dad, Bobby 'two cakes' Harvey, my hero, slipped away peacefully with my brother and me by his side. His ten-year fight with prostate cancer over.

His final week was an emotional roller-coaster. We sat together in the dark in his bedroom, laughing and remembering some of the adventures we'd squeezed in.

He talked fondly of his Ceilidh Band and he told me the story of when he spotted Mum at 'the dancing' for the first time: 'She was the most beautiful thing I'd ever seen.'

To start with, he didn't want me to help him empty his urine leg bag; by the end, we were sharing jokes as his tiny frame sat frustrated and bent double on his commode.

There were no boundaries left to cross and we were both fine with that.

Nicola Dunne, our district nurse, and her team were superb, as were the home care team who popped in every morning and night

307

to ensure his wish to remain at home could be fulfilled. Thank you.

The difficult funeral chat became comical when Dad asked what his options were. I replied jokingly, 'I can turn you into a firework if you'd like?'

His face lit up (no pun intended) and he said, 'YES! Do it!'

One Google search later gave him a hilariously unexpected dilemma: 'Shall I be a big rocket or a small colourful display, Toots?'

He chose the multi-coloured display! On Hogmanay, surrounded by friends, Bobby Harvey will light up the sky like the brightest star he was, is, and forever shall be.

We shall toast his 'nauseatingly positive' existence and be eternally thankful for having this joyous force of nature in our lives.

Please remember him as I will. Always kind, always laughing and eating cakes. Two at a time . . .

Thank You

I'd like to thank all 'the girls' for their ongoing support and friendship, my brother Scott and his family and of course my dad.

This year my Fitbit and I must say a special thank you to my lockdown walkers. The friends I've regularly pounded the streets with, in hail, rain and shine keeping me healthy and happy and encouraging this book every step of the way.

They are Andrew Agnew, Karim Baaziz, Lynsey Brown, Lynn Cameron, Michelle Evans, Trish Fraser, Alyson Gray, Joanna Kaczynska, Lizanne Lambie-Thomson, Johnny Mac, Steph MacDonald, Dolina Macfarlane, Geraldine McCartney, Michelle McManus, Denise Mair, Stuart Martin, Joe O'Loughlin, Annie Paterson, Debbie Paterson, Louise Robertson, Peter Samson and Steven Thomson. Not forgetting Bea, Betsy Mac, Buddy, Harry and Sherlock the borrowed dugs!

Also indebted to Joe, Mrs P, Garry Spence and Ellen and Roberto MacDonald for the endless homemade food parcels and to Michelle, my lockdown bubble buddy, thanks for all the chats and dinners.

Special mention to my Bauer radio dream team of Graham Bryce, Victoria-Easton Reilly, Producer Michael and Producer Carnage for persuading me once again that life with Ewen Cameron would never be dull.

Given that I'm on radio, I'm also going to squeeze in a shout-out to Sal, Emma, Debbie, Grace and all of the Cash for Kids team in Scotland for embracing my book and Ali, Campbell and the wonderful team at Black & White Publishing for making it happen.

Finally, to Ewen Cameron. My radio partner in crime. You, my friend, are unique. I know your story. I am proud watching you survive and thrive. One day you will tell your tale, until then be the star of mine!

Once again, my gratitude goes out to everyone who reads this book and listens to *Ewen and Cat at Breakfast*. You are the ketchup to our square sausage. Nope, I'm not even sorry for that one.

I hope you have enjoyed my collection of uplifting stories and thank you for choosing to help support children in your local area struggling with poverty issues.